An Introduction to Contemporary Epistemology

B

An Introduction to Contemporary Epistemology

JONATHAN DANCY

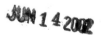

BLACKWELL
Oxford UK & Cambridge USA

First published 1985
Reprinted 1986, 1987, 1989, 1991, 1992, 1993,
1994 (twice), 1995, 1996 (twice), 1997, 1998, 1999, 2000, 2001

Blackwell Publishers Ltd
108 Cowley Road
Oxford OX4 1JF, UK

Blackwell Publishers Inc.
350 Main Street
Malden, Massachusetts 02148, USA

British Library Cataloguing in Publication Data
A CIP catalogue record for this book is available from the British Library

Library of Congress Cataloging in Publication Data
Dancy, Jonathan
An introduction to contemporary epistemology
Bibliography: p.
Includes index.
1. Knowledge, Theory of—History—20th century.
I. Title.
BD161.D29   1985   121   84–28334

ISBN 0–631–13622–3 (pbk)

Typeset by System 4 Associates, Gerrards Cross, Buckinghamshire
Printed and bound in Great Britain by T. J. International Ltd, Padstow, Cornwall

This book is printed on acid-free paper

for
Sarah

Contents

Part II JUSTIFICATION

Preface

This book is an expanded version of a course on epistemology which I have been giving for some years at the University of Keele. It is of course the product of many conversations with students and colleagues. I am grateful to all of them, but special thanks are due to David Bakhurst, David McNaughton and Richard Swinburne, who read the whole book, sometimes in several drafts, and were kind enough to offer detailed comments and suggestions. My father, John Dancy, also cast an elegant eye upon the whole. Angus Gellatly, Hanjo Glock, Peter Hacker and Cathy McDaniel read parts of the book and made helpful criticisms. I am grateful to all of them, and to four anonymous reports commissioned by Basil Blackwell Ltd, for their attempts to improve the text; also to Charles Swann for consistent and welcome support. John Thompson persuaded me, both explicitly and by example, that I should start writing; I think I am grateful to him too.

But my main debt is to my wife Sarah, who provided a never-failing source of encouragement after the bad days and a willing ear after the good ones. I have often been somewhat sceptical about authors' protestations of gratitude to husband, wife, friend or whoever, without whom. . . Never again. To have to live with someone whose thoughts are occupied by one topic to the exclusion of most other things is more than one can reasonably ask; it was certainly not in the original contract.

Introduction

As its title indicates, this book is intended to provide an introduction to the main topics currently discussed under the rather unclear heading of 'epistemology' or theory of knowledge. Epistemology is the study of knowledge and the justification of belief. Central questions to which epistemologists try to provide answers include 'Which beliefs are justified and which are not?', 'What, if anything, can we know?', 'What is the difference between knowing and having a true belief?', 'What is the relation between seeing and knowing?'. Questions like these are at the heart of epistemology, but of course the subject spreads, like all philosophical enquiry, and its boundaries are fuzzy.

The book is intended for undergraduates in their second or third year of a philosophy degree, but this need not necessarily deter readers with other backgrounds; e.g., my father claims to be able to understand it, though perhaps he would not thank me for the suggestion that he is representative. Although the book is an introduction, I have seen no reason to conceal my own opinions; which anyway are not particularly idiosyncratic. I think it an advantage to a student to have something to react against, but this has not led me to struggle to reach firm conclusions on every topic. Some of the material used here has appeared in print before, and I am grateful to the editors of the *American Philosophical Quarterly* and of *Analysis* for permission to reprint it.

The approach which I take to the subject is one concerned almost exclusively with the Anglo-American tradition, though Hegel is allowed into the last chapter, at the end of which I give some references to sample writings in the continental tradition, especially critical theory. The tradition within which I work contains a choice between two approaches to the questions of epistemology. The first, associated with Descartes, starts by considering the challenge of scepticism, the claim that knowledge is impossible; and hopes in answering this challenge to be driven to expose the nature of what it is to know, from which the possibility of knowing will follow. The second, which I associate with Grice (1961), holds that Descartes distorted philosophy into an unhealthy obsession with a non-existent person called 'the sceptic'. Instead we should investigate the nature of knowledge (if knowledge has a nature) and of justification directly, and hope by our results in this area to provide a conclusion, one way or the other, about the possibility of knowledge. On this second approach, the refutation of scepticism is not the intention, and need not be the result, of a successful epistemology.

Of these two approaches I have adopted the first, formally at least, since my first chapter is concerned with scepticism, and there are constant if sporadic references to one form of sceptical argument throughout the book. My reason or excuse for this is that interest in scepticism has revived. The topic returns to the forefront of attention in the final chapter, in which I discuss the very possibility of the enterprise I have been engaged in for the previous fourteen.

The book falls into three parts, the first on knowledge, the second on justification, the third on forms of knowledge. There are various complaints one could make about this division, most of which are justified. One is that scepticism is not restricted to doubt about the possibility of knowledge; most interesting sceptical arguments, as I suggest in chapter 1, involve an equal doubt about the possibility of justified belief. So the chapter on scepticism which occurs in part I has an equal right to be in part II. Another complaint is that it is not clear that all the matters discussed in part III, perception, memory, induction and a priori knowledge, are *forms* of knowledge. Some have been held to be *sources* of knowledge. Knowledge, we might say, is *derived* from what is given in perception; what perception provides is not itself knowledge, but becomes knowledge after some transformation. Induction, on the other hand, seems more like a form of inference than a form of knowledge. Many writers escape these difficulties by offering chapters on *objects* of knowledge: the external world, the past, the future, the necessary, other minds and so on. But this approach seems to me to contain difficulties of its own, not the least being that each object of knowledge is knowable in more than one of the different ways. So I have spoken instead of forms of knowledge, and allowed the various possible objects of knowledge to surface where they will. The topic of other minds, for instance, occurs exceptionally in chapter 5.

After the introductory chapter on scepticism, the first part contains a chapter on the nature of knowledge and its relation to true justified belief, and another concentrating on one particular theory. The former can do no more than skim the surface of an area which has recently been very heavily mined; the latter is included because I think that this theory, though recent, is more than a passing fashion and contains some insights into the nature of knowledge.

I examine in part II the comparative merits of two approaches to the nature of justification, foundationalism and coherentism. In chapters 4 and 5 I expose defects in the crudest form of foundationalism, and in chapters 6 and 7 I argue that we have a more general reason to avoid any sort of foundationalism, a reason derived from considerations in the theory of meaning. This obviously raises questions about philosophical priority; is the theory of meaning able to be prior to epistemology and to provide a court of appeal for epistemological debate? But quite apart from that, these two chapters are perhaps more difficult than their surroundings, and I recommend that they be omitted from a first reading. If you move straight from chapter 5 to chapter 8 you will get a stark contrast between two theories of justification, and all you need to know for the moment is that I take the intervening chapters to provide a reason against any form of foundationalism. The final two chapters, 14 and 15, are to some extent dependent upon what is said in chapters 6 and 7. So I suggest that they also be omitted from a first reading, leaving chapters 1 – 5 and 8 – 13 inclusive.

The third part is dominated by two chapters on perception, which perhaps constitute the centre of the book. This topic seems to me both the most important and the most difficult in epistemology.

Each chapter ends with a short addendum entitled 'Further Reading', which comprises two sections. (There are also references in the body of the text, some of which are picked up at the end of the chapter.) The difference between these two sections is that the former is supposed to show you where you should start pursuing the main themes of the chapter. The latter provides references to background reading, allows me to talk around the area concerned, and offers bibliographical suggestions on every topic that arises in the chapter so that you have some idea where to go next if you want to pursue any particular aspect. Items mentioned in the first section are at roughly the same level of difficulty as the chapter they accompany. Items in the second section may be harder. All references are by the author-date system (e.g., 'Grice, 1961') and are collected in the References at the end of the book.

Finally, the index is intended to remedy one defect of the book, which is that topics, theories and approaches recur at different places as we go along. For instance, anti-realism is discussed in chapter 1 and recurs in chapter 9; anti-realist approaches to perception are discussed in chapters 10 and 11, to memory in chapter 12 and to induction in chapter 13. This can be confusing; it would have been nice if each topic could have been dealt with in one place only. If you are confused about what has happened or curious to know what will happen to a topic, consult the index; if I have got it right, the index will tell you the story.

I have permitted myself throughout the useful abbreviation 'iff' for 'if and only if'.

Part I
KNOWLEDGE

1
Scepticism

Scepticism in its most interesting form always depends on an argument; the better the argument, the stronger the scepticism it generates. Since it depends on an argument, it must be able to be expressed as a conclusion. The sceptical conclusion is that knowledge is impossible. No one *does* know, because no one *can* know.

There is a contrast between the sceptic who offers an argument which has this as its conclusion and two other sorts of sceptic. The first is the person who responds to every assertion with the question 'How do you know that?' and then, whatever is offered, merely repeats the question until answers dry up. This repeated question is very successful in reducing others to furious but impotent silence, but there is very little to be learnt from it as it stands until we know what lies behind it. There are of course interesting possibilities here, for instance the following propositions:

1   No one knows that p unless he can say how he knows that p.
2   The attempt to answer the question 'How do you know that p?' by simply reasserting that p cannot be successful. It begs the question.

A sceptic who peddles the question without being willing to make an appeal to propositions such as these is not presenting an interesting philosophical position. Once the appeal is made, however, we are back with a scepticism that depends on an argument. It is worth pointing out in this connection that the two propositions above are dubious. The second, for instance, amounts to an assertion that one cannot answer the question 'How do you know that you are in pain?' by simply saying 'Because I am in pain'. Someone who gives this answer clearly takes it that in some cases it works, and we must not beg the question against him.

The second contrasting sceptic offers not so much an argument or a question but rather an attitude. This sceptic is a hard-nosed person who claims that most people allow themselves to be persuaded by what is really rather weak evidence, but that he needs more than that to convince *him*. This sceptic claims to have higher evidential standards than the rest of us; he stigmatizes others as gullible or as too easily persuaded. His position develops into scepticism proper (i.e. the view that knowledge is impossible rather than merely rarer than one thinks) when the standards are set so high that they cannot be fulfilled. But in order to become philosophically interesting (rather than simply an intellectual freak) he must do more than assert that higher standards of evidence are better. He must have some argument that the normal standards are inappropriate in some way. And that argument must be justified by appeal to our standards as well as his. There is then the danger of incoherence; is it consistent to provide an argument justified by normal standards of evidence, to the effect that those standards are inappropriate?

The conclusion is that with which we started; scepticism in its most interesting form always depends on an argument. In the next section we shall consider three sceptical arguments which are strong enough to be worth taking seriously. First we need to look at some distinctions between types of sceptical argument.

The first and least important distinction is between local and global sceptical arguments. Local scepticism maintains that, even if knowledge is possible elsewhere, it is for special reasons not available in this or that selected area. Favourite areas for local scepticism are ethics, religion and the future. We can know how things are in front of our noses, maybe, but it is not possible to know that an altruistic act is morally good, nor that God exists, nor that you will have eggs for breakfast tomorrow. Obviously local scepticism hopes to feed on special features of the areas it is concerned with. But my experience is that it is very hard to keep one's local scepticism local. A local ethical scepticism, for instance, tends very quickly to spread out and become a general scepticism about the unobserved or about the possibility of scientific knowledge. The problem is to find a convincing argument for local ethical scepticism which has no expansionist tendencies.

If local scepticism tends to collapse into global scepticism, this may be an advantage, since global sceptical arguments are generally more convincing and effective than their local counterparts. And the same is true of the second distinction I want to draw. Some sceptical arguments attack the notion of knowledge directly but leave other related notions, crucially that of justified belief, untouched. Thus I might argue that to know you must be certain, but that one can never be really certain and hence one can never really know. Ignoring for the moment the force of the word 'really' in this argument, we can still feel confident that even if we give up talking of knowledge, granting that a necessary condition for knowing is unfulfilled, we can happily continue to talk about justified belief, distinguishing some beliefs as justified or as more justified than others and others as less justified or even completely unjustified. None of this talk of justification is threatened by the present sceptical argument. We may feel that the argument exposes idiosyncrasies in the concept of knowledge but that we can get by very well both for practical and philosophical purposes with the surviving notion of justified belief. A stronger form of sceptical argument would, however, threaten both notions at once and claim that any defect in the notion of knowledge is equally present in that of justified belief. Such stronger forms are available, as we shall see, and they are always more interesting than their weaker counterparts. The claim that none of our beliefs about the future are ever justified is more important and more interesting than the claim that although our belief that the sun will rise tomorrow is quite probably both true and justified, we cannot really be said to know that the sun will rise tomorrow.

The third distinction is even more important. We can distinguish sceptical arguments which, although they attempt to deprive us of knowledge (or even of justified belief) still allow that we *understand* the propositions whose truth we are no longer allowed to know, from those which claim that the reason why we don't know their truth is that we cannot understand them. An obvious instance would be the contrast between the suggestion that although we understand the proposition that God exists, we could have no evidence that it is true, and the suggestion that the proposition is incomprehensible to us, and hence *a fortiori* we can neither know it to be true nor be justified in believing it.

Of course the distinction drawn above only remains if we assume that it is possible for us to understand a proposition which we would or could never be justified in believing or could never come to know to be true. On a theory of understanding which linked what we can understand with what we could come to recognise as true, the distinction collapses and all the relevant sceptical arguments will be of the strongest type; that is, will claim that we do not even understand the propositions we claim to know.

It might seem that an argument to the effect that we don't understand the propositions we claim to know must be local rather than global. For a global argument would claim that we understand nothing, which is ridiculous first because we clearly do understand something and second because crucially we understand (and are expected to understand) the sceptical argument itself.

1.2 THREE SCEPTICAL ARGUMENTS

Brains in Vats

You do not know that you are not a brain, suspended in a vat full of liquid in a laboratory, and wired to a computer which is feeding you your current experiences under the control of some ingenious technician/scientist (benevolent or malevolent according to taste). For if you were such a brain, then, provided that the scientist is successful, nothing in your experience could possibly reveal that you were; for your experience is *ex hypothesi* identical with that of something which is not a brain in a vat. Since you have only your own experience to appeal to, and that experience is the same in either situation, nothing can reveal to you which situation is the actual one.

Is it possible, however, that though you do not know that you are not a brain in a vat you still know many other things, perhaps more important? Unfortunately if you do not know this there is not much else that you can know either, it seems. Suppose that you claim to know that you are sitting reading a book. You presumably also know that if you are sitting reading, you are not a brain in a vat. We can surely conclude that if you know that you are sitting reading, you know that you are not a brain in a vat, and hence (by simple *modus tollens*) that since you don't know that you are not a brain in a vat (agreed above) you don't know that you are sitting reading.

The principle on which this argument relies can be formalized as the principle of closure under known entailment:

$$PC^k: [Kap \& Ka(p \rightarrow q)] \rightarrow Kaq.$$

This principle asserts that if a knows that p and that implies q, a also knows that q; we always know to be true any propositions we know to be the consequences of a proposition we know. (It is a standard practice to express principles of this sort in logical notation, but for our purposes each logical formula will be followed by its English equivalent, as here. It is worth working through the logical notation, however, for ease of reference later. PC^k is a *closure principle* because it says that a move from something known to something known to be implied by it does not take us outside the closed area of knowledge.) The principle, then, given that a does not know that q ($\sim Kaq$), and that a does know that p implies q ($Ka(p \rightarrow q)$), allows us to infer that a does not know that p ($\sim Kap$). It seems therefore to show, more generally, that since you don't know that you are not a brain in a vat you cannot know any proposition p of which you know that if p were true, you would not be a brain in a vat. And there are similar slightly different arguments, for instance Descartes' version which takes q = you are dreaming and argues that since you don't know that you are not dreaming you don't know any proposition p of which you know that if p were true you would not be dreaming (see the first *Meditation* in Descartes, 1955).

How should we map this argument using the distinctions of 1.1? It is not entirely global; it admits that knowledge is possible, e.g. that you can know that $p \rightarrow q$, and indeed uses this fact as a lever. In fact its grip is restricted entirely to those propositions whose truth would mean that you were not a brain in a vat. It is however a strong argument in the sense that it aims to attack the notion of justified belief in just those areas where it attacks the notion of knowledge. This has not been shown yet, but it can be shown by running a complete analogue of the argument. All we need is to show that your belief that you are not a brain in a vat cannot be justified since nothing in your experience can count as evidence for that proposition, and then appeal to an analogue of PC^k:

PC^j: $[JBap \ \& \ JBa(p \rightarrow q)] \rightarrow JBaq$

which holds that if a is justified in believing that p and that p implies q, a is justified in believing that q. PC^j seems just as convincing as PC^k, if not more so.

However the argument does nothing to suggest that you do not understand the proposition that you are sitting reading a book. You are still allowed to understand it even if you can neither know it nor be justified in believing it. The argument only turns into an argument about understanding if we take a special view about understanding, as mentioned earlier.

The Argument from Error

You have sometimes made mistakes even in areas where you felt most confident; simple mistakes in arithmetic, for example. But nothing you can point to in your present situation tells you that this situation is not one in which you are mistaken. For all you can tell, it is relevantly similar to situations in which you have made mistakes. Since you clearly did not know then, how can you say that you know now? For all you can tell, the new situation is no better than the old.

This argument relies on an epistemological version of the principle of universalizability familiar in ethical theory (cf. Hare, 1963, pp. 7 – 16). A judgement that an action is morally good is universalizable in the sense that by making such a judgement one commits oneself to holding that any relevantly similar action is morally good. When a new and relevantly similar action occurs, one must either call it good or take back one's judgement that the first one was good. What makes a new action relevantly similar to an old one? An action is relevantly similar if it too has the properties which constituted one's reasons for the judgement in the first case. Being relevantly similar is not the same, then, as being completely indistinguishable. There is at least this restriction on the properties that count here, that they must be properties whose presence or absence can be registered by the person making the judgement. A difference between the two actions which that person is unable to recognize cannot justify a difference in judgement. The principle of universalizability tells us, then, that in the absence of an available difference we must make the same judgement again. There must be something we can pick out if a difference in judgement is to be justified.

There may perhaps be properties which are evidence-transcendent, by which we mean that it is always possible that they be absent even though we have the best possible evidence of their presence. Goodness is such a property, perhaps; and this is why the principle of universalizability has teeth in ethics. We cannot suppose that one action is good and another not good unless we can pick out a further relevant difference between them.

The argument from error exposes the consequences of this approach for epistemology. Suppose that I claimed yesterday to know that it would rain in the afternoon, on the normal grounds (weather forecast, gathering clouds, etc.), but that it turns out that I was wrong. At the time of my claim the fact that it was not going to rain was evidence-transcendent, as all claims about the future must be. And this means that if on the same grounds I claim today to know that it will rain in the afternoon, I must continue to assert that I knew yesterday that it would rain that afternoon (in the teeth of the evidence). If, on the other hand, I abandon my claim to have known yesterday, I cannot make the claim to know today. For the only fact which would justify such a difference in claim is one which is not available to me; facts about the afternoon's weather are evidence-transcendent in the morning. Hence my acceptance that yesterday I did not know prevents me from claiming knowledge today.

We can run through the argument again from the point of view of an outside observer. There is the possibility that though *I myself* would not be justified in making different claims, another person might perhaps be justified in saying that yesterday I did not know, while today I do. This might be so after today's rain, for instance, when the facts about the rain have ceased to be evidence-transcendent to all. Although I couldn't tell the difference at the time, I was in fact wrong yesterday and right today, and this is sufficient to ground a difference in the outside observer's description of me as knowing today but not knowing yesterday. But it is easy to see what the sceptic will say at this point, quite apart from the implied oddity that there is a claim which I could not be justified in making but which another can be justified in making for me. For what is being suggested is that I knew today and not yesterday, despite the fact that there was no difference between the two days that I could tell at the time. But this shows that today, for all I knew, it was not going to rain, and how can we allow that I know that it will rain when for all I know it won't?

The conclusion seems to be that if I recognize that I have once wrongly claimed to know that *p*, then I cannot ever claim to know that *p* unless I can show a relevant difference between the two cases. And no one else can say of me that I know in one case and not in the other, because for all I know I am wrong both times.

So far, however, we have restricted the argument unnecessarily to cases where I have in fact made mistakes in the past. But we do not need to rely on actual mistakes in the past. For our purposes, possible mistakes will do just as well. This can be seen in the ethical case. An imaginary example can be so described that I am willing to say that the action it recounts is good. And that judgement of mine is as much universalizable, as binding on my future judgements about relevantly similar cases, as if the example had been real rather than merely imaginary. Similarly, an imaginary case in which I would claim to know that p, but where p is false, will succeed in preventing me from claiming to know that p in a new case which is not relevantly (i.e., discernibly to me) different. So imaginary cases are as effective in the argument as actual ones.

It was of course a hallmark of our first sceptical argument that it started from an imaginary case in which you are a brain in a vat, which is not discernibly different from your present case. So the argument we have now reached seems to be a complex defence of the first part of that first sceptical argument. It seems to show that the imaginary case in which you are a brain in a vat being fed the experiences of reading a book is perfectly effective in showing that you do not know that you are reading a book. The difference between the two arguments seems to be in the route they pursue thereafter. The first uses PC^k to show that you don't know anything of which you know that if it were true you would not be a brain in a vat. The second argues more generally that since we have made mistakes, or would make them in imaginarily similar circumstances, we do not know now.

How strong is the scepticism which the argument from error would create if successful? If, as I shall argue in 4.2, there is no separable area in which we make no mistakes, then the argument from error will be global rather than local. But it is not immediately obvious how to write a similar argument against the notion of justified belief. We cannot argue straightforwardly that a false belief cannot be justified. So unless we can say, as we said above for knowledge, that you cannot claim your belief is justified unless you can tell the difference between cases where such beliefs are true and cases where they are false, it will be impossible to conclude that your true belief here is unjustified.

Perhaps, however, we can make this claim by appeal to the initial moves of the argument that you are not justified in believing that you are not a brain in a vat. There we claimed that if nothing in your experience could count as evidence that you were not a brain in a vat, your belief that you are not a brain in a vat cannot be called justified. The belief is unjustified because nothing that you can point to suggests that you are rather than are not a brain in a vat. And equally in our new case we can say that your belief is unjustified because nothing you can point to suggests that this is a case where your belief is true rather than one of the (admittedly rarer but still) indistinguishable (to you) cases where it is false. If this move is sound, our second sceptical argument attacks the notion of justified belief at least as much as the first argument does; in fact even more, because it is more global.

We must allow, too, that this argument as it stands leaves our understanding untouched. As before, unless we have a theory of understanding which links the possibility of understanding with the availability of justified belief, or of knowledge, our understanding survives the loss of justified belief. Such a theory might claim, for instance, that to understand a proposition is to be able to tell the difference between circumstances in which one would be justified in believing it and those in which one would not. There are such theories; more on them below.

The Justification of Arguments from Experience

Do we have any knowledge of events which we have not experienced or are not now experiencing? We normally suppose that our experience is a reliable guide to the nature of those parts of the world which we are not observing, and that in favourable cases it gives us knowledge. Thus I can know what is in the bottom drawer of my desk, or what I shall eat for breakfast tomorrow, by some form of inductive inference from what I have observed or am now observing. David Hume (1711 – 76), the Scottish historian and philosopher, raised in a special way the question of whether this is really so (Hume, 1955, ch. 4.2). He argued that I cannot know that my diary is in the (closed) bottom drawer of my desk unless I have reason to believe that my experience makes that proposition probable; we can suppose, perhaps, that my relevant experience is that I remember having put the diary there five minutes ago and that I do not remember having touched the drawer since, together with my general knowledge of the consistent behaviour of the experienced world. But I only have reason to believe that my experience makes that proposition probable if I have reason to believe quite generally that events which I have not observed are similar to events which I have observed. And Hume's point is that it is impossible to have any reason for that last belief. For that belief is not analytically or necessarily true; no contradiction is implied by supposing it false. And I cannot suppose that experience itself has given me reason to believe that the unobserved will resemble the observed, since the appeal to experience begs the question asked; it argues not *to* but *from* the crucial belief that our experience is a reliable guide, or that the unobserved will resemble the observed. Therefore I can have no reason to believe that my experience is a reliable guide, and hence have no reason for any belief about events beyond my experience and so cannot have knowledge of them.

It is worth stressing that Hume's argument does not attempt to derive a sceptical conclusion from the fact that I might be wrong (as in a way the first argument does) nor from the fact that I have been wrong (as the second argument does). Instead, he maintains that our general belief that experience is a reliable guide cannot be justified, since all promising justifications assume what is at issue by supposing that experience can reveal that our experience is a reliable guide. There is an obvious weakness in this attempt to use an argument from experience to justify all arguments from experience.

The scepticism which Hume's argument creates is not global, since it concerns only our knowledge of the unobserved. The argument clearly attacks the notion of justified belief as well as that of knowledge in that restricted area, since it maintains that we have no reason in what is observed for any beliefs about the unobserved. It leaves the notion of understanding untouched; Hume seems to agree that we understand propositions about unobserved objects, although he does argue on independent grounds that they are mostly false.

<h3 style="text-align:center">1.3 A SHORT WAY WITH THE SCEPTIC</h3>

None of the three arguments mentioned above is of the strongest type, since none attacks our notion of understanding. There are local sceptical arguments of this strongest type, as we shall see in chapter 5 (our knowledge of other minds); and in our discussion of our knowledge of the past and of the future (chapters 10 and 11) we shall have to bear in mind arguments that it is impossible to conceive of an event as other than present, i.e. as being in the past or in the future. But we might suppose it impossible to provide an effective global argument of this type. It is not just that we clearly do understand *something*; rather we know in advance that it is only by understanding the sceptic's argument as we are clearly expected to, that we could be led to believe that we understand nothing. And even if we don't understand the argument, we surely understand the conclusion; and so the conclusion must be false.

This short way with the global argument can be copied with any global sceptical argument, whether it attacks knowledge alone or justified belief as well. Thus we might say that the sceptic implicitly claims to know his conclusion that knowledge is impossible, or that he claims that his premises justify his belief that justified belief is impossible. The former suggestion seems unconvincing, but the latter is quite effective. What is the point of arguing that justified belief is impossible, for if you were right there could be no reasons for your conclusion?

These defences against the sceptic attempt to avoid detailed examination of the arguments put forward and focus instead merely on the conclusion. They do this in one of two ways. Either they dispute the sceptic's right to assert the conclusion, or to assert it as a conclusion; or they suggest directly that the conclusion cannot be true, and that hence they are excused from considering any suggested reason for believing it. Instances of the first sort have already been mentioned. An instance of the second sort could be derived from the claim that to understand this or any proposition is to know under which conditions it is true and under which it is false. If the sceptic's conclusion were true we could not have such knowledge; so if the conclusion were true we would not be able to understand it. It is impossible for us to understand the conclusion, then, without realizing that it is false. It is clear, I think, that this argument would, if successful, turn the argument against a global scepticism about understanding into an argument against a weaker but still global scepticism about knowledge. Since we do understand what the sceptic is saying, we must have the sort of knowledge required for that understanding.

In my opinion the sceptic should be entirely unworried by such arguments. He should insist that they provide no justification whatever for an unwillingness to consider his arguments seriously for what they are. To take the weakest case first; even if the sceptic were unwise enough to admit that any assertion involves a claim to knowledge and that he is asserting his conclusion that knowledge is impossible, he can still maintain his position. He takes himself to have true premises and a valid inference to a true conclusion; the premises might include the proposition that in the past he has made mistakes. He may admit (unwisely again) that in using that proposition as a premise he is implicitly claiming to know it to be true. But he insists that it follows from it and others of the same kind that knowledge is impossible. His argument then can be rewritten as follows: if I know this − and this is a central case of the sort of thing I know if I know anything − then I know that knowledge is impossible, and so if I know anything I know nothing. This argument can be seen in two ways. Either it is an instance of a proof by *reductio ad absurdum*, in which we assume something true in order to prove it false; or it is a way of exposing a paradox within the concept of knowledge, for the sceptic can surely insist that if a central concept such as that of knowledge can be used to take us validly from true premises to a false or impossible conclusion, something is wrong with the concept; there is probably some internal tension which should be exposed rather than swept under the carpet. An answer which merely consists in pointing out the falsehood or impossibility of the conclusion must, therefore, be missing the point.

1.4 ANOTHER REPLY

One common reply to the first two sceptical arguments is to say that we have no reason to worry ourselves about them. Since it is admitted, or rather insisted, that as far as you are concerned there could be no difference between the hypothesis that you are currently sitting reading and the hypothesis that you are a brain in a vat being fed the experiences of one sitting reading, then it cannot matter to you which is really true and which is false. Nothing of any genuine interest or importance can depend on whether you are a brain in a vat or not.

This reply comes in a stronger and a weaker form, but in either form it has clearly got some point. It maintains that what the sceptic takes to be his strength is in fact his weakness. The sceptic insists that there is a difference between the two hypotheses, but that it is evidence-transcendent, i.e. that it is a difference which you cannot tell; and he concludes from this that you don't know which situation you are really in. The reply admits that the difference is evidence-transcendent, and uses that fact against the sceptic. But that fact can be used in two ways.

The weaker way is to say simply that although there is a radical and obvious difference between the two hypotheses, it is not one which could make any difference to you, and so that you can be exempted from paying any attention to it. This is rather like an attitude one might take to the philosophical discussions about whether we have free will or not. One might attempt to reject that entire discussion on the grounds that whether we have free will or not can make no difference to the way we live our lives. We act and will continue to act as if we have free will, whether our actions are determined or not. There seems to me to be something very wrong-headed about this move, both in the areas of free will and of scepticism. But we need not pause to examine its defects, since there is a stronger and more interesting move with which it may be confused.

The sceptic says that there is a difference between the two hypotheses but that you cannot tell it since it is evidence-transcendent. Our weaker move admitted this, but the stronger move denies it. The stronger position denies the existence of evidence-transcendent truth and evidence-transcendent differences, and so denies the sceptic the contrast he needs between his two hypotheses. If the difference suggested is one which *could* make no difference to us, then it is empty and does not exist.

The weaker move, then, says that there is a difference which does not matter. The stronger move says that there is no difference to matter. We could call the former a *realist* position; the realist believes that there are evidence-transcendent truths, truths whose obtaining lies beyond our powers of recognition. The stronger move could be called *anti-realist*; it denies the existence of evidence-transcendent truth and holds that differences which we are in principle incapable of recognizing do not exist.

Anti-realism of this sort does not arise gratuitously, nor is it intended initially as a method of countering scepticism. But its general thrust is clear. The realist and the sceptic think of the world as one on which we have at best a tentative grasp. There are many facts about the remote past and the remote future which we shall have no means ever of recognizing or verifying. And it is always possible that unknown to us the present world differs radically from the way it appears to us. The anti-realist does not believe in the existence of this further 'real' world which lies behind the world that we know and which may come apart from our world in ways which of course we could not recognize if they occurred. For him our world, the recognizable world, is the only world. So for the anti-realist the enterprise of epistemology is easier, since the objects of knowledge are brought closer to us; and there is no yawning gap between evidence and truth, since there can be no evidence-transcendent properties. For the question whether a property is present here can never be different from or lie beyond the question whether we have the best possible evidence that it is present.

Anti-realism is the theory of understanding which has been mentioned at various points in this chapter. (Its name and recent development are owed to Michael Dummett.) The anti-realist holds that our understanding of the sentences in our language must have been acquired in situations which we learnt to take as warranting the use of those sentences; situations in which those sentences are to count as true. It follows from this that if there is no such thing as justified belief, there is no such thing as understanding. For to understand a sentence is to be able to pick out situations which justify us in believing that sentence to be true.

It might seem, then, that the anti-realist is in a peculiarly weak position. Every sceptical argument against the possibility of justified belief is an argument of the strongest form, and leaves us devoid even of the understanding we thought we had of our own language. But in fact the reverse is true. The sceptical arguments which would have this effect all require a move which the anti-realist would disallow, and hence never reach the annihilating conclusion. They all require us to make sense of the realist thought that it is always possible that, unknown to us, the world differs radically from the way it appears to us, and argue from this that we cannot know that the world really is the way it appears to us. But the anti-realist rejects this as impossible. For him, the sense of a sentence is determined by the sorts of situation we count in favour of the sentence being true, in such a way that the sentence with that sense (i.e. as we understand it) cannot be false if the sort of situation we count as making it true occurs. So anti-realism offers a perspective from which not only is there no possibility of a global scepticism about understanding, but also (and for the same reasons) there is no room for a global scepticism about justified belief either.

The trouble here is that the implausibility of the truth of scepticism is about as great as the implausibility of the truth of anti-realism. To see this, we need to see how much anti-realism requires us to give up and how strong our realist intuitions are.

One area which seems to demand a realist approach is that of other minds, which will be discussed in chapter 5. Our realist intuition here is that the sensations and thoughts of others, which do occur, are hidden from us. We observe their behaviour, of course, but the question whether they are actually experiencing sensations as we suppose is, for us, evidence-transcendent. It is always possible that despite all the behaviour there are actually no sensations going on there at all, or at least different ones from those we imagine. So there is a real question whether or not there are sensations which are not ours, but it is evidence-transcendent.

Another is that of the past. Whatever we may think of the future, we think of the past as having been in its time as determinate as the present now is. But we suppose that there are many propositions about the past whose truth is for us evidence-transcendent. Despite our lack of grip on these truths, we do take there to be a transcendent fact of the matter at stake, one that lies now beyond all possibilities of being recognized by us. And this attitude about the past is a realist attitude.

These two areas will be considered in greater detail in later chapters. The point of our discussion of them so far is that the attempt to rebut scepticism by constructing an anti-realist alternative to the realism espoused by the sceptic is not going to be easy, even if it is possible. If there are some areas where anti-realism is comparatively easy to accept, well and good. But so long as there remain others where realism seems compelling, in those the sceptic's challenge bites. We may be unable to buy our way generally out of scepticism in the anti-realist market; the cost would be too high.

1.5 A BETTER RESPONSE

If no short way with the sceptic is possible, we have no alternative but to get involved directly with the arguments presented. Where might we look for help in a critical offensive? One hope might be that a satisfactory account of what knowledge is would have the effect of exposing errors in the sceptic's reasoning. And I shall be considering an account which claims to do this in chapter 3.

Meanwhile we should perhaps consider what state we would be in, were we to agree that the sceptic's argument is effective. It has sometimes been suggested that epistemology could survive the loss of the concept of knowledge, because all the important epistemological questions can equally profitably be rephrased using instead the concept of justified belief. Thus instead of asking whether we ever know what will happen in the future, we ask in which if any circumstances our beliefs about the future are justified. And the problem of other minds (ch. 5) can be presented as the problem of how, if at all, my observation of the behaviour of human bodies justifies my belief that those bodies are people; little extra is gained by asking whether and how I *know* that they are people.

The difficulty with this suggestion is that all the sceptical arguments presented, and indeed any interesting sceptical argument, seem to be directed as much against the notion of justified belief as against that of knowledge. And this means that the easy compromise position is unavailable. It really does seem to matter for epistemology that we find some reply to the sceptic.

FURTHER READING

Descartes' dreaming argument is in the first of his *Meditations*; use the Haldane and Ross edition (Descartes, 1955) or any reputable alternative.

Hume's questions about induction are raised in his *Inquiry Concerning Human Understanding*, section 4, part 2 (Hume, 1955; or any reputable alternative).

Stroud (1984, ch. 1) offers a very readable account of Cartesian (i.e., Descartes') scepticism.

The argument about brains in vats is given in Nozick (1981, pp. 167 – 71). His account will be examined further in ch. 3.

Stroud (1968) gives a helpful account of the anti-sceptical move considered in 1.3, commonly called transcendental. He links it to verificationism (the 'verification principle'), an earlier form of anti-realism.

Dummett, architect of anti-realism as successor to verificationism, offers the most introductory account I know in Dummett (1978, ch. 10) but if you are new to this area you would do better to wait until you have read ch. 9 of the present book before attempting it.

2
Knowledge

2.1 THE TRADITIONAL ACCOUNT

The standard account of knowledge, around which all recent work has been done, defines knowledge as justified true belief; it holds that a knows that p if and only if

1 p,
2 a believes that p,
3 a's belief that p is justified.

Because there are three parts to this definition it is called the tripartite definition or the tripartite account; it defines propositional knowledge, knowledge that p; it does not define knowledge by acquaintance as in 'a knows James' nor knowledge-how, e.g. knowledge how to ride a bicycle, unless these can be shown to reduce to knowledge-that.

The tripartite definition has obvious attractions. The first clause, that if a knows that p then p is true (which can be read as $Kap \rightarrow p$), is normally seen as stipulative. The second clause, that if a knows that p then a believes that p (we can read this as $Kap \rightarrow Bap$), seems minimal, and the third, that if a knows that p then his belief that p is justified ($Kap \rightarrow JBap$), is there in order to prevent any lucky guess from counting as knowledge if the guesser is sufficiently confident to believe his own guess. It is worth noticing, however, a consequence of this justification of clause 3; this is that a belief is not generally considered to be justified by the mere fact that it is true, for otherwise clause 3 would be unnecessary. If I decide on the toss of a coin which investment will provide the greatest yield, and fortunately turn out to be right, we suppose that my choice is vindicated by the outcome perhaps, but not justified by it; I had no real justification for making the choice I did. (Alternatively we could distinguish between two forms of justification, justification before the event and justification after it, and run the tripartite definition in terms of the former; but then the question would be whether these really are two forms of the same thing.)

What are the problems for the tripartite definition? One might think that clause 2 is insufficient: to believe that p is not so strong as to be certain that p, and to know one must be certain, not just believe.

The best reason for wanting some account of certainty in our analysis of knowledge is that people are rightly hesitant to *claim* knowledge when they are less than certain. This hesitation seems to be due to something about what knowledge is, and there is no obvious way to explain it if knowledge is as the tripartite conception claims it to be. Thus although it is commonly suggested that the notion of certainty is relevant to the analysis of *claims* to knowledge, but not to the analysis of knowledge itself (e.g., in Woozley, 1953), this leaves us with no method of explaining why certainty should be required before one can claim knowledge when it is not required for knowledge itself, i.e., for the existence of what one is claiming.

Since we are going to discover other reasons for rejecting the tripartite definition, we have no reason to pursue this point here. The moral to be drawn is that if we are to give an account of knowledge which does not include a requirement of certainty, our account should make room for the notion of certainty somewhere; if it sees certainty as a requirement for a knowledge claim it needs to be able to explain in its own terms why that should be so.

But why should we be reluctant simply to change clause 2 to '*a* is certain that p'? The answer is that we are prepared, in circumstances that are not particularly unusual, to allow that someone does in fact have knowledge when that person is so far from certain that he would not claim the knowledge himself. The classic example offered is that of the diffident schoolboy, who has learnt the dates of, say, the English kings the previous night but who is so alarmed by his hectoring schoolteacher that he becomes completely unsure that the answers that suggest themselves to him under questioning are in fact the right ones. Supposing, however, that those answers are correct, would we not allow that he knows them, even though he himself might not make that claim? And surely our reasons for allowing this are close to those suggested by the tripartite definition; he has the right answer, and not by luck.

There is a weakness in this appeal to the diffident schoolboy, which concerns clause 2 again. To the extent that the schoolboy is less than certain of the answers that occur to him, can we allow that he still believes them? If we are not careful, use of this example to defuse the pretensions of a certainty condition will result in our losing the belief condition we were trying to defend.

2.2 GETTIER COUNTER-EXAMPLES

Henry is watching the television on a June afternoon. It is Wimbledon men's finals day, and the television shows McEnroe beating Connors; the score is two sets to none and match point to McEnroe in the third. McEnroe wins the point. Henry believes justifiably that

1 I have just seen McEnroe win this year's Wimbledon final.

and reasonably infers that

2 McEnroe is this year's Wimbledon champion.

Actually, however, the cameras at Wimbledon have ceased to function, and the television is showing a recording of last year's match. But while it does so McEnroe is in the process of repeating last year's slaughter. So Henry's belief 2 is true, and surely he is justified in believing 2. But we would hardly allow that Henry knows 2.

This sort of counter-example to the tripartite account of knowledge is known as a Gettier counter-example, after E. L. Gettier (1963). (I owe this particular example to Brian Garrett.) Gettier argued that they show the tripartite account to be insufficient; it is possible for someone not to know even when all the three clauses are satisfied.

Gettier here is not quarrelling with any of the three clauses. He allows that they are individually necessary, and argues only that they need supplementing.

It is worth formalising the situation, for reasons which will emerge later. Reading 1 as p and 2 as q, we have:

$\sim p$, Bap, JBap, $p \rightarrow q$, JB$a(p \rightarrow q)$, q, Baq, JBaq.

So a Gettier counter-example is one in which a has a justified but false belief by inference from which he justifiably believes something which happens to be true, and so arrives at a justified true belief which is not knowledge.

What response should be made to these infamous but slightly irritating counter-examples? There seem to be three possible routes:

1 find some means to show that the counter-examples do not work;
2 accept the counter-examples and search for a supplement to the tripartite analysis which excludes them;
3 accept the counter-examples and alter the tripartite analysis to suit rather than adding anything to it.

The remainder of this section is concerned with the first route.

On what principles of inference do these counter-examples rely? Gettier himself exposes two. For the examples to work, it must be possible for a false belief still to be justified; and a justified belief must justify any belief which it implies (or is justifiably believed to imply). This last is just the principle of closure PC^j mentioned above in the discussion of scepticism (1.2). So if we could show PC^j false this would have the double effect of undermining the Gettier counter-examples and (part at least of) the first sceptical argument. It might be possible, however, to construct new variants on the Gettier theme which do not rely on inference or on an inference of this sort, as we shall see in the next section, and if so no complaints about PC^j or other principles will be very effective.

One thing we cannot do is to reject Gettier counter-examples as contrived and artificial. They are perfectly effective in their own terms. But we might reasonably wonder what point there is in racking our brains to find an acceptable definition of 'a knows that p'. Is this more than a mere technical exercise? What, if anything, should disconcert us if we cannot come up with a trouble-free definition? Many of the innumerable papers written in response to Gettier give the impression that responding to Gettier is a kind of private philosophical game, which is of no interest except to the players. And hasn't Wittgenstein shown us anyway that a concept can be perfectly healthy without being definable, arguing that there need be no element common to all instances of a property (e.g. instances of knowledge) other than that they are instances (e.g. that they are knowledge)? (Cf. Wittgenstein, 1969b, pp. 17 – 18, and 1953, §§ 66 – 7.) So what on earth could depend on our success or failure to discover necessary and sufficient conditions for knowledge?

In many ways I sympathize with the general tenor of this

complaint, as may quickly become apparent. What sustains me in the search for a response to Gettier is the feeling that it may be possible to find an account of what knowledge is which will have a substantial effect on what we are to say about justification in later parts of this book. This could happen in either or both of two ways. We might find an account of what knowledge is which would suffice to undermine crucial sceptical moves, and hence confirm the possibility that some of our beliefs are justified; the account to which I give tentative support in chapter 3 has pretensions in this direction. Or we might hope to define justification in terms of knowledge. For instance, we might suppose that a belief is justified iff in certain circumstances (to be spelled out) it would be knowledge. (Jennifer Hornsby gave me this idea.) In the meantime we must consider some accounts of knowledge which seem less fruitful.

2.3 RESPONSES TO GETTIER

I rather obviously avoided, so far as I could, offering even the most tentative diagnosis of the defect in the tripartite analysis which Gettier exposed. This is because the different responses to Gettier all stem from different diagnoses of the way in which the tripartite analysis is lacking; once we know what is missing, it should be quite a simple matter to add it.

The Presence of Relevant Falsehood

The most obvious diagnosis is simply that the initial belief that p, from which the true justified belief that q is inferred, is false. So we might add to the tripartite analysis the fourth condition that nothing can be known which is inferred from a false belief, or from a group of beliefs of which one is false.

This simple suggestion has two defects. First, variants on the Gettier theme can be written in which, though there is falsehood, there is no inference. Suppose that I believe that there is a sheep in the next field because of what I see. I am not inferring from what I see that there is a sheep in the field; I take myself simply to see that there is one. The animal I see is a large furry dog, but my belief is not false, because there is a sheep there too, unknown to me, hidden by the hedge. Here we might admit that my belief is true and justified but refuse to grant that I know there to be a sheep in the field. (This example comes from Chisholm, 1977, p. 105.)

A reply might be that surely I am inferring that I see a sheep in the field from my knowledge of my own present sensory states. This reply raises large issues; but chapter 5 contains a lengthy argument that if there is any non-inferential knowledge, some of it concerns things other than our sensory states — so why not sheep, for instance?

The second defect is that the suggestion is too strong and is likely to make it impossible for any of us to know anything at all. As we shall see, this is a danger with a number of responses to Gettier. In the present case, we all of us suffer from numerous false beliefs which have some role in our inferential processes, and so on this suggestion none of our present true justified beliefs would count as knowledge.

To eliminate these defects we must remove the reference to inference and tighten up the relation specified between the false beliefs and the true justified ones which are not to count as knowledge. Thus we could simply require an absence of relevant falsehood. This would get round the example of the sheep in the field because I presumably believe (falsely) that the animal I can see is a sheep even though this belief is not used in inference. But as a suggestion it seems rather to name the difficulty than to solve it: which false beliefs are to be counted as relevant?

An answer might be that a false belief that p is relevant in the required sense if, had the believer believed instead that $\sim p$, his belief that q would cease to have been justified. Not all false beliefs are relevant in this sense. Some will be so distant or insignificant that whether one believes them or their opposite would have no effect on what one believes here. For instance, among the beliefs in virtue of which I claim to know that Napoleon was a great soldier there may be one which is false, but which is so insignificant that my justification for believing that Napoleon was a great soldier would survive my changing my mind on that particular point. Such a false belief would not be relevant in our present sense.

But the new account faces difficulties, which can best be illustrated by an example. Suppose that I expect a colleague to give me a lift home this evening, but that her car has a flat battery; this won't stop us, however, because a friend's car is parked conveniently near with some jump leads which we can use to get her car to start. I now believe that she will give me a lift this evening, and this belief is justified. Do I know that she will give me a lift? The requirement that there be no relevant false beliefs suggests plausibly that whether I know depends on what other beliefs I have. But this suggestion raises difficulties. If, for instance, I merely believe

1 she will give me a lift home this evening,

I may be allowed to know this, but if I believe both 1 and

2 her car battery is not flat,

I may not, since I have a relevant false belief. But if, as well as believing 1 and 2, I happen also to believe

3 there is a friend's car conveniently near with jump leads,

then this apparently gratuitous belief makes it the case again that I know that I will be given a lift. For if I had believed the opposite of 2, my belief 1 would not be justified unless I also believe something like 3. It seems then that our present suggestion has the effect that whether I have knowledge will depend commonly on which other apparently gratuitous beliefs I may have. There is something unsatisfactory about this, and more work needs to be done to defend the account against complaints of this sort.

Defeasibility

A slightly different approach diagnoses the Gettier counter-examples as arising because there are some truths which would have destroyed the believer's justification had he believed them (cf. Lehrer and Paxson, 1969; Swain, 1974). Thus, for instance, suppose that Henry had believed that he was watching a recording of last year's final, as he was; in that case, his justification for his belief that p and thus by PC^j for his belief that q would have been destroyed. The suggestion then is that a fourth clause be added requiring that there be no other truth such that Henry's believing it would have destroyed his justification for believing that q. This is the defeasibility suggestion; we require for knowledge that the justification be indefeasible, i.e. that the addition of further truths should not defeat it.

This will not imply that a false belief will never be justified, since the suggestion is that although some beliefs are defeasibly justified, we require indefeasible justification for knowledge. However, it is in danger of rendering the first condition for knowledge ($Kap \rightarrow p$) redundant. It looks as if a false belief could never be indefeasibly justified since there would always be some truth (even if only the negation of the false belief) whose addition would destroy the justification. But perhaps this is a strength in the theory rather than a weakness, since the new quadripartite analysis will have a coherence that was previously lacking; it provides an explanation in the fourth clause of what was before included by mere stipulation, that knowledge requires truth.

The defeasibility suggestion could be said to provide an extension of the earlier requirement that there be no relevant falsehoods; we now look beyond those propositions actually believed by the believer to propositions which would have an effect if they were believed. But this extension is no real advantage. The sort of difficulty facing the notion of defeasibility can again best be illustrated by an example. Thus, perhaps, I believe that my children are at present playing in the garden at home, and I have good reasons for this belief. However, unknown to me, a neighbour rang up after I left home this morning to invite the children round for the morning. And if I had known this my justification for believing that they are playing at home would be defeated, because I also believe that they normally accept such invitations. However, my wife has become concerned about the health of one of them and refused the invitation. Do I know that my children are playing in the garden at home? If your intuition is that I do, you must reject the defeasibility criterion as formulated at present. If it is that I do not, on the grounds that had I heard about the invitation my justification would have been defeated, you have a duty to give some account of why the (unknown to me) truth that my wife has refused the invitation does not somehow redress the balance. Either way the defeasibility proposal needs to be altered.

The problem seems to lie, as it lay for the requirement that there be no relevant falsehood, in the way in which new true beliefs can be added piecemeal and overturn the existing justification, while there remain yet further truths waiting in the background to overturn the overturning. First we want to ask anyway whether there isn't likely always to be some truth which, if it alone were added and all others excluded, would defeat my justification. Even if this won't always happen, it will certainly happen often enough for the range of my knowledge to be considerably reduced, and this itself is some sort of an objection. Second, we need to find a way to counter the way in which the piecemeal addition of further truths seems to switch me into knowledge and out again.

We might achieve the second task by altering our account of defeasibility so that instead of talking about some one other truth (which caused the problem of piecemeal addition) we talk about all truths whatever. Thus we could require as our fourth condition that our justification would remain even when every truth is added to our belief set, all at once. This new notion of defeasibility seems to allow (probably) that I now know that my children are playing in the garden, because the second added truth negates the defeating powers of the first. But there remain problems for this new notion of defeasibility. First, in talking of adding all truths at once we seem to have moved firmly into the realm of fiction. Indeed, do we have any suitable conception of 'all the truths'? Second, it seems on this criterion that we shall never have more than the slenderest of reasons to believe that we know something; for in believing this we are believing that when all the truths are in, our justification will remain, and it looks as if much more is required to support that belief than is required to support an ordinary claim to know.

Reliability

A different approach diverts our attention away from the relation between the proposition claimed as knowledge and other false beliefs which should have been true or other truths which should have been believed. It is sometimes suggested that a justified true belief can be knowledge when it derives from a reliable method (see Goldman, 1976; Armstrong, 1973, ch. 13; Swain, 1981). In the Gettier example, Henry does know that the Wimbledon final is being played that afternoon; this justified true belief derives from the reliable method of reading the newspapers, which are normally right about this sort of thing. However, his belief that q clearly derives from a method that is less than reliable. It would have led him badly astray here, had McEnroe suffered an unexpected lapse and succumbed to the efforts of Connors for once.

The reliability approach can be made more elaborate; in some ways it is closely related to the causal approach considered next, because we are clearly owed an account of what reliability is, and a causal answer is tempting (see, e.g., Goldman, 1979). However, we can already see difficulties for any variation on this approach. It is in danger either of making knowledge impossible or of walking straight into one of our sceptical arguments.

We may mean by 'reliable' that a suitable method, if properly followed, is perfectly reliable and never leads to a false belief. But, quite apart from the general difficulty of distinguishing between a defect in the method and a defect in the manner in which the method has been applied, it seems improbable that there are any perfectly reliable methods of acquiring beliefs. Man is fallible, and his fallibility is shown not just in the manner in which the methods are used but in the belief-gathering methods available to him. Hence if knowledge requires an infallible or perfectly reliable method, it is impossible.

But if we retreat from the notion of perfect reliability and require only that the method be generally reliable, we invite sceptical arguments of our second type. How is it that a method which has failed elsewhere in relevantly similar circumstances suffices to yield knowledge this time? If we had any hope that our eventual account of knowledge would help us to reject the sceptical arguments, this particular account seems to make matters worse rather than better. Of course this won't show that the account is wrong. It may be that the correct account of knowledge does unfortunately give the sceptic the opening he is looking for. But we should not accept that this is how things are until we are convinced that there is no other account of knowledge which offers the sceptic less leverage. We can still hope for one which makes life harder rather than easier for him.

A final retreat would be to require only that the method be reliable *this* time. This has the effect of diverting our attention away from previous cases where the method has failed and hence of escaping the sceptical argument which takes its start from those cases. But we might reasonably doubt whether the requirement that the method be reliable this time amounts to any genuine addition to the tripartite account. If reliability is defined in terms of the production of truth, it adds nothing to the first condition once we restrict our attention to the particular case. If it is defined in terms of justification, it adds nothing to the third. And no other accounts seem very inviting. (It may be, however, that the causal theory amounts to a notion of justification in the particular case; see 2.4)

Conclusive Reasons

A different approach diagnoses Henry's failing in the Gettier case as due to the fact that his reasons were less than conclusive. If we require for knowledge that the justified true belief be based on conclusive reasons, all the Gettier cases, and indeed any case in which the believer is right by accident, fall to the ground.

All the work in this approach must go into a persuasive account of what it is for reasons to be conclusive. One suggestion would be that where beliefs A – M constitute conclusive reasons for belief N, A – M could not be true if N is false. This will exclude the counter-examples, but it will also make knowledge a rare phenomenon at best. Empirical knowledge, anyway, looks impossible now; in the empirical realm, our reasons are never conclusive in this sense.

A weaker account, owed to F. Dretske (1971), suggests that someone's reasons A – M for a belief N are conclusive iff A – M would not be true if N is false. This is weaker because to say that A – M *would* not be true if N is false is not to say that they *could* not be true if N is false, as the stronger account demands. It is so weak as not really to provide a genuine sense of 'conclusive', but this doesn't really matter. This weaker account seems to me promising in its general approach, and the theory I shall be supporting in the next chapter is distinctly similar. But it differs in not talking about reasons; and this is a virtue because it does seem possible that there should be justified belief without reasons. My belief that I am in pain may be justified, perhaps, but I can hardly be said to base it on reasons, conclusive or otherwise. I don't base it on reasons at all.

The Causal Theory

A. I. Goldman proposes a causal supplement to the tripartite definition (Goldman, 1967). An initial diagnosis of the Gettier counter-examples may be that it is just luck that Henry's justified belief is true. This diagnosis cannot itself provide a suitable answer. We cannot merely stipulate that there be no luck involved, because we all of us rely on luck to some extent. For instance, the fact that our reliable belief-gathering method provides here a true belief rather than a false one, as it sometimes does, will be just luck as far as we are concerned. And of course the fact that luck is always involved somewhere gives the sceptic a toehold too. But the diagnosis can suggest a better answer. Goldman's suggestion is that what made the belief true in the Gettier case is not what caused Henry to believe it. So he proposes, as a fourth condition for knowledge that *p*, that the fact that *p* should cause *a*'s belief that *p*. This excludes the Gettier cases because in them it is coincidental that the belief is true. We want a link between belief and truth to prevent this happening, and a causal link looks promising.

Attractive though this approach is, it faces difficulties. The first is that we may find it hard to suppose that facts can cause anything; surely they are too inert to affect the way the world goes, even where that world is the merely mental world of beliefs. What, after all, are facts? One's first idea is that facts are similar to, if not identical with, true propositions (which would explain why there are no false facts). But can true propositions cause anything? Surely facts (or true propositions) reflect the world rather than affect it. The prevalent analyses of causation seem justifiably only to allow events and possibly agents as causes. Second, there is a problem about knowledge of the future; Goldman's suggestion seems to require that here either we have an instance of backward causation (the future causing the past) or that knowledge of the future is impossible since causes cannot succeed their effects. Third, there is the problem of universal knowledge, or more generally of knowledge by inference. My belief that all men are mortal is caused, but not by the fact that all men are mortal; if any facts cause it, they are the facts that this man, that man, etc., have died. And these men are not caused to die by the fact that all men die (which would restore the causal analysis, with an intermediary cause); rather, all men die because those men do (among others). How then can the causal analysis show that I know that all men die?

There are answers to some of these criticisms, of course. We are more used to talking about facts as causes than the first criticism allows. The fact that philosophers have not yet persuaded themselves that they understand the idea that facts can be causes should not cause us to rule out all appeal to fact-causation as philosophically unsound. (The preceding sentence is a case in point.) The second criticism, too, might be answered by complicating the theory by allowing facts to be known in cases where fact and belief are different effects of a common cause. The third criticism, however, seems more intractable. The admission that facts can be causes will not much improve our willingness to suppose that universal facts can cause universal beliefs.

There are promising aspects about the causal theory, and the theory which I shall support can in fact be seen as a generalization from it.

2.4 CONCLUDING REMARKS

The various proposals considered in the previous section were presented as if they were additions to the tripartite analysis, it being admitted that Gettier had shown that analysis to be insufficient. But we can find among them at least one which can be seen as a direct defence of the tripartite analysis. Any proposal which amounts to a new theory of justification may succeed in showing that in the Gettier cases the relevant true beliefs were not justified at all. And we could take the causal theory in this way. The causal theory could be telling us that a belief is only justified when caused (directly or indirectly) by the facts. It would then be adopting route 1, as distinguished in 2.2. (Some versions of the reliability proposal could also be seen in this light.) Moving this way, then, we would be starting from a causal theory of justification; the causal theory of knowledge would simply be one of its consequences.

A possible way of arguing against a causal theory of justification would be to claim that we have no guarantee that there is only one way in which beliefs come to be justified, and in particular no real reason for supposing that any acceptable way must somehow be causal, so that all justified beliefs that p must be caused by relevant facts. Surely we don't want to rule out in advance the possibility that some moral beliefs, say, are justified, doing so just because we don't want to admit the existence of moral facts (if we don't). And we might still be doubtful of the existence of causally effective mathematical facts, without wishing to say that no mathematical beliefs can therefore be justified.

More importantly, however, the suggested causal account of justification is false because it denies the possibility that a false belief be justified. A false belief that p has no fact that p to cause it. This objection can only be evaded by finding a different account of the justification of false beliefs from that which is offered for true ones. But that cannot be right. Justification must be the same for true as for false beliefs, if only because we can ask and decide whether a belief is justified (e.g. a belief about the future) before we decide whether it is true or false.

This criticism leaves open the possibility of a different sort of causal theory, on the lines suggested at the end of 2.2. With a causal theory of knowledge and the thesis that a belief is justified iff if true it would be knowledge, we can give a causal account of justification which is not vulnerable to the existence of false justified beliefs.

FURTHER READING

Central papers in the area are Gettier (1963), Dretske (1971), Goldman (1967) and Swain (1974).

Perhaps the earliest discussion (and rejection) of the tripartite definition is in Plato's *Theaetetus* (Plato, 1973, 201c – 210d).

The enormous industry recently generated by perceived defects in the tripartite account is painstakingly analysed in Shope (1983), with copious references. There are of course many approaches and variants on approaches to the Gettier problem which I have not discussed, including Shope's own.

Most of the papers referred to in the present chapter are collected in Pappas and Swain (1978), which also contains an analytical introduction to the area.

Prichard (1967) gives an interestingly different account of the relations between knowledge, belief, certainty and truth.

An important question which we have not discussed is whether knowledge implies belief. For this, cf. Ring (1977).

The papers by Gettier, Prichard and Woozley are collected in Phillips Griffiths (1967).

3
The Conditional Theory
of Knowledge

3.1 THE THEORY

This theory, which we owe mainly to Robert Nozick, takes its start as others do: from the defects which Gettier exposed in the tripartite analysis. Nozick suggests that the reason why we take the justified true beliefs in those examples not to have been known is that a would have believed them even if they had been false. The reason why Henry's belief that McEnroe is this year's champion was too lucky or too luckily true to count as knowledge is that his route to this lucky truth was such that even if it had been false, he would still have ended up believing it. Nozick takes it therefore that for a to know that p we require that a would not have believed that p if p had been false.

This gives us, so far, the standard two conditions:

1 p
2 a believes that p,

with

3 if p were not true, a would not believe that p.

But Nozick argues that although this account may cope with the examples Gettier offers, there are other similar examples which would escape what we have so far. There are two ways in which it can be a coincidence that a's belief is true, and both need to be ruled out. The first is that if it were false, a would still believe it; we have dealt with this already by the addition of clause 3. The second is that there may be slightly different circumstances in which it remains true, but a no longer believes it. Many examples are coincidental (lucky) in both senses. Suppose that I believe that there is a police car in the road outside because I can hear a police siren. There is in fact such a car outside, but the siren I hear is on my son's hi-fi in the next room. I do not know that there is a police car outside, for two reasons. First, I would still have had the belief even if the car had not been there. Second, I would not have believed the car was there if my son's hi-fi had been silent, even though the car itself remained outside. We rule out this second way in which a true belief may be too luckily true to count as knowledge by adding a fourth clause to the initial three:

4   if, in changed circumstances, p were still true, a would still believe that p.

These four conditions, comprising the conditional theory of knowledge, can be symbolised as follows:

1   p
2   Bap
3    $\sim p \ \Box\!\!\rightarrow \ \sim Bap$
4    $p \ \Box\!\!\rightarrow \ Bap$

where the box-arrow '$\Box\!\!\rightarrow$' is used to symbolise the subjunctive conditional construction in English 'If it were the case that..., it would be the case that...'. The theory which they comprise is an attempt to articulate the feeling that, for a belief to be knowledge, it must be peculiarly sensitive to the truth of the proposition believed; it must *track* the truth (Nozick's term) in the sense that if the proposition were in changed circumstances still true, it would still be believed, and if it were not true, it would not. In the case of the police car, my belief fails to track the truth in both ways, and so is not knowledge.

3.2 SOME COMMENTS

(a) The requirement that the belief that p should track the truth of p is a requirement that the first two clauses of the theory should be related in a certain way. This is similar to the way in which the causal theory worked, but in that case the relation required was specifically a causal relation. The conditional theory is less demanding, and hence escapes some of the difficulties which the causal theory faced. But it includes the causal theory as a special case, since we might think that if the fact that p does cause a's belief that p, then the two subjunctive conditionals will be true (but not vice versa). So the conditional theory is a generalisation of the causal theory. While the causal theory suggests that there is only one way in which justified true beliefs can get to be knowledge (by being caused by the facts), the conditional theory is willing to countenance any way, causal or not, which preserves the truth of the two subjunctive conditionals.

In fact the conditional theory adopts some of the best points of several of the theories found wanting in the previous chapter. For instance, it is close to Dretske's version of the 'conclusive reasons' approach.

(b) We considered whether the causal theory of knowledge either rested on or made available a causal theory of justification. So we should ask the same questions of the conditional theory. Can we offer a conditional definition of JBap, thus:

$$\text{J}Bap \equiv (p \ \Box\!\!\rightarrow \ Bap \ \& \ \sim p \Box\!\!\rightarrow \ \sim Bap)?$$

This would be to hold that a justified belief is one which tracks the truth. But the same sort of difficulty arises. A false belief may nevertheless be justified. If so, JBap is consistent with ($Bap \ \& \sim p$). But ($Bap \ \& \sim p$) is inconsistent with ($p \ \Box\!\!\rightarrow \ Bap \ \& \sim p \ \Box\!\!\rightarrow \sim Bap$); a false belief does not track the truth. Hence the conditional definition of justification fails.

Such a theory would have been attractive, however. For someone who takes his belief that p to be justified is surely close to taking it that his belief tracks the truth of p. We can, if we want, restore the possibility of a conditional theory of justification by a move like the one made in 2.4. The suggestion there was that we derive the account of justification from that of knowledge, thus: a is justified in believing p iff in certain circumstances a would know that p. As an illustration, we can offer this instance of that approach:

$$\text{J}Bap \equiv (p \ \Box\!\!\rightarrow \ Kap).$$

Here the crucial phrase 'in certain circumstances' is read in the simplest possible way, as 'if p were true'. If a theory like this were available, we would have reintroduced in a roundabout way the possibility of a conditional theory of justification.

(c) Another point which I take to be in favour of the theory is that it begins to make some theoretical sense of the intuitive feeling that what was wrong in the Gettier cases was that there was too much luck around. The theory gives an account of what it is for a belief to be luckily true, as follows: the extent to which a's belief is luckily true is the extent to which even if it had been false, a would still have believed it, or if it were in changed circumstances still true, he would still not believe it. The importance of this account will emerge in the next section.

(d) The theory does seem to have some resources with which to explain the link between certainty and knowledge. Someone who claims that he knows that p is claiming that if p were not true, he would not believe it and if p were true he would believe it. But this claim is precisely one which he would not make if he were not certain that p. What the diffident schoolboy has lost is the confidence that his beliefs are tracking the truth; he takes it that, although he does believe that p, it is at least as probable that he is wrong as that he is right. The theory therefore analyses the certainty required for a knowledge claim as the belief that the two subjunctive conditionals are satisfied. It uses this analysis to explain the otherwise puzzling fact that the diffident schoolboy does know but cannot claim to know.

3.3 THE PRINCIPLE OF CLOSURE AND THE FIRST SCEPTICAL ARGUMENT

The conditional theory of knowledge can show that you do not know that you are not a brain in a vat. For a necessary condition for such knowledge, 3 (that if it were not true that you are not a brain in a vat, you would not believe that you are not a brain in a vat) fails. We can simplify this conditional as follows: if you were a brain in a vat, you would not believe that you are not a brain in a vat. This is false because if you were a brain in a vat (being fed your current experiences), you would still believe that you are not a brain in a vat. Therefore, if the conditional theory of knowledge is on the right lines, you do not know that you are not a brain in a vat. A necessary condition for such knowledge is not satisfied.

Despite this, Nozick's account can be used to show that you do know that you are currently sitting reading a philosophy book (please sit down first). For the four conditions are all satisfied. It is true that you are sitting etc., you believe that you are sitting etc., if you were not sitting etc. you would not believe that you are, and if you were sitting etc. you would believe that you are.

The account also shows, in similar fashion, that you know that if you are sitting reading a philosophy book, you are not a brain a vat. And so it emerges that on the conditional theory of knowledge it is possible to know that p and to know that p implies q without knowing that q. But doesn't this conclusion directly breach the principle of closure $[Kap \ \& \ Ka(p \rightarrow q)] \rightarrow Kaq$? It does; but Nozick is able to show more generally that on his account that principle fails, and (which is perhaps more important) to explain its failure. The explanation relies on the broad sweep, but not the details, of a theory about the conditions under which subjunctive conditionals such as 3 and 4 are true.

The theory uses the notion of a possible world in order to give its account of truth conditions for subjunctive conditionals. A possible world is to be thought of as a complete way in which the world might have been. The thought that the world might have been different in a certain respect is taken to be the thought that there is a possible world which does differ from the actual world in that respect (and probably others too). Possible worlds vary in their degree of resemblance to the actual world. Some are close to our world, others much more remote. But it may not be possible to order worlds according to their closeness to the actual world, for two reasons. First, the notions of closeness, resemblance and similarity are too imprecise to support the sort of precise comparative judgement which such an ordering would require. Second, for any possible world we can reasonably expect to be able to find another which resembles the actual world to the same degree. For both these reasons we need to think not in terms of individual possible worlds but of groups of possible worlds, all worlds in a group being equally close to or distant from the actual one. If there is even a vague or sketchy ordering, it will be an ordering of groups of equally similar worlds rather than of individual worlds.

Nozick gives an initial account of truth-conditions for a subjunctive conditional $p \ \square\!\!\rightarrow q$ as follows:

$p \ \square\!\!\rightarrow q$ is true in the actual world iff $p \rightarrow q$ is true throughout a range of groups of worlds reasonably close to the actual world.

(This is not the final theory but a first approximation.)

Although this theory is expressed formally it can easily be given intuitive support. Suppose that we want to know the circumstances which would justify assertion of the subjunctive conditional 'If

Mrs Thatcher had waited longer, she would have lost the election'. What we do is to picture the current situation altered to the extent that Mrs Thatcher delays the election. Other things will have to be altered as well, of course, for the date of the election is not an isolated fact (there are no isolated facts, which is why there cannot be a world similar to ours in every respect except one). We will have also to change all those things which would not have happened if the election had been delayed, e.g. Mrs Thatcher's age at election time. Then, holding everything else constant so far as we can, we form a judgement about what will most probably happen. If we take it that a Conservative defeat is most probable, we assert the subjunctive conditional. If not, not.

The formal theory implements this informal approach by saying that we consider the nearest groups of worlds in which the antecedent p is true and ask whether in those worlds q is true also. If q is probable given p, then p & q is more likely than p & $\sim q$; and therefore in the nearest worlds where p is true, q will also be true. There will of course be some remoter worlds where we have p & $\sim q$, but they do not matter. For we are deciding what would (most probably) happen, not what might (within the bounds of possibility) happen.

This distinction between what would happen and what might happen is crucial for what follows. To take David Lewis' example (D. Lewis 1973), 'if kangaroos had no tails, they would topple over'; it is of course always true that they *might* not topple over – they might be given crutches by a grateful and tourist-conscious government. But this doesn't affect the fact that they would topple over, for in worlds most similar to ours tailless kangaroos do topple over and are not given crutches.

Nozick's account can now be used in two ways. First, it can reinforce our intuitions that you know that you are sitting reading etc., that you know that if you are sitting reading etc. you are not a brain in a vat, and that you do not know that you are not a brain in a vat. With the conditional theory of knowledge, and the above explication of clauses 3 and 4, you can be said to know that you are sitting reading because (3) in the nearest worlds in which you are not sitting reading you do not believe that you are, and (4) in the nearest worlds in which you are sitting reading you do believe that you are. However, you do not know that you are not a brain in a vat because it is not the case that (3) in the nearest worlds in which you are a brain in a vat you believe that you are a brain in a vat. I emphasise again that it is only the *nearest* worlds in which the antecedent is true that count. It is admittedly possible, for instance, that you should believe you are sitting reading when in fact you are not. But such a world is vastly more remote from the actual world than is a world in which, when you are sitting reading, you believe that you are. We are interested not in what *might* be the case (of course anything is possible) but in what *would* be the case, and the theory captures that interest by focusing only on the nearest relevant worlds.

The theory also provides a direct disproof of the principle of closure. This can be done in two ways, either by giving a description of a world for which the principle fails and and proving formally that the description is consistent, or informally by appeal to a counter-example. We already have such an example: the case where a = you, p = you are sitting reading, and q = you are not a brain in a vat. But this example is contentious. It needs support from an explanation, in terms of the conditional theory, of how there can be such counter-examples. This can now be done.

An important preliminary task is to distinguish the principle of closure, which is false, from the following much more reliable instance of *modus ponens*:

$[Kap$ & $(Kap \rightarrow Kaq)] \rightarrow Kaq.$

So long as these two principles are kept apart, it should be easy to see why the principle of closure fails. The reason lies in the subjunctive conditionals and the possible worlds held relevant to the assessment of those conditionals as true or false. The worlds relevant to assessing the left-hand side of the principle of closure are the nearest group in which p is true, the nearest group in which p is false, the nearest group in which $p \rightarrow q$ is true (which may be distinct) and the nearest group in which $p \rightarrow q$ is false. The worlds relevant to assessing the right-hand side of the principle of closure are the nearest group in which q is true, and the nearest group in which q is false, i.e. completely different sets of worlds one of which may be, as in our actual example, far more remote from our world than are any of the first four groups. Hence it is hardly probable that a group of remarks about the first four groups could place any restriction on the nature of the two later groups, and thus there is a lot of room for an invalidating counter-example to the principle of closure. The more distant one of those later groups is, the more likely we are to be able to construct a counter-example; as is revealed in our own example where $\sim q$ = you are a brain in a vat.

By way of final illustration, we can apply Nozick's refutation to Descartes' sceptical argument about dreaming, and hence perhaps do better than Descartes did on the last page of the *Meditations*. Here a = you, p = you are sitting reading, q = you are not in bed dreaming that you are sitting reading. Can we have Kap, $\sim Kaq$ and $Ka(p \rightarrow q)$? Yes. Kaq is false because in the nearest group of worlds in which q is false (you are in bed dreaming etc.) you still believe that q is true. Kap is true because in the nearest worlds in which you are sitting reading you believe that you are sitting reading, and the nearest worlds in which you are not sitting reading are either worlds in which you are standing/kneeling/lying reading or worlds in which you are sitting knitting/watching TV, etc., but not worlds in which you happen to be asleep dreaming that you are sitting reading. Hence you can know that you are sitting reading even though you do not know that you are not asleep in bed, dreaming that you are sitting reading.

3.4 HAS NOZICK REFUTED THE SCEPTIC?

One purpose of the preceding section was to show that an interest in the strengths and weaknesses of the tripartite condition can yield genuine philosophical profit. The conditional theory is attractive ir :s own right as a promising account of knowledge which escapes Gettier-type objections. And it has the secondary virtue that it destroys a prevalent type of sceptical move, and does so in a way that explains the attraction of that move.

According to Nozick, however, all sceptical arguments rely on the principle of closure and the invalidation of that principle serves therefore as a general response to scepticism (Nozick, 1981, p. 204). But apart from the general implausibility of this suggestion, there is surely one sceptical argument which he cannot reject in this way. This is the argument from error (1.2).

The argument is that we or others have made mistakes in the past or would make them in circumstances which, so far as we can tell, are not relevantly different from our present circumstances. We cannot therefore, admitting that we or they did not know before, insist that we do know now, since that would be to make different claims in circumstances that show no relevant difference.

This argument turned out to be the one that forced us to admit in the first place that we do not know that we are not brains in vats. Nozick needs this conclusion to generate the sceptical problem that he is attempting to dissolve. For his sceptic argues that the consequent Kaq of PC^k is here false, and hence, via the admitted truth that $Ka(p \rightarrow q)$, that Kap is false. Nozick wants to unroll this sceptical argument while admitting its first move, and it is the argument from error that forces that admission. So it is only if he admits the strength of the argument from error that he can think he is getting anywhere by refuting PC^k.

Nozick might claim that his conditional theory also proves the same point, that we don't know we are not brains in vats. And he is right; our belief here would not track the truth. But if we had no independent reason for accepting this conclusion, such as the argument from error provides, we would take it as a point *against* his theory that it shows we don't know the most central and obvious things such as that we are not brains in vats, that there is a material world or that the world began more than five minutes ago. So he cannot cast off the argument from error and rely entirely on the conditional theory to show that Kaq is here false.

Second, there is something right about an argument which holds, as does the argument from error, that for the very same sort of reason that you don't know you are not a brain in a vat, you don't know, e.g., that *The Times* will be published tomorrow, nor whether you are sitting reading. Surely it is implausible to suppose, taking Russell's example, that I do know what I did yesterday but I don't know that the world did not begin five minutes ago replete with archaeological and other traces (Russell, 1921, p. 159). Nozick wants to show us that we can suppose this; but I am not sure that I really want to (or ought to want to). The argument from error has here a plausible consistency, while the point which Nozick takes to be his strength begins to look like a weakness. (This remark could be promoted to form the basis of a general argument against the conditional theory of knowledge.)

Third, the argument from error cannot be attacked for relying on PC^k. This is not because PC^k is valid, particularly. Even if it were valid, I can see no reason for supposing that the argument relies upon it. Nozick anyway could not hold that it does, because his position relies on the independent proof it provides that you don't know you are not a brain in a vat. Without that proof, we would hold it against the conditional theory that it cannot even show that we know that we are not brains in a vat. With it, Nozick can and does find independent support for his theory; he wants to say that the theory gets things right here. But if the argument from error does rely on PC^k, which on his theory is invalid, he lacks that independent support and with it a considerable degree of plausibility. And I do not know of any other argument, not relying on PC^k, which Nozick could use to show that we do not know we are not brains in a vat without showing that we do not know most other things either.

Fourth, the argument cannot be rejected on the similar grounds that it argues directly from the fact that you might be wrong to the conclusion that you do not know. Such an argument would be invalid, as Nozick can show. But the argument does not proceed directly in this fallacious way, but indirectly via the principle of universalizability.

3.5 INTERNALISM AND EXTERNALISM

So far we have it that Nozick's account of knowledge succeeds in defusing one sceptical argument but not another. Is this a conclusion which Nozick must simply accept, abandoning his claim to total success and pointing merely to the admitted partial success?

There remains a complaint which Nozick could and probably would make. He could say that his conception of knowledge is an *externalist* conception, while our sceptical argument from error is an *internalist* one. If externalism is a sound stance, then the argument from error is irrelevant; for it does no more than elaborate on a defective (though traditional) approach to epistemology or if it does more, it succeeds only in showing how that defective approach must lead to scepticism.

What is meant by an 'externalist' and an 'internalist' conception here? The answer to this question can best be given by example. The causal theory of knowledge, which defines 'a knows that p' as equivalent to

1   p is true
2   a believes that p
3   a's belief 2 is justified
4   a's belief 2 is caused by the fact that p is true

is an externalist conception, because condition 4 is one which a might be entirely incapable of recognizing or pointing to when asked whether he does know that p. The externalist says, in this case, that so long as condition 4 does in fact hold, whether a is able to point it out or even to understand it or not, a does know that p (given conditions 1 – 3, of course). The internalist would claim that for the causal clause to turn justified true belief into knowledge, it must not only be true but be believed by a to be true. Thus the internalist would add:

5   a believes 4.

There are arguments in favour of externalism and arguments in favour of internalism. The externalist can point out how difficult it is going to be for the internalist to provide a satisfying account of knowledge. Surely, he might say, if we are to add clause 5 we should also add

6   a's belief 5 is justified,

and then presumably

7   a's belief 5 is caused by the fact that 5 is true.

But we have surely now generated an infinite regress, which will mean that internalism is doomed to scepticism. What is more, the regress does not depend on the causal element of the example used. We could create the same regress by starting from the traditional tripartite conception and adding, on internalist grounds,

4   a believes 3

and then presumably requiring

5   a's belief 4 is justified

and then

6   a believes 5

and so on.

The internalist can respond by pointing out how great our natural intuition is to favour the internalist conception. Suppose that we work with the causal example; it is required for knowledge that the fourth clause be true, but not that a have any inkling that the fourth clause be true. Doesn't this show that, for all a knows, he doesn't know that p? And how can he know that p when for all he knows he doesn't?

In my opinion neither of these arguments is effective in destroying its opponent. The first merely points out the difficulties with scepticism; the internalist would accept this and say that these difficulties have to be faced and not ignored. The second seems to amount more to a statement of the internalist position than an independent argument against externalism. In fact I doubt that there can be a conclusive argument in favour of either of these approaches; the approaches are so different that there is a danger that any argument will simply beg the question.

Now Nozick's position is intended to be externalist (Nozick, 1981, pp. 265 – 8 and 280 – 3). Conditions 3 and 4 are obvious evidence of externalism, and there is no suggestion that we need to add anything like

5   $Ba(\sim p \,\Box\!\!\rightarrow\, \sim Bap)$.

As an externalist, would he not be justified in simply dismissing the argument from error as an irrelevant expression of internalism? I do not think so, for two reasons. First, again, Nozick relies on the argument, internalist or not, to provide the independent support for something which would otherwise look like a counter-intuitive consequence of his theory. Second, in taking the argument to be necessary Nozick tacitly accepts that his theory is not as purely externalist as it might initially appear, and hence he cannot claim immunity from an attack merely on the grounds that it is internalist.

We will return to the contrast between internalists and externalists in 9.3, and examine it in greater detail. Meanwhile, where has our discussion of the conditional theory left us? We still have no answer to the sceptical argument from error. We have mentioned, but not adopted, two positions which show promise in this respect: externalism and anti-realism. But those who find these positions unattractive will have to look further if they want to say that there are such things as knowledge or justified belief. The argument from error will recur as a persistent threat. I shall venture my own response to it in the final chapter.

FURTHER READING

The conditional theory and its consequences for scepticism are expounded in Nozick (1981) pt 2, especially pp. 172 – 8 and 197 – 227.

   Stroud (1984, ch. 2) considers a similar argument against the sceptic's attempt to generalize from the fact that we do not know we are not brains in a vat. He continues the discussion in his ch. 7.

Counter-examples to the conditional theory are given in Garrett (1983); Gordon (1984) attempts an answer. Shope (1984) offers more than counter-examples.

D. Lewis (1973) gives a pioneering account of truth-conditions for subjunctive conditionals (which he calls "counterfactuals") in terms of possible worlds. I discuss an important difference between Nozick and D. Lewis in Dancy (1984b).

References to the internalism/externalism debate are given at the end of ch. 9.

Part II
JUSTIFICATION

4
Foundationalism

Perhaps the most influential position in epistemology is the one I shall call classical foundationalism. Discussion of justification, of what it is for a belief to be justified, begins with this theory; other theories will be described in terms of their relation to or divergence from this one. It offers a compelling picture of what the aims of epistemology are; in short it amounts to a definition of the epistemological enterprise.

The classical foundationalist divides our beliefs into two groups: those which need support from others and those which can support others and need no support themselves. The latter constitute our epistemological foundations, the former the superstructure built on those foundations.

This distinction between foundations and superstructure, between basic and non-basic beliefs, is a structural one. But classical foundationalism gives the distinction content by adding that our basic beliefs are beliefs which concern the nature of our own sensory states, our own immediate experience. Such beliefs are able to stand on their own feet, without support from others. Other beliefs need support, and hence must get it from our beliefs about our sensory states.

Classical foundationalism thus gives expression to the central tenet of empiricism, the view that all our knowledge is derived from our experience. It does this by insisting that a belief which is not about our own sensory states (immediate experience) must, if it is to be justified, be justified by appeal to beliefs which are about our own sensory states.

How is it that beliefs about our present sensory states need no support from others, while all other beliefs require such support? The answer comes from the third element of classical foundationalism;

this is that our beliefs about our present sensory states are infallible. It is because of this that they can play the role ascribed to them in this form of empiricism; beliefs about our present sensory states can be our basis – can stand on their own two feet and support the rest – because they are infallible.

We can now see what epistemology is, according to classical foundationalism. It is a research programme which sets out to show how it is that our beliefs about an external world, about science, about a past and a future, about other minds, etc., can be justified on a base which is restricted to infallible beliefs about our sensory states. It is suggested that if we can do this, the demands of epistemology are satisfied. If not, we relapse into scepticism.

In this chapter and the next we shall examine classical foundationalism in some detail, and find reason to reject almost every part of it. But first we should turn to investigate the motives and arguments which lead or have led philosophers in this direction. We have already seen that classical foundationalism is an expression of empiricism. But there are other expressions of empiricism, as we shall see. Why should we opt for this one?

Probability and Certainty

C. I. Lewis, the most eminent classical foundationalist of this century, held that "unless something is certain, nothing else is even probable" (see C. I. Lewis, 1952). This view can be best understood by approaching it from a (very slight) knowledge of the probability calculus. In this calculus, probability is always assessed relative to evidence. We do not ask what the absolute probability of a hypothesis h (written $P(h)$) would be. Instead we ask about h's conditional probability given evidence e (written $P(h/e)$). The probability of h given e is expressed as correlations generally are, on a scale from 0 to 1. If $P(h/e) = 0$, then given e, h is certainly false. If $P(h/e) = 1$, then given e, h is certainly true. If $P(h/e) = .5$, then it is as probable that h is true, given e, as that it is false, since $P(h/e) + P(\sim h/e) = 1$ in the calculus.

The main point is that in assessing the probability of h given e we do not question e; we assume temporarily that e is certain, and we ignore the chance of e not being true. But e itself has a probability relative to further evidence e', and so on indefinitely. And unless we can find in the end a proposition or set of evidence e'' which has somehow in its own right the probability 1, all these probabilities will have nothing to rest on. We need to find something certain which can function as the unquestioned evidence by appeal to which the probabilities of other things are to be assessed.

In this argument it is suggested that a proposition with probability 1 is *certain*. But certainty and infallibility are not identical, and we are trying to explain a theory which takes its basic beliefs to be infallible. The move from one to the other is easy, however. If a proposition, being certain, has a probability of 1, then there is no chance that a belief in that proposition will be false; so the belief will be infallible.

There is an oddity in the argument, which starts by insisting that we speak only of probability relative to evidence, and ends by talking of a proposition having a probability of 1 in its own right. Probability theorists escape this oddity by defining absolute probability in terms of relative probability: they say that the absolute probability of $h =$ the probability of h relative to a tautology. $(P(h) = P(h/qv \sim q).)$ Whether this manoeuvre is more than a technical device is dubious.

The Regress Argument

All agree that some of our beliefs are justified by their relation to other beliefs. Standardly that relation is thought of as inferential; one belief is inferred from another or others. Thus my belief that striking the match will light it is justified inferentially. I have inferred it (not consciously, of course) from other beliefs, probably beliefs about similar occasions in the past.

The regress argument is an argument that as well as the inferentially justified beliefs, there must be some beliefs which are justified non-inferentially. The general thrust can be seen intuitively by supposing that inference is basically a matter of moving from premises to conclusion along an acceptable path. If the premises are unjustified, there will be no justification for the conclusion – at least, not by *this* inference. We can suppose, then, that only justified beliefs can justify others; and it is this thought which generates the regress.

Suppose that all justification is inferential. When we justify belief A by appeal to beliefs B and C, we have not yet shown A to be justified. We have only shown that it is justified if B and C are. Justification by inference is conditional justification only; A's justification is conditional upon the justification of B and C. But if all inferential justification is conditional in this sense, then nothing can be shown to be actually, non-conditionally justified. For each belief whose justification we attempt there will always be a further belief upon whose justification that of the first depends, and since this regress is infinite no belief will ever be more than conditionally justified.

The only way round this conclusion is to suppose that instead of the chain of justification stretching away to infinity, it turns round on its tail and joins up with itself at some point, forming a circle. But this will not mend matters, for it will still be the case that the justification of all members of the loop is conditional. The loop will never succeed in removing the conditionality.

The regress argument therefore drives us to suppose that there must be some justification which is non-inferential if we are to avoid the sceptical consequence of admitting that no beliefs are ever actually justified. And the claim that there are two forms of justification, inferential and non-inferential, is the core of any form of foundationalism in the theory of justification.

There is a variety of possible responses to the regress argument, apart from straight capitulation. A central one will be suggested in 9.1. Meanwhile we should ask if the regress is as damaging as it might seem. Not all infinite regresses are vicious. Some are *virtuous*, i.e. we can live with them and do not have to find some way to stop them. For instance, the regress generated by the remark that there is a point between every pair of points may be virtuous, even when we take it to concern points in time rather than in space. Equally we might accept the temporal regress caused by supposing that for each moment in time there is a moment that precedes it, or the causal regress derived from the propositions that every event has a separate cause and that every cause is an event. We might even accept the regress caused by the suggestion that when we believe that p we believe that p is probable (the regress comes by taking $q = $ 'p is probable'). Can we not then simply accept that justification continues *ad infinitum*? I think that the regress of justification, once it has been allowed to start in the way I have outlined, is vicious in the sense that it will show that no belief is ever actually justified. There is a bad reason for thinking this, which involves taking the regress as temporal; *before* I can justify A, I have to justify B and C, and so on *ad infinitum*, and thus I can never get started. But I do not take the regress argument to be concerned with temporal relations between acts of justification. A better approach merely underlines what was said above, that the regress shows that if all justification is inferential, no belief is ever more than conditionally justified. If knowledge requires more than conditional justification, as it seems to, then the only way to escape the sceptical thrust of the regress argument is to conclude with the foundationalist that some beliefs are justified non-inferentially.

If we are to avoid this foundationalist conclusion we shall have to show that the regress argument is fallacious. I shall give later (in 9.1) a non-foundationalist answer to it. At present I only wish to draw attention to a possible ambiguity in a crucial move. The sentence 'We have only shown that A is justified if B and C are' could mean, as was pretended above, that we have shown A's justification to be conditional on that of B and C; but it could also mean that if B and C are in fact justified, we have shown that A is, i.e. that the success of our demonstration is conditional, not the justification we have demonstrated. The argument as I have presented it seems to require the first reading of this crucial sentence; on the second reading we get, not a regress of justification, but a demonstration of justification which is only successful in certain conditions.

Our regress argument differs from Lewis' argument about probability and certainty, despite the great structural similarities (they are both regress arguments, really). The difference between them is that the first regress can only be stopped by certain (= infallible) beliefs, while the second insists merely on the existence of beliefs which are non-inferentially justified.

Infallibility and Justification

The two previous arguments are brought together as a joint argument for classical foundationalism by the claim that any infallible belief would be non-inferentially justified. An infallible belief would be justified but would not derive its justification from any relation in which it stood to other beliefs; it would not need any support from elsewhere. For surely a belief whose chances of being false are nil is unimpeachable. Nothing could reduce its probability, and hence there could be no reasons for supposing it false. So if there are any infallible beliefs we have no need to worry about the threatened regress of justification. Infallibility in the base will stop the regress.

We shall see in 4.3 that even if all infallible beliefs are non-inferentially justified, the reverse is not true; this is what opens the door for foundationalisms other than the classical variety. One can abandon the view that we have any infallible beliefs and find other ways of supposing that some beliefs are non-inferentially justified. But we cannot just announce that this is the case, e.g. with our beliefs about our sensory states. We have to produce some account of how it is that a belief can achieve this status and play this special role. Classical foundationalism says, plausibly, that our beliefs about our sensory states can do this because they are infallible. In the next section I offer an argument that this cannot be right, and if the argument is sound we shall have to find some other way of showing how any of our beliefs can be non-inferentially justified and thus can stand on their own feet.

4.2 PROBLEMS FOR CLASSICAL FOUNDATIONALISM

One of the main reasons for wanting one's own basic beliefs to be infallible is that this would guarantee that they are all true. But is there any real purpose in seeking this guarantee? The principles of inference by which we are to move from basic to non-basic beliefs are fallible, in the sense that they take us sometimes from true beliefs to false ones. (Remember Russell's chicken (Russell, 1959, p. 35), whose true beliefs about the regularity with which it had been fed so far led it into a false belief about the security of its future.) If there is this source of contamination necessarily present in the procedure, why should we insist that the input to the procedure be completely sterile, i.e. devoid of any taint of falsehood?

But the main objection to classical foundationalism is that there are no infallible beliefs. The *fallibilist* holds, correctly in my opinion, that we are nowhere entirely immune from the possibility of error.

Are our beliefs about our present sensory states infallible? Champions of infallibility tend to concede that there is room for a mistake in the *description* of one's sensory states (see Ayer, 1950). I might mistakenly describe my sensory state as being an experience of pink (things look pink to me here) when in fact it is an experience of orange. But this is dismissed as a merely verbal error. Of course I can be mistaken about the meanings of the words I use, but this will not show that I have any mistaken beliefs about my present sensory states. On the contrary, I must know how things look to me: my only error lies in choosing the wrong words to describe it. The description I use may be false, but I, the describer, am in this case infallible. My *beliefs* − the things I use words to express, with more or less success − must be true.

Similarly, we may say that merely verbal errors can be corrected in standard ways. You can show me or remind me of the difference between orange and pink, perhaps by showing me a colour chart. When I have grasped this (the difference, not the colour chart), I can apply it to my present experience in order to see whether the experience is one of pink or of orange. But in order to do this I must be aware of the nature of the experience already, before I compare it with others in order to get the right words to describe it. I don't change my beliefs about how things look, only about how to describe them.

Third, although some comparison between my present experience and others is necessary for me to know what words to use in description, and although such comparison, especially in the case where the objects compared are a past and a present experience, is fallible (since memory is fallible), still the comparison is not what I am trying to express when I try to express my beliefs about my present experience alone. For my experience would have been this way no matter how other experiences might or might not have been. So the fallibility of the comparison does not extend to show the fallibility of the belief expressed; it only shows the fallibility of the expression of belief.

Finally, if a comparison is possible at all, this can only be because ultimately we have non-comparative knowledge of the two things compared. We compare them in order to see not what each is like but in what respects they are like each other.

What reply should the fallibilist make to this argument? First, what is the content of such an infallible belief? It cannot really be that the way things are looking to me now is pink, since I could be wrong about whether that way is pink or not. What is more plausibly infallible is a belief that things *look that way* now to me. But what does such a belief amount to? What content does it have? It isn't an internal and somehow non-verbal description of how things look; it doesn't say which way they look. All such a belief amounts to is a gesture towards something; and a very strange sort of gesture too, for gestures are normally only comprehensible as public acts with publicly observable objects, while here the gesture is a private act with a private object. If gestures draw one's attention to something, can we see ourselves as somehow drawing our own attention to how things look to us?

The infallibilist may insist that I cannot be wrong in believing that the way things look to me is pink, though I can be wrong in supposing that 'pink' is the word to use to describe the way things look. This is the 'merely verbal error' move. But it seems to misuse the notion of an error which is *merely* verbal. There are several sorts of such errors (a study of the life of Warden Spooner is instructive here, though one can be pardoned the suspicion that some of his errors were deliberate). But the case where, choosing my words carefully with full consciousness of what I am doing, I deliberately pronounce on the nature of my present sensory state is not one of them. Here if I am wrong, my error is substantial, for in being wrong about whether 'pink' is the word to describe my present experience I am wrong about what pink is and hence about whether my experience is of pink rather than of orange. Here then the error is both verbal and substantial.

If the content of a putatively infallible belief is merely that things are looking that way to me now, there is clearly less room for error than if I were to risk the belief that that way is pink. The less the content, the less the risk, and greater the chance of infallibility. It seems probable, then, that a belief can only be genuinely infallible if it has no content at all. This is the strong fallibilist conclusion. But even if this conclusion is not justified, we can say that infallible beliefs must have vanishingly small content. And the point of this is that the infallible beliefs are intended, within the programme of classical foundationalism, to act as those by appeal to which all others are to be justified. They are the *basic* beliefs which ground all others, our epistemological foundations. And to perform this role they need to have sufficient content to be used rather as premises in inferences. With the reduction in content required to keep them infallible, it seems unlikely that any interesting beliefs about the past, the future, the unobserved or even the present material surroundings could ever be justified by appeal to the basic. Our basic beliefs must have sufficient content to support the superstructure in which we are really interested, and no belief with that amount of content is going to be infallible.

This diagnosis of the infallibilist's errors can be confirmed by considering briefly the arguments of Chisholm, a leading contemporary foundationalist. Chisholm distinguishes between comparative and non-comparative uses of the phrase 'appears white' (Chisholm, 1977, pp. 30 – 3). In the comparative use, 'X appears white' is short for 'X appears the way in which white things normally appear'. But in the non-comparative use, which is found in the sentence 'white things normally appear white', things are different. The latter sentence would be tautologous if we expanded 'appear white' in it as for the comparative use. But it is not tautologous, and hence there must be another non-comparative use of the phrase 'appears white' – a use in which we make a genuine attempt to describe, without comparison, the way in which white things generally appear. And Chisholm claims that in the non-comparative use, appear-statements express what is 'directly evident'. A directly evident proposition is one, in Chisholm's terminology, which is either identical with or entailed by a true contingent proposition which is all but certain. (A contingent proposition is one which might or might not be true, and might or might not be false.) A belief in a directly evident proposition is not quite the same as an infallible belief, but they share the characteristic with which we are here concerned, that all of them are true.

Chisholm considers various objections to his thesis that there is a non-comparative use of 'appears white' which expresses what is directly evident (and therefore true). Some of his remarks have been echoed in the arguments for infallibilism given above. The last objection he considers runs as follows (Chisholm, 1977, p. 33):

> (a) in saying 'Something appears white' you are making certain assumptions about language; you are assuming, for example, that the word 'white', or the phrase 'appears white', is being used in the way in which you have used it on other occasions, or in the way in which other people have used it. Therefore (b) when you say 'this appears white', you are saying something not only about your present experience, but also about all of these other occasions. But (c) what you are saying about these other occasions is not directly evident. And therefore (d) 'this is [*sic* — should be 'appears': JD] white' does not express what is directly evident.

Chisholm comments correctly that in this argument the error is the step from (a) to (b). I agree that this step is invalid. (b) should be (b¹): "When you say 'This appears white', what you say cannot be true unless certain propositions about experiences other than your present ones are true." This creates a much stronger argument, but what interests me here is Chisholm's reason for holding that (b) does not follow from (a). He says:

> We must distinguish the belief that a speaker has about the words he is using from the belief that he is using those words to express. A Frenchman [may believe that] "potatoes" is English for apples...; from the fact that he has a mistaken belief about "potatoes" and "apples" it does not follow that he has a mistaken belief about potatoes and apples.

It is clear here that Chisholm is following the traditional line that all apparent error in beliefs about our sensory states is verbal error, and that verbal error is to be distinguished from substantial error. This confirms our original diagnosis of the infallibilist's mistaken move. Chisholm does make that move, and provides no new reason for believing in infallibility.

4.3 FOUNDATIONALISM WITHOUT INFALLIBILITY

In the absence of infallibility, the programme of classical foundationalism collapses. But we saw no reasons to suppose this to be the only, nor necessarily the best form of foundationalism. What weaker versions are possible?

The first characteristic foundationalist thesis embodies the response to the regress argument:

> F^1: There are two forms of justification, inferential and non-inferential.

But there is a further thesis involved in acceptance of the regress argument:

> F^2: Basic beliefs are never justified, even in part, by appeal to non-basic beliefs.

F^2 rules out the suggestion that the non-inferential justification of basic beliefs is only partial, and needs supplementing by appeal to other beliefs. This suggestion might tempt those who notice that although we do normally accept without query a person's description of his own sensory states, we sometimes object by saying, for instance, 'Surely that traffic light doesn't look orange to you. It's the top light, and the top lights are always red'. If non-basic beliefs such as these can reduce the justification of basic beliefs, they can presumably also increase it, and in this case there would be the possibility that although our beliefs about our sensory states are always partially justified just because of their subject matter, they are never completely or satisfactorily justified unless there is confirming or at the least a lack of disconfirming evidence at the non-basic level. But this idea is not available to anybody convinced by the regress argument. Foundationalists suppose that there are two sorts of justification, and that the inferentially justified beliefs are justified by appeal to the non-inferentially justified ones. If we go on to admit that the latter are partially justified by appeal to the former, we reintroduce the circle of conditional justification whose sceptical consequence was that nothing was ever actually justified. Foundationalists must keep the direction of justification all one-way, from the non-basic to the basic, or else renounce any use of the regress argument.

So the only sort of foundationalist who could retain F^1 without F^2 would be one who accepted F^1 for other reasons than those provided by the regress argument. We might hold that our beliefs about our sensory states are always justified to some degree just because of their subject matter (non-inferentially, therefore), whereas most other beliefs are justified inferentially if at all; one could suppose this in an attempt to make sense of the empiricist idea that our beliefs about our present experience have a stability which other beliefs lack, in virtue of which they are able to justify those other beliefs and thus meet the empiricist demand (vaguely expressed here) that all our knowledge be grounded in our experience. This new sort of foundationalist, who will be considered further in chapter 6, could escape the demands of F^2, but only at the cost of abandoning the foundationalists' favourite weapon, the regress argument.

Any foundationalist has a duty to make sense of the possibility that there be non-inferentially justified beliefs. What might these be like? The formal requirements of the regress argument would be satisfied if there were beliefs of any of the three following types:

1 beliefs which are justified by something other than beliefs;
2 beliefs which justify themselves;
3 beliefs which need no justification.

It would be harsh to rule 3 out just because the argument demands that only justified beliefs can justify others; if we can give a reasonable sense to the notion of a belief standing on its own feet, as it were, rather than on those of others, we could easily see 3 as a special case of 2.

We should think of 1 – 3 as formal properties; beliefs with these properties would stop the regress, but any such formal property needs to be grounded in a more substantial 'epistemic' property. Infallibility is such a property, as was remarked earlier. The classical foundationalist supposed perhaps that infallible beliefs would be of type 2. In the absence of infallibility, what similar moves are available?

C. I. Lewis used to claim that basic beliefs were 'certain' or 'incorrigible' (Lewis, 1952 and 1946, ch. 7); it is not always clear whether he thought of these as the same as being infallible or not. In similar vein others (Descartes, perhaps) have held that they are or could be 'indubitable'. We could define incorrigibility and indubitability thus:

A belief is *incorrigible* if and only if no one could ever be in a position to correct it.

A belief is *indubitable* if and only if no one could ever have a reason to doubt it.

Is either of these two properties able to provide us with a slightly weaker but still attractive form of classical foundationalism? In my view, once we have admitted that our beliefs about our sensory states are not infallible and may be false, incorrigibility would be a vice rather than a virtue. The thought of some basic beliefs being incorrigibly false is too horrific to countenance. Equally, we could ask how a fallible belief could be indubitable. For the basic beliefs stand in inferential relationship with more interesting beliefs about public objects, and these beliefs are certainly dubitable; there is always a possibility that someone should have a reason to doubt them. But, if so, it is hard to see how the dubitability of the non-basic beliefs which they support would not rub off onto the basic ones which support them; surely falsehood in a non-basic belief would be a reason to doubt the basic beliefs which support it, once we have admitted that basic beliefs *can* be false.

So neither incorrigibility nor indubitability can provide us with an alternative form of foundationalism. But other possible forms remain. We could suggest that there could be beliefs of type 1 if there were beliefs which were justified by appeal to the facts and that a belief could be so justified if it was caused by the facts. Austin mooted the idea that on occasion what justifies my belief that there is a pig before me is just the pig (Austin, 1962, pp. 115 – 16). But this idea is not easily generalizable unless we suppose that the justification is achieved less by appeal to the pig than by appeal to the fact that there is a pig before me; the fact, in this instance, causes the belief. This move should call to mind some remarks made in 2.4 about the causal theory of knowledge. We accepted there the idea that facts can be causes; the difficulty there that universal facts cannot cause universal beliefs doesn't matter here, because universal beliefs are unlikely to be basic.

Another possible version of foundationalism holds that there are some beliefs which are given us as 'data', and which are fully justified unless something arises to defeat their justification (cf. the use of defeasibility in 2.3). We could call this a 'defeasible' or 'prima facie' justification; it is weaker than that provided by indubitability, because it countenances the possibility that there be reasons against a basic belief. But it still accepts both F^1 and F^2.

A final version has already been mooted. Weaker than the last, it holds that beliefs given us as 'data' are never fully justified merely for that reason, but that all such beliefs are already partially justified, quite apart from any further support they may receive from other beliefs. Without that further support, however, their justification is insufficient. This is the foundationalism which accepts F^1 but not F^2.

These different versions of foundationalism remain unharmed by the absence of infallibility. In the next chapter we turn to consider a different problem for foundationalism, which may have more damaging effects.

FURTHER READING

C. I. Lewis (1952) and Ayer (1950) defend forms of infallibilism.

Alston (1976) gives a good account of the regress argument, as does Armstrong (1973, ch. 11).

Firth (1964) maps weaker forms of foundationalism from the point of view of its rival, coherentism.

The notion of infallibility used in this chapter needs careful attention. Alston (1971) analyses the differences between infallibility, incorrigibility, indubitability etc.

C. I. Lewis (1952) is a response to Reichenbach (1952) and Goodman (1952), both of whom argue against his view that unless something is certain nothing is even probable.

Most of the above, with many other important papers on topics discussed in this chapter, are reprinted in Chisholm and Swartz (1973).

The foundationalism of Chisholm (1977) explicitly relies on the regress argument at pp. 16 – 20.

The attack on Ayer in Austin (1962) is still well worth reading, especially ch. 10.

Sellars (1963, ch. 5) is an extremely influential attack on the 'myth of the given' embodied in classical foundationalism. This paper is difficult but rewards study.

5
Foundationalism and Other Minds

In the last chapter classical foundationalism was presented as a response to three demands; those of two regress arguments and those of empiricism. The double response consists in the claims that there are infallible basic beliefs, and that those beliefs concern the nature of one's own sensory states. In 4.2 I gave reasons for doubting the existence or if not the existence the usefulness of infallible beliefs. Now I want to examine the other half of the story.

There is a strong tradition in philosophy which holds that we start from knowledge of our own sensory states and build up from there. Descartes never questioned his beliefs about how things seemed to him at the time; he asked instead how he could know other things, such as the existence of God or of a material world. John Locke perhaps set the classic pattern. He held that a person is directly aware only of the nature of his or her own ideas; everything else is known indirectly if at all. And this approach has been standard in epistemology since. We know the nature of our own sensory states, perhaps, but how can we build from there to gain knowledge of a past, a future, or the sensory states of others?

A questionable aspect of this approach which does seem genuinely Cartesian is the suggestion that epistemology is concerned with the individual. There is no interest here in stressing the growth of knowledge through the generations, and our rich inheritance from earlier investigators. Instead, each of us is thought of as starting more or less from scratch and the philosophical questions are how we can come from such a state, via our awareness of the passing show of sensory experience, to the sophisticated knowledge which we all have as members of a modern society.

In this chapter I shall give reasons for rejecting this approach, or if not for rejecting it then for supposing that the questions it raises can never be answered and so that it leads directly to scepticism. There is in fact a sceptical tendency in foundationalism of this sort, just because it leads us to see as problematic everything other than our knowledge of our own sensory states; it acknowledges the danger that we might be unable to construct the superstructure which the foundations are intended to carry.

5.2 THE PROBLEM OF OTHER MINDS

One such area where ignorance threatens is the area of other minds. Each of us knows the nature of his or her own sensory states; but can we know the nature of the sensory states of others, or even that there are any other minds to have the sensory states which are not ours?

Calling the problem 'The Problem of Other Minds' of course enshrines the foundationalist approach; our knowledge of ourselves is secure, while that of outsiders is problematic. (In the same way the traditional name for another problem, 'Our Knowledge of an External World', enshrines a certain sort of epistemological approach, without which there might not be a problem, or at least not *that* problem. The approach may create the problem rather than solve it.) But for the moment we shall go along with this way of looking at things. It will not last.

There is no doubt that on the traditional approach we are going to have difficulty in countering the arguments for scepticism about other minds. The argument from error can be used to show that we know of cases where others have successfully concealed their states of mind, or pretended to be in a state of mind other than their own (these possibilities are not really distinct). What then tells us that this new case is not another such?

Now there is nothing wrong with this argument as it stands, but it is weak; it assumes that there are other minds than our own, and argues only that we may be mistaken about their states, thinking someone to be happy when she is really sad, etc. To use the argument from error without that assumption we would have to point to cases when we mistakenly took there to be another mind present. There may perhaps now be such cases, with the development of increasingly sophisticated technology, and machines which answer back or play chess too well.

But it is normally an appeal to possible rather than to actual cases that is used to generate scepticism about the existence of minds other than our own. Mightn't it be the case that those other bodies with which we seem to have personal relations of friendship, dislike etc., actually have no mental states at all; that there is no internal life, but only the external behaviour? A world in which the behaviour of others was the same, but the mental life blank or absent, would be, to us, indistinguishable from our present world. How then do we know that there are other minds? For all we can tell, there are none.

5.3 THE ARGUMENT FROM ANALOGY

The argument from analogy with which we shall be concerned here admits that it is *possible* that the objects we call persons are, other than ourselves, mindless automata, but claims that we none the less have sufficient reason for supposing this not to be the case. There is more evidence that they are not mindless automata than that they are.

The classic statement of the argument is found in J. S. Mill. He writes (1867, pp. 237 – 8):

> I am conscious in myself of a series of facts connected by an uniform sequence, of which the beginning is modifications of my body, the middle is feelings, the end is outward demeanour. In the case of other human beings I have the evidence of my senses for the first and last links of the series, but not for the intermediate link. I find, however, that the sequence between the first and last is as regular and constant in those other cases as it is in mine. In my own case I know that the first link produces the last through the intermediate link, and could not produce it without. Experience, therefore, obliges me to conclude that there must be an intermediate link; which must either be the same in others as in myself, or a different one; . . . . by supposing the link to be of the same nature. . . I conform to the legitimate rules of experimental enquiry.

We could start by complaining that this argument, as an inductive argument, is very weak, since of necessity it argues from a single instance. But this criticism is not really to the point. By the nature of the case, the hypothesis that other apparent persons enjoy feelings which are like ours but which are necessarily unobservable by us is not one that we could have any evidence against. If Mill's argument succeeds in showing that there is even only a little evidence in its favour, there will be more evidence in favour than against; and we should therefore accept the hypothesis.

The difficulties for the argument derive from two assumptions which it makes, (a) about separability and (b) about understanding.

It accepts without demur (a) the *separation of the mental* (unobservable) *from the behavioural* (observable) on which the sceptical argument trades. The sceptic suggests that the two are only contingently related, i.e. that it is quite possible for there to be the one without the other, and that in fact for all we know this is how things are. The argument from analogy concedes the first half of this but denies the second, claiming that we have at least some evidence to the contrary. In conceding the first half, it shows why an argument from analogy is necessary. It is necessary because we cannot see the mental and the behavioural as related in a non-contingent way. If there were, for instance, a *conceptual* link between mental state and behaviour such that we could not conceive of the behaviour being present without the (or some) mental state, the argument from analogy would be unnecessary.

The argument also assumes (b) that *I can understand what it is for others to have mental states*. And it gives a rudimentary account of how I can do this. I learn from my own resources what pain is, in the best and the only possible way; that is, by feeling it. But the concept of pain which I have acquired in this way is such as to be applicable to others, by simply supposing that they have a sensation which is like the one I have (Mill: "by supposing the link to be of the same nature").

The main criticism of the argument from analogy is that these two assumptions are inconsistent. This criticism is due to Wittgenstein; Malcolm (1958) expounds. If there is no non-contingent link between behaviour and mental state (that is, if we accept (a)), we shall never be able to show (b) to be true, and hence we shall be at the mercy of a local scepticism of the very strongest form (cf. 1.1). So if the argument from analogy is necessary, by (a), it is doomed to failure with respect to (b). If however we can show (b), we can only do so by denying (a), and making the argument from analogy unnecessary.

All this is programmatic until we have shown what the crucial sceptical argument is. It must be different from those mentioned already, since they show no reason for doubting our ability to understand propositions about other minds. So far we have assumed that we understand the suggestion that there are minds other than our own, and asked merely how much evidence we have in its favour. The argument we are now to consider tries to show that this assumption (characteristic of a weak scepticism) is false.

5.4 CAN YOU UNDERSTAND PROPOSITIONS ABOUT MINDS OTHER THAN YOUR OWN?

Why does the separation of the mental from the physical make it impossible to show that we understand what it is for there to be other minds than our own? The argument from analogy supposes that you can construct from your own case a concept of pains which can be felt by others rather than by you. But is it so easy to conceive of a pain which is not hurting you? You have to start from a pain of yours and conceive of there being something like this which hurts but which does not hurt you, and also that there could be something which is like you but not you for such pains to hurt. Both of these ideas are very dubious. How can you conceive of something as painful, as hurting, without conceiving of it as hurting you? Surely, in conceiving of something that hurts, you necessarily conceive of it as painful to *you*. Your conception of pains which are not yours is not a conception of something which is like your pain, since it hurts, but which is not one of yours. Equally, how easy is it for you to conceive of another subject of experience, one who is not you? If you cannot do it by constructing the notion of pains which are not yours, you cannot do it any other way. For you cannot subtract from the conception of your pain that part of it which is you, the subject, and substitute the notion of another subject (something like you but not you) while supposing that the remainder (the painfulness) stays unchanged. Any pain you can conceive of as hurting in just the same way as yours hurt must be conceived of as hurting you.

This sceptical argument is crucial. It shows that it is no use simply announcing that you can conceive of another's pain on the grounds that you can suppose that what he has is the same as what you have. This easy remark (see (b) above) begs the question against the relevant argument.

Nor is it any use to insist that you can conceive of what it is like for a knee which is not yours to be hurting. A pain conceived of as being in another body is not yet conceived of as hurting another person. And in fact, if the argument above is sound, to conceive of a knee other than yours hurting in the way in which yours hurts is to conceive of it as hurting you. We might admit, then, so far as that goes, that you can conceive of its hurting you in someone else's knee (a new sense of 'His knee is hurting me') but you cannot conceive of its hurting anyone else there.

The sceptical argument therefore claims that you cannot make sense of the idea of a subject of experience other than yourself. You cannot conceive of experiences which are not yours (generalising now from the simple example of pain) and you cannot achieve in any other way a conception of a subject of those experiences who is not you. It drives us directly from foundationalism (for it was in foundationalist terms that the argument was formulated) to the most interesting form of *solipsism*, the view that you must take yourself to be the only subject of experience – in fact *the* subject of experience – since you can have no conception of another such.

Why does this show that the argument from analogy, by making assumption (a), cannot account for (b), our understanding of statements about others? It does this because it shows how if we start from our own case alone, and concentrate entirely upon a conception of mental states which is independent of behaviour, we cannot move from our conception of ourselves as subjects of experience to a conception of other subjects. The concept of a mental state in which the argument trades, and on which the sceptical argument relies, is too restrictive to make the move possible.

The proper conclusion from all this is not that scepticism, indeed solipsism, is inevitable, but that the terms in which the sceptical argument was presented, assumption (a), must be rejected. But in rejecting that assumption we render the argument from analogy redundant.

How then are we to find a conception of mental states other than that on which the sceptical argument trades? One such conception is *behaviourism*, which provides a conceptual link between behaviour and mental states by saying that the mental state of my being in pain in my knee just is the behavioural state of my wincing and holding my knee, taking greater care of it and so on. Or there are weaker forms of behaviourism which attempt to make allowances for concealed mental states; for instance, one might hold that my being in pain in my knee is for me to be *disposed* to behave in a certain way, whether I actually do so or not. To conceal the pain, I have to repress my desire (disposition) to wince, hold my knee, etc.

The obvious difficulty with behaviouristic accounts of mental states is that, although in a way they do provide what was wanted, i.e. an account of mental states in which they are non-contingently related to behaviour, still they appear to ignore everything that is characteristically mental. In the case of pain they ignore the way pain *feels*, for instance. This may not be *all* there is to the concept of pain, but it is certainly part of it. Even if we are able to show that it is not possible for there to be people who feel as we do but have no disposition to behave as we do, or vice versa, the behaviourist way of doing this seems too extreme. We are looking for a compromise position between behaviourism, which identified mental states with some function of behaviour, and the approach common to the sceptical argument and the argument from analogy, which separates them too much. Successful compromises are rare in philosophy, because often they share the defects of both extremes with the virtues of neither. We must hope none the less that one can be found here.

The criticism of the argument from analogy which I gave above is due to Wittgenstein. Its conclusion is that we can only hope to show that we understand propositions about the mental states of others if we take there to be a non-contingent relation between mental states and behaviour, and thus remove the possibility that the two should come apart. Wittgenstein's own method of achieving this is expressed using his much-disputed notion of a *criterion*. Here is a tentative account of that notion:

> A is a *criterion* for B iff the truth/occurrence of A is necessarily good but defeasible evidence for the truth of B, and in the absence of contrary indications sufficient evidence. Hence in favourable cases the truth/occurrence of A perfectly justifies the belief/assertion of B.

and

> To know this is part of competence with the concept of B; part of what it is to know the meaning of 'B'.

This notion of a criterion could be used to show the argument from analogy to be unnecessary. For, using it, we can say that anyone who understands the concept of pain knows that certain sorts of behaviour are criteria for pain-ascription. It is not possible, therefore, for there to be beings who behave just as we do but lack mental states such as pain. For in cases where there are no contrary indications such behaviour counts as conclusive evidence that the behaver is in pain. It is possible, of course, for someone to pretend to be in pain or to act pain. In many such cases the evidence created by the satisfaction of the criteria is defeated by other evidence; for example, we see him wincing and holding his stomach, but we know that he has done this at this point in the play every evening this week, and hence we are not justified in believing here what similar evidence of the same sort would perfectly justify elsewhere. But the crucial point about pretence or acting is that these are activities for which there are criteria too. They need a background and this may not be available. If in battle I see an explosion and my comrade, having lost half a leg, is doubled up in agony, there is no possibility that he is acting or pretending.

Thus Wittgenstein's notion of a criterion seems to provide the sort of compromise we are looking for. It is, however, extremely idiosyncratic, quite apart from scholarly doubts as to its exact formulation. We don't *need* to take Wittgenstein's way out here; or at least, we don't need to yet. All we have at the moment is that there must be *some* non-contingent link between mental state and behaviour if we are to understand talk about other minds. In the absence of such a link we seem to be committed to solipsism.

5.5 THE PRIVATE LANGUAGE ARGUMENT: RULE-FOLLOWING

Solipsism is not a tenable position; in fact it suffers from multiple incoherence. This is one of the conclusions of a family of arguments in Wittgenstein known collectively as the private language argument. The solipsist is in the position of claiming that he has a language in which he describes his present and past experiences, and perhaps speculates about the future. But this is a *private* language; no one else could learn it, because the experiences by appeal to which the terms in it get their meaning are private to the speaker. Wittgenstein argues effectively that such a private language is impossible. The solipsist cannot have even that limited knowledge of his own experiences.

The interpretation of the private language argument is highly contentious. I shall begin with an account due, in the main, to Saul Kripke (Kripke, 1981).

How does the solipsist acquire his language? He claims to learn from his own case what, for example, pain is. He experiences a sensation of a certain sort, and decides to apply the word 'pain' to every sensation like the first (every sensation of the same sort). Given that he remembers correctly what the original sensation was like, he has developed a concept of pain which will tell him, of each new sensation, whether to call it pain or not.

The thrust of the private language argument is that the solipsist cannot even get started in this way. Nothing that he can do in the way of concentrating on the original sensation and uttering the word 'pain' will succeed in endowing that word with a meaning. For a word to have a meaning is for there to be rules for its use: rules in virtue of which the application of the word can count as correct in some cases and incorrect in others. It is in virtue of such rules that we can make sense of the idea that we are objectively correct to call the new sensation a pain. Because a rule has actually been set up, there is something which the solipsist could misapply. He could think he was following the rule, when he was in fact not doing so; the new sensation could seem to resemble the original one, when it does not resemble it in fact. If there is to be objectivity here, we cannot have it that 'everything that seems right is right'. How, then, does concentrating on the original sensation enable the solipsist to create a rule in virtue of which it can be objectively true that the new sensation is a pain? It doesn't.

Kripke's interpretation of the private language argument holds that a negative answer to the last question is a consequence of more general considerations about rules and objectivity.

Let us move away from the special case of solipsism and sensation terms, and consider a case which may seem simpler (actually it is the hardest case in which to make the point plausible). The example used is that of a mathematical rule; the rule for $+2$. We suppose that if you know the rule for $+2$, you know, for any number n, the number which is $n + 2$. The rule creates a series; 0, 2, 4, 6..., and at each step in the series there is an objectively correct answer as to how to go on.

The question is what there is about what we learnt when we learnt the rule for $+2$ which makes the continuation 20,002, 20,004, 20,006 objectively correct, and 20,004, 20,008, 20,012 objectively incorrect. What could we point to if someone chose the latter continuation, to show that he was wrong? We suppose that this person takes it that the rule he learnt demands this continuation rather than the one we favour (which is of course the right one). What makes us right and him wrong?

There seems to be nothing in the early stages of the series which could support one continuation against the other. For there is a formula which generates the 'deviant' continuation from the same early stages; since both series start in the same way, we cannot appeal to the way in which one starts in order to justify our preference for its way of going on.

We might suggest that in conceiving the rule for $+2$, we somehow already conceived all the instances, and this is what makes it the case that the 'correct' interpretation is correct. But this suggestion is very unconvincing. Even if by chance we happened to conceive of just these members of the series, it is surely not in virtue of that fact that they count as correct continuations. And anyway, what about all the other equally correct continuations which never crossed our mind until we came to them?

In a similar spirit, we might say that in conceiving the rule, we simply conceived that we should add 2 every time. But this ploy fails, partly because such a conception fails to tell us what is to count as 'adding 2', and partly because it relies upon a smooth interpretation of 'every'; but we could ask about 'every' the same questions as we are asking about ' + 2', for there is always the possibility that someone should after a while begin to use 'every' as we would use 'every other', maintaining that he was the only one in step.

The last possibility seems to be that our original conception of the rule amounted to the creation of a disposition to carry on the series in one way rather than another. But what fact is there in virtue of which the disposition then created was a disposition *now* to go on one way rather than another? The content of my original disposition seems to be determined by the way I now find myself driven to go on, rather than vice versa.

We seem now to have exhausted all possible answers to our question. Should we then conclude that the apparently arbitrary scepticism which underlies the question in fact has no answer, and that there is no objectively right way of following the rule? This would fly in the face of our intense conviction that 20,002, 20,004, 20,006 *is* the right way and all others are just wrong. But this seems to be one of those cases where thinking cannot make it so. Luckily there remains one possibility which our search has overlooked. For we concentrated entirely on resources internal to the individual rule-follower, on things which a solipsist could point to.

Kripke therefore sees the conclusion of the argument to be that if we are to find a ground for our belief that there is an objectively correct method of continuing the series, we must look beyond the individual to the community of rule-followers. Eventually the ground of objectivity lies not in the past, in the nature of early members of the series or in our early grasp of the rule, but in the present behaviour of our linguistic or mathematical community. What makes our continuation of the series correct is that the community agrees on it. What makes the deviant interpretation incorrect is that it would be the only one in step, for in this case correctness just is being in step with the others. It is easy to see why Kripke's interpretation is called 'the community interpretation'.

These thoughts about rule-following in the mathematical case can be generalised to provide the argument against solipsism that we are looking for. The solipsist admits no community to ground his belief that it is objectively true that this new sensation is a pain. But this means to say that he has no rule that takes him one way rather than another in a new case. As far as rules go, he can say whatever comes into his head and it will be as correct as anything else. But in that case his words lose their meaning and become empty. If it doesn't matter what you say, you would be better silent. It is impossible, therefore, for there to be a private language of the sort which the solipsist needs. All possible languages are necessarily public, since they have no meaning unless they are used by a community.

5.6 ANOTHER INTERPRETATION

The community interpretation of the private language argument sees it as a direct consequence of Wittgenstein's thoughts about rules, rule-following and objectivity. Towards the end of his discussion of rule-following, Wittgenstein says (Wittgenstein, 1953, § 202):

> And to *think* one is obeying a rule is not to obey a rule. Hence it is not possible to obey a rule 'privately': otherwise thinking one was obeying a rule would be the same thing as obeying it.

And Kripke takes this early statement to be a brief foretaste of the private language argument proper, which seems officially to begin some 40 sections later.

But there is an alternative interpretation, owed to Baker and Hacker, which sees the relationship between the rule-following considerations and the private language argument rather differently (Baker and Hacker, 1984). On their account, the thrust of the rule-following considerations is that rule-following is a practice, a custom or a way of behaving. To follow a rule, e.g. the rule for use of the word 'pain' (the rule embodied in the concept of pain), is not to check, as it were within oneself, on whether this new sensation resembles the original one and, if it does, to think of it as a pain. Obeying a rule is a matter of public behaviour, not the operation of a private mechanism. Thus it is important that the section quoted above actually begins: "And hence also 'obeying a rule' is a practice. And to *think* one is obeying a rule. . .". But if rule-following is a practice, which must be public only in the sense of being a way of behaving rather than in the sense of being regulated by a community, how are we to derive from that thought the conclusion that the solipsist's private language is impossible? For why should it not be a practice which could be operated alone, apart from any community? And, equally, what answer can Wittgenstein give on this interpretation to Kripke's questions about objectivity? Surely those were good questions which need answering, and to abandon the community interpretation deprives us of the only possible answer.

The first of these objections to the Baker – Hacker interpretation can be answered by saying that although the practice which constitutes knowing and following the rule for pain could be operated away from any community (on a desert island) if it could be set up, the problem is not in the operation but in the institution of the practice. The solipsist, that is to say, cannot get the practice started in the way in which he pretends, by concentrating on the nature of the original sensation and inventing a word to refer to this sensation and to others like it.

We have seen some argument to this conclusion already in discussing the community interpretation. This is not surprising because both interpretations agree on this starting point, that the original sensation cannot serve to ground the practice (create the relevant concept). But more argument is needed now, to the extent that Kripke's version depended too heavily on his account of the relation between thoughts about rule-following and the private language argument. Luckily Wittgenstein's text bristles with such arguments. The problem is not to find them, but to select and order them comprehensibly.

First, he points out that the process of ostensive definition, whereby the solipsist attempts to give a meaning to the term 'pain' by pointing (mentally) to a sensation, is one which only works when we already have a background of conceptual knowledge, and cannot be used to construct such knowledge from a blank sheet. Suppose that I point at a chair and say "By 'chair' I mean *that*", nothing in what I have done creates the desired meaning for the word 'chair' unless I can further characterise what it is about the object I am pointing to that I am taking as relevant; for example, I might say 'that sort of furniture', and this would improve matters, but I have to have the concept of furniture first. Equally with a sensation, saying "by 'pain' I mean *that*" will only achieve the desired effect if we have some means of separating characteristics which are to be relevant from those which are not. In virtue of what are the duration, intensity, location, cause and ownership of the sensation to be deemed irrelevant? In general, then, ostensive definition relies upon the previous existence of conceptual knowledge, and cannot be the first source of such knowledge. And this means that there can never be such a thing as the sort of pure private ostensive definition that the solipsist (amongst others) is relying on.

Second, let us suppose that we do need a formulatable rule for the word 'pain', which contains explicit reference to the initial sensation, as in 'pain = sensation like this'. The rule is supposed to be something we can use in order to check whether the new sensation is also a pain. But if we are tempted to call it 'pain', what is the content of the suggested check on this temptation, the check which we operate in order to see whether it is justified? Wittgenstein suggests that all we can do is to look again to see if we are really tempted to call it pain. But this is no independent check: it is rather like buying a second copy of the same newspaper in order to check on whether the first was telling the truth. Our temptation to call the new sensation 'pain' just is the temptation to think of it as similar to the original one. We cannot check this independently by re-examining the original one, not because we cannot re-examine the original one but because everything we can do in the way of a re-examination is just doing again what we have already done in thinking of the new sensation as relevantly similar to the old one.

This is not the point that the only checks we can make on what we are tempted to say are fallible checks. If there were a check, one need not require it to be an infallible one; the fact that we might always be wrong about how the original sensation was (a sort of memory scepticism) is not a part of the argument at all. The argument is not that the check is fallible, for if it were we might still hope that enough memories could be got to prop each other up, as Ayer suggests (Ayer, 1954). The point is rather that the so-called independent check is a mere repetition of the procedure which it is supposed to be checking.

This conclusion should not be affected by any view we take about whether the use of memory constitutes a re-examination of the original sensation or a mere inspection of how that sensation now seems to us to have been. Whichever of these two (not very clear) alternatives we adopt (see 12. 2 – 3), the point remains that whatever memory does provide is not a separable check on our taking it that the new sensation resembles the old. All that memory can provide contributes already to our feeling that in calling this sensation 'pain' we are going on in the same way, following the rule. And hence we cannot check on whether we are following the rule by recalling the original sensation.

Finally, Wittgenstein makes the point that if the language is ever

ist programme espoused by the classical foundationalist. This
an be made in two ways. First, Wittgenstein sees this sort
dationalist as a form of sceptic, who admits the difficulty
ving that we are ever justified in believing that other persons
ut he sees this foundationalist as a weak-kneed sceptic, who
n consistency to go further; who ought, in fact, to doubt
r he understands the proposition that other minds exist, and
t to be a solipsist. Criticisms of solipsism should therefore
s criticisms of the weak-kneed scepticism embodied in foun-
lism. Suppose, however, that we resisted Wittgenstein's
t to push us from weak-kneed scepticism to solipsism;
d the relevant argument (see 5.4) unconvincing, perhaps.
nstein's point can still be made in another way. For the
l foundationalist programme of starting from one's own case
ving outwards suffers from all the radical defects which face
psist's attempt to set up a language in which to describe the
nces which form his subject matter. Neither the founda-
t nor the solipsist can make the *first* move. Their approach
rmined by their mistaken belief that we know what experien-
rds ('pain', 'looks red') mean by direct acquaintance with
gs they stand for.

5.8 PROSPECTS FOR FOUNDATIONALISM

in 4.3 that there are foundationalist theories other than the
l variety. How do they fare if we accept Wittgenstein's
nts?

dationalism takes it that there are two types of justification:
ial and non-inferential. This tenet is untouched by the private
ge argument. This asymmetry involved in the distinction
n two types of justification only becomes dangerous when
pposes that all basic (non-inferentially justified) beliefs
n the nature of the believer's present sensory states. As far
rivate language argument is concerned, foundationalism is
ssible as long as it avoids the traditional view that
ology is the enterprise of starting from one's own case and
g on that.
ed not come as a surprise to learn that Wittgenstein is in
n way a foundationalist. He writes (Wittgenstein, 1969a,

to be used for communication, the terms in it cannot get their
meanings from objects private to one user of the language. He
compares the suggested scenario with a group of people who have
boxes; in each box there is something (or nothing in some, perhaps)
and each calls what is in his box his 'beetle'. If the term 'beetle'
gets its meaning from what is in the box, it cannot be used for
communication with others, who being ignorant of that beetle's
nature will not be able to understand the term. If the term has a
meaning independent of the nature of the object, then it can be used
for communication (perhaps it means 'whatever is in the box') but
the private object in the box drops out of consideration as irrelevant
— an idle cog.

This last argument seems to be of little use against the solipsist,
who is not interested in communication with others. There may
however be a way of adapting it to say that the solipsist will be
unable to use the term 'beetle' to communicate with his later self
(in a diary, perhaps), since what gives the term its meaning to him
now cannot be what was then in the box (an object to which he
now has no access) but what he now thinks was in the box.

It seems, then, that the private language argument can live a life
independent of Kripke's interpretation of the rule-following considerations. Instead of saying that in the absence of a community
there can be no rules, we say that what is wrong with the solipsist's
rules is that they cannot be set up in the way he pretends, by using
a private experience as a sample. And this point is independent of
the *number* of private language users there are. If, *per impossibile*,
the language could be set up, it could be operated in the absence
of a community to regulate it. What is wrong with the solipsist's
language is not that there is no community to control it; Robinson
Crusoe *can* talk to himself and keep a diary on his desert island.
But his language is not the solipsist's; it is not set up by ostension
of private sensations which serve as samples.

What, however, about the second objection to the Baker–Hacker
interpretation, that they cannot answer Kripke's sceptical questions
about objectivity? Here they take an intransigent line, denying that
Wittgenstein was at all impressed by such questions. His main aim
with scepticism is to reject its assumptions, not to answer them,
and in this case the assumption is that we need any ground for the
objectivity of our rule-following practices. *Nothing* supports such
practices. Sceptical doubts about objectivity make good sense *within*
a practice; there are objectively correct answers to questions how
to go on, and if challenged in a particular case, we can support our

choice by appeal to the rule ('Why did you write 20,002?' 'Because you told me to go on adding 2'). But questions about the objective consistency of a practice, asked as it were from outside that practice, make no sense. (What justifies me in writing 20,002 after 20,000 when I am adding 2? Nothing justifies that; this is what we *call* 'adding 2'). And the sceptical questions which Kripke takes as central are all external questions of this sort. They involve separating the rule from its instances and asking what justifies us in taking the instances to be instances of that rule. But if you take the instances away from the rule in this way there is no rule left to ask this question about. The instances are the practice and the practice is the rule; a rule is 'internally related' to its instances, and the sceptic's attempts to plant a gap between them simply betray a misconception of what it is to follow a rule.

There is more to Wittgenstein's attitude here than a straightforward refusal to play the philosophical game. His position is that we should think of rules as practices, as ways of behaving, and not suppose that to support this way of behaving there must be some internal interpretation of the rule which tells the rule-followers how to work the rule. For if we suppose this we shall fall into an infinite regress; we shall find ourselves looking for a further interpretation. Rule-following as a practice must therefore be able to carry on without anything to support it, and we must attempt to wean ourselves away from the feeling of vertigo which is engendered by our recognition of the lack of support. And similarly we must not allow ourselves to look for something below that practice on which we can ground the feeling that the practice is going on in an objectively correct way. Objectivity is a part of the practice, not something that grounds or supports the practice from beneath. Objectivity is that element of the practice which involves checking, reassessing, abandoning old positions, complaining about others, etc. But nothing else is needed in the way of a ground to make these activities somehow justifiable.

5.7 COMMON CONCLUSIONS

Given the differences between the two interpretations of Wittgenstein's arguement, we should stress their similarities.

First, they agree that the concept of 'pain' which has served as our example throughout this discussion is not special in any relevant way. We might feel tempted to say that Wittgenstein's account may

be true of sensations; but that there is n(of blue, and so there is no reason why a start by naming the way things look to the more difficult talk of the way things a pretations would see this attempt at escap relevant difference between sensations a1 of awareness'. This can be checked by arguments. Nothing was said there wh characteristic of pain. And of course we l wanted to show it impossible that there sl like us but have no sensations or differen ours. And he wanted to make similar rem that though we use the same language a1 which to describe the colours of the objec for all we know *see* the objects comple that causes in me what I call a sensatio what I would call a sensation of blue, t this since we will continue to agree on \ act in our differently coloured environr red traffic light, for instance). According belief is as incoherent as the solipsist's a private language, since it relies upon t(behaviour (including linguistic behaviou

Second, they agree on the conclusion of concentrating on an experience and matter how fervently, cannot succeed i1 the solipsist can follow in a new case. the sensation can create a rule; the ru sensation, by enabling us to conceive of \ might resemble others. Until we have su describe the original sensation to oursel for the concept of the sensation has no been set up.

This conclusion is similar to the cri tionalism which was made in chapter foundationalist's beliefs about his sens would have to have vanishingly small (to no more than an incomprehensibl between the two prongs of the attack o1 looks pleasing.

It is worth reminding ourselves, the criticism of solipsism is intended to be a

> when Moore says he *knows* such and such [for instance that he has two hands: JD] he is really enumerating a lot of empirical propositions which we affirm without special testing; propositions, that is, which have a peculiar logical role in the system of our empirical propositions.

and this view that some propositions (beliefs) play a special role in our belief set is symptomatically foundationalist.

Wittgenstein is not an ordinary foundationalist. The beliefs which, he suggests, play this special role for us now include the belief that I have two hands, that men do not fly to the moon, that the sun is not a hole in the sky, that the earth has existed during the last century and that our hands do not disappear when we are not paying attention to them. He agrees that we can ask what justifies these beliefs; but to do so would mean that we no longer treated them as having this special status. The special status they have is not one which needs grounding or justification. It is just that we do treat them as propositions which need no justification but which can justify others. We don't ask or even think of asking what justifies them.

If Wittgenstein can still be a foundationalist after the arguments of this chapter, it is clear that the ultimate prospects for foundationalism are not yet decided. I shall offer in chapter 7 a reason for rejecting all forms of foundationalism.

FURTHER READING

Wittgenstein (1953, §§ 143 – 242) on rule-following, and §§ 243ff., on private languages.

Hacker (1972, chs 7 – 10) gives a fuller account of Wittgenstein's position.

Kripke (1982) is an expanded version of Kripke (1981), including a chapter on Wittgenstein and other minds. Baker and Hacker (1984) explicitly attack Kripke's interpretation.

Extreme behaviourism is normally associated with B. F. Skinner. For one of the less contemptuous discussions of Skinner's behavourism, see Dennett (1978, ch. 5).

Ryle (1949) is another attempt to find a way between extreme behaviourism and the mental/physical separation.

Space has sadly precluded any discussion of Wittgenstein's positive views on epistemology, for which see Wittgenstein (1969a). Much more could be made of Wittgenstein's contribution here.

The notion of a criterion is discussed in Albritton (1959); a new approach to the role of criteria is McDowell (1982), to which Wright (1984) responds.

6
Empiricist Theories of Meaning

6.1 THE RELEVANCE OF THEORIES OF MEANING
TO EPISTEMOLOGY

There is an intimate connection between epistemology and theory of meaning which has shown its head already in previous chapters. In chapter 1, for instance, we considered the effect which different theories of understanding might have on certain sceptical arguments; and a theory of understanding is only a theory of meaning under another name. Equally, anti-realism as a response to the sceptic relies on the view that we cannot understand propositions whose meaning is such that they express (or purport to express) evidence-transcendent facts. And we saw in 1.2 and again in 5.4 that the strongest sceptical arguments attack understanding as well as knowledge. Finally, in chapter 5 a theory of meaning was used to discredit a certain programme in epistemology. It is worth taking time to see exactly how this came about.

Wittgenstein's criticism of solipsism, or of foundationalism with stronger knees, was that the solipsist cannot, despite his pretensions, develop a language. This criticism depends on a view about what competence with a concept is, a view about what it is to know the meaning of a word, about what it is to know the rules for the application of that word, rules that take you from one instance to the next. Wittgenstein argued that the solipsist cannot develop rules in the way required, and hence cannot construct a language; and we conclude from this that a certain programme in epistemology is not going to be available. So in a way the basic error underlying classical foundationalism is an error in the theory of meaning.

We know that there are other forms of foundationalism than the classical one. Can we now discern a theory of meaning which, if correct, would force us towards some form of foundationalism? If we can, there might be two ways in which this would help. First, we might use it to persuade ourselves that the errors Wittgenstein found in classical foundationalism don't really infect all forms of foundationalism. Second, we might see something right about that theory of meaning or something wrong about it, and use this to determine our attitude to foundationalism in general; thus we might avoid the need to consider all the different varieties one by one.

This is what my strategy will eventually be. I shall argue that the attractions of foundationalism, whatever they may be, do not derive from the theory of meaning which underlies it; in fact, the most acceptable form of theory of meaning is noticeably lacking in the features characteristic of foundationalism, and supports instead an alternative epistemology, coherentism.

6.2 LOGICAL EMPIRICISM AND THE EVIDENCE OF ONE'S SENSES

I suggested in 4.3 that foundationalism should be defined by its response to the regress argument:

F¹: There are two forms of justification, inferential and non-inferential.

But there is another characteristic strand to foundationalism, that of empiricism. Foundationalism, viewed quite generally (though here we must exclude Wittgenstein), can be seen as the expression of the empiricist thought that verification and justification, telling whether something is true and backing up one's claims about what is true, must rely eventually upon the evidence of one's senses; not in the first instance, maybe, but at the end of the day. What else could we appeal to, to tell us whether something is true, than the evidence of our senses? This is a good sound empiricist question. So the evidence of our senses is what we start from when we need to construct a justification for our beliefs, on this approach.

The crucial point now is that the evidence of one's senses is not just what we appeal to in justification and verification. It is also what we start from in learning a language. Here again we can ask what else we could possibly start from other than what is given, that is to say the evidence of our senses. So this notion of the evidence of one's senses is held by empiricists to be basic in epistemology, and also to be basic in the theory of meaning. An empiricist theory of meaning will be one which enshrines this dependence of all language-learning, and thus of all meaningful language, on the evidence of one's senses.

Led by the thought that the evidence of our senses is basic both in epistemology and in the theory of meaning, positivists such as Ayer proposed as a theory of meaning what they called the verification principle of empirical significance (see Ayer, 1946, and Schlick, 1936):

> VP: a statement has empirical meaning iff its truth would make a difference to the evidence of our senses,

which, since a statement is verifiable, on this approach, iff its truth would make a difference to the evidence of our senses, is equivalent to:

> VP^1: a statement has empirical meaning iff it is verifiable.

And from this account of empirical meaning there naturally arises an account of what it is for someone to understand a statement, or to know its meaning:

> UP: a knows the meaning of p iff a knows how to verify p.

This could be expanded to read:

> UP^1: a knows the meaning of p iff a knows what difference the the truth of p would make to the evidence of a's senses.

And from this we naturally derive an account of what the meaning of a particular statement S is:

> MP: the meaning of S is the difference that the truth of S would make to the evidence of one's senses.

This was sometimes, not perhaps very helpfully, read as:

> MP^1: the meaning of S is its method of verification.

All three of these principles, as can be seen, are acceptably empiricist. Indeed, VP^1 was and is the core of the position known as logical empiricism, or logical positivism.

What is meant by the word 'verify' in these principles? A distinction is traditionally drawn between strong and weak verification (see Ayer, 1946, p. 9). Strong verification is conclusive verification; a statement is conclusively verifiable if, once we have the best possible evidence for it, there remains no possibility that the statement be false. Weak verification is less than conclusive. A weakly verifiable statement is not itself strongly verifiable, but is confirmable or disconfirmable by appeal to other statements which are conclusively verifiable; that is, strongly verifiable statements can count as evidence for or against it.

This distinction can help us to give the best version of logical empiricism. We could insist that 'verifiable' in VP^1 means 'strongly verifiable'. But this would rule out so many of our statements as insignificant that it would be self-defeating. On the other hand empiricists are not normally tempted to suppose that there are no strongly verifiable statements at all. Rather, they take it that statements which simply report the evidence of one's senses, whatever that may be, can be conclusively verified when one's senses do in fact produce that evidence. It seems then that the most plausible form of logical empiricism holds that statements can be divided into two classes, those that are strongly verifiable and those that are not strongly verifiable themselves but are confirmable and disconfirmable by appeal to the strongly verifiable ones.

One can see here how close the relation is between logical empiricism and foundationalism. The foundationalist claim that there are two sorts of justification, inferential and non-inferential, is mirrored by the claim of logical empiricism that all significant statements are either strongly or weakly verifiable.

Which statements are conclusively verifiable, or in other words which statements report the evidence of one's senses? Which statements are 'observation statements' to use Ayer's term, and which report states of affairs beyond those which can, strictly speaking, be observed? Logical empiricists differ on this question, just as foundationalists differ on the nature of basic beliefs. Ayer, for instance, takes the classical line that observation statements are those which describe the nature of our present sensory states. But this position is not obligatory; which is just as well since I take the arguments of chapters 4 and 5 to have refuted it. Quine on the other hand takes the evidence of one's senses to concern not what is internal to the observer but what is external to him, that is to say the presence of certain (public) stimuli (Quine, 1975a, p. 73). An observation statement is one made in response to certain stimuli and strongly verifiable by appeal to the occurrence of such stimuli.

So the notion of an observation statement, which reports nothing but the evidence of one's senses, is in dispute among logical empiricists. What is not in dispute is the distinction between strong and weak verification and its relevance to the theory of meaning. Quine's version of logical empiricism would support a version of foundationalism not vulnerable to the arguments of chapter 5, since for him the observation statements basic to justification, verification and language-learning do not concern the nature of one's own sensory states.

6.3 THREE VERIFICATIONIST THEORIES

What exactly is the relation between observation statements and the others, which form the vast majority? We have suggested that the latter are confirmable or disconfirmable by appeal to the former; but how are the two related so that such confirmation can take place? We have to give an account of this which is consistent with the verification principle. In fact, this means that our answer will amount to an account of what it is for a non-observation statement to be significant, and what it is that makes one such statement mean something different from what another one means. We shall consider three answers to the question, which form a sort of spectrum.

Phenomenalism

Phenomenalism, as a theory of the meaning of non-observation statements, held originally that such statements are equivalent in meaning to a (probably very long) list of statements about what would be observed under different circumstances, all linked by conjunction. For instance, what it is for there to be a red rose in this darkened room is for it to be the case that if I were to turn the light on, I would make a certain observation, and if I were then to move to another place, I would make an observation rather different, and if you were to come in, you would observe such and such, and so on. This theory had enormous attractions both in metaphysics and in epistemology. For phenomenalists such as Ayer tended to take it that observation statements report the nature of the observer's sensory states. And if this is so we get the delightful result that instead of there being at least two radically different sorts of things in the world, sensory states and material objects, there is only one sort of thing, sensory states, and all putatively other sorts of thing are reducible to complexes of actual and possible things of the first sort. This is the metaphysical advantage of phenomenalism. The epistemological attraction is, of course, that knowledge of the 'external' world of material objects is genuinely possible. Such objects do not lie beyond our grasp, as the sceptic might suggest; for we can hope that every member of the set of statements about what would be observed should be conclusively verified, and in such a case there would remain no further possibility that the material object statement should be false. Phenomenalism of this sort, then, would be a form of anti-realism (see 1.4).

If we could precisely specify and conclusively verify every member of the set of observation statements which together make up the meaning of a non-observation statement, that non-observation statement would, in accordance with the verification principle, have its own determinate meaning and in certain circumstances be determinately true or determinately false. This situation would be the phenomenalist's ideal; all such non-observation statements would be strongly verifiable, and sceptical doubts about them shown to be impossible. But things are not like this, for two reasons. First, it seems possible that in most cases the conditional statements about what would be observed in certain circumstances cannot *all* be verified, because there will be cases where if you verify one you lose the chance of verifying another. If only some can be verified, the non-observation statement will be no more than weakly verifiable. Second, it is not clear that conditional statements are strongly verified simply by showing that both antecedent and consequent are true. You can read English and you are reading this book, but it is not true that if you can read English you are reading this book. So if the meaning of a non-observation statement is given by a set of statements about what would be observed if..., it is unlikely that they will be strongly verifiable. (They might still be strongly falsifiable.)

This means, of course, that the advantages against the sceptic are not so dramatic as was claimed. But something would still have been gained, for we would not be claiming to know on the basis of experience the nature of a world which is independent of experience. Phenomenalism narrows the gap between the world we experience and our experience of it.

I have expressed phenomenalism so far as if all phenomenalists agree that observation statements report the nature of the reporter's own sensory states. But such a phenomenalism is only one form of reductionism. We might instead hold that observation statements report the nature of the immediately surrounding world, and define all other statements in terms of these (taking them as conditional upon the location of the observer). This would be a similarly reductionist theory, compatible with the demands of empiricism and the verification principle, but it would not perhaps have all the metaphysical and epistemological attractions of the traditional theory.

A crucial problem for phenomenalism of either sort is that few philosophers have attempted, and none have remotely succeeded, in showing what such a reduction would look like in detail. As soon as it was tried, the theory was shown unworkable. Quite apart from any other difficulties, it seemed implausible to suppose that a statement about a red rose in the dark did have exactly these or those consequences for possible observation. So, as well as being probably infinite in length, the list of conditional observation statements was probably rather vague in content. As Ayer said, "what is required to verify a statement about a material thing is never the occurrence of precisely this or precisely that sense-content, but only the occurrence of one or other of the sense-contents that fall within a fairly indefinite range" (Ayer, 1946, p. 12). And with this admission, phenomenalism loses one of its advantages. For to the extent that the range concerned is vague, to that extent non-observation statements have an indeterminate meaning and the range of circumstances under which they are determinately true or determinately false is greatly reduced, perhaps to nothing. This really meant the abandonment of the original reductive theory, since it could no longer be claimed that a non-observation statement was exactly equivalent in meaning to any collection of observation statements, however complex and conditional that collection might be.

Carnap's Relaxation

Rudolf Carnap was perhaps the only philosopher to attempt a full-scale reduction of non-observation statements to explicitly laid out complexes of observation statements. His attempts failed, and he came to the conclusion that the best that could be achieved was to specify, so far as one could, which observation statements were implied by which non-observation statements (see the preface to Carnap, 1967, and Quine, 1969, p. 77). This would never yield anything like a reduction of one to the other, but Carnap supposes that it still allowed us to claim that the concept of a material object could be reduced to 'autopsychological concepts', those which concern the nature of one's own sensory states.

But if all we can do, in our attempts to specify the meaning of a non-observation statement, is to state some implications of that statement at the observational level, it seems that there will always be some aspects of that statement's meaning which will escape us and remain unspecified. But this merely increases the sense in which the meaning of a non-observation statement is indeterminate. It gives a good sense to the idea that a weakly verifiable statement can only be confirmed or disconfirmed, and never conclusively verified. But it leaves us admitting that if we ever want to say that such a statement is determinately true, we must admit that there are facts in virtue of which it is true but which lie beyond the possibility of verification. The verificationist who is unwilling to admit the possibility of such facts (in this he is a consistent anti-realist) must therefore say that such a statement, though perhaps it may be determinately false when one of its consequences is observed to be false, still cannot achieve determinate truth.

Quine

Quine's position is more radical. He argues that we cannot hope even to specify observation sentences which are consequences of given non-observation sentences.

There are three distinct inputs to Quine's eventual position here. The first is Quine's thesis that theory is underdetermined by data (evidence). No matter how much evidence we may have, there will always be different theories which explain and assimilate the data equally well. For instance, it is compatible with the results of all actual and possible measurements to hold either that the universe is of a fixed size or that it is expanding at a constant rate. No theory, then, is ever entailed by the data. Different theories can have the same observational consequences.

The second is the claim that non-observation sentences face the tribunal of experience not singly but in groups. Quine says that this thesis is owed to Pierre Duhem; we can call it Duhem's thesis (Quine, 1969, p. 80). Duhem is suggesting that individual non-observation sentences cannot be conclusively verified or conclusively falsified by observation, by the evidence of our senses. The reason is that such sentences do not somehow occur alone, in limbo; they occur as part of a more general theory. And because of this we have a choice where to alter the theory when things go wrong at the observational level. There will always be more than one way of doing this; we are never forced by recalcitrant experiences to alter just this non-observation sentence. Equally, individual non-observation sentences are never confirmed by experience. Experience can confirm theories, and thereby confirm the sentences of which the theories are constructed, but it cannot confirm those sentences singly and directly. No matter how well experience goes, it is only able to confirm a non-observation sentence in the light of the theory that surrounds it; alter the theory, and the non-observation sentence might not be confirmed by experience at all.

These two inputs are separate. The second says that individual non-observation sentences cannot be verified or falsified on their own. The first says that the things which can be verified, theories, can never be conclusively verified. (They can of course be conclusively falsified.)

The third input we have already seen. It is the empiricist theory of meaning MP:

MP: the meaning of S is the difference that the truth of S would make to the evidence of one's senses.

Quine says of this theory that "one has no choice but to be an empiricist so far as one's theory of linguistic meaning is concerned" (Quine, 1969, p. 81).

Quine uses these three inputs to argue against the notion of individual non-observation sentences having a separate meaning all their own. By MP, in specifying the observational consequences of S we are specifying the meaning of S. But, by Duhem's thesis, no individual non-observation sentence has its own observational consequences. For if it had, then when those consequences failed we would know exactly where to revise. But we always do have such a choice and hence no sentence has observational consequences all its own. And this means, by MP, that no non-observational sentence has a meaning all its own; for there is no such thing as *the* difference *its* truth would make to observation.

The meaning of a given sentence, so far as it has one, is not some determinate characteristic which it carries around with it. Since meaning is a matter of observational consequences, and such consequences belong to theories and not to sentences, Quine's conclusion becomes inevitable: meaning belongs to theories rather than to sentences. And since one partial theory can be played off against another in the same way that sentences can, we have eventually to hold, with Quine, that 'the unit of empirical significance is the whole of science'.

This conclusion can be re-expressed in two ways, both of which will be needed for future discussions. Quine holds, against Carnap, that a non-observation sentence does not have its own observational consequences (Quine, 1953, pp. 40 – 1). This shows that there is nothing which the sentence means, taken all by itself. To the extent that we can say what it means, our answer is dependent upon the nature of the remainder of the theory surrounding the sentence. There is no determinate object, then, which we can call the meaning of this sentence.

So at the non-observational level, sentential meaning is indeterminate. There are no facts of the matter about what individual sentences mean. This is the thesis of the *indeterminacy of sentential meaning*.

So far as non-observation sentences are concerned, Quine's theory of meaning can be called *holistic*. Atomism, opposed to holism, holds that each sentence has its own meaning, which it can carry about with it from theory to theory. Holism is the view that the meanings of sentences are interdependent, so that what one means depends upon the meanings of others, and can be changed by a change elsewhere. Meaning is something born primarily not by the parts but by the whole theory, since the whole theory is the only thing that has its own observational consequences. Nothing other than the whole theory is conclusively falsified by untoward experience.

Quine uses the perspective we have now reached to argue, further, that no sentence in our theory is completely immune from revision (Quine, 1953, pp. 41 – 3). We can see the whole theory as a sphere, with observation sentences on the periphery and non-observation sentences in the interior, starting from comparatively mundane sentences about material objects, moving through more theoretical sentences to laws of physical science and finally, at the centre, the laws of logic. If there is a disturbance at the periphery we already know some observation sentences which we have to revise, and we must also make a revision in the interior, for our original theory has been proved false. Our normal response is to look for a comparatively minor adjustment near the periphery; if we cannot see the cake when we expected to we would normally suppose, perhaps, that someone has eaten it, rather than that cakes now have a tendency to dematerialize. We do this because such an adjustment leaves the general structure of our theory untouched. Sentences nearer the centre are more resistant to revision, then, than are sentences further out. The laws of logic, lying at the centre, are the most resistant of all. We would need extraordinary circumstances to arise before we abandoned laws like the Law of Non-Contradiction. But no sentence is completely immune to revision. Laws of logic, even, *can* be revised in response to empirical investigation. It may be that the simplest change in the theory, given awkward observations, would be a general structural change at the very centre rather than a whole series of alterations further out. For instance, Heisenberg's indeterminacy principle has been held to be a reason to reject the Law of Excluded Middle.

This conclusion is the final nail in the coffin of the notion of sentential meaning. Given that notion, we might hold that most sentences, when true, are made true by a combination of what they mean and how the world is. We need to know more than what they mean to know whether they are true. Such sentences are traditionally called 'synthetic'. But there might also be, and were traditionally held to be, sentences that are true solely because of what they mean. These 'analytic' sentences can be recognized as true by someone who knows nothing other than their meaning. And such analytic sentences would be unrevisable. There is no possibility that they become false, unless their meaning changes. Quine's position has the consequence that there are no such analytic sentences. The sense in which we can talk of the meaning of an individual sentence is not determinate enough to make it possible that a sentence be unrevisably true in virtue of that meaning. There are no analytic truths.

Overall, then, Quine argues that the empiricist theory of meaning MP, together with Duhem's thesis and that of the underdetermination of theory by data, has the effect of collapsing the notion of sentential meaning which it was supposed to explain. But this is not an argument against MP. Empiricists must accept MP. The situation is saved by the holistic claim that the unit of empirical significance is the whole of science.

FURTHER READING

Quine's classic paper 'Epistemology naturalised' is in Quine (1969, pp. 69–90).

Quine's doubts about analyticity are first voiced in his 'Two dogmas of empiricism', essay 2 in Quine (1953). Quine's arguments are discussed in Putnam (1975, essay 2).

Ayer (1946), introduction to the second edition and ch. 1, was a brash but influential statement of logical positivism as an expression of extreme empiricism.

Quine (1975a) is "a summary statement of my attitude towards our knowledge of nature".

Follesdal (1975) is a helpful account of Quine's epistemology and its relation to his theory of meaning, by an *aficionado*.

Berlin (1939) is a good example of the sort of response generated by Ayer (1946).

Ayer (1969, pp. 240 – 3) gives a fuller expression of phenomenalism. C. I. Lewis (1946, ch. 8) also argues the phenomenalist case. Chisholm (1948) criticises phenomenalism as a theory of meaning.

7
Holism and Indeterminacy

Sentential meaning is indeterminate, according to Quine. There are no facts of the matter about what an individual sentence means. It seems to follow that just as the notion of the meaning of a single sentence is indeterminate, so the notion of two sentences having the same meaning is indeterminate. Translation is the enterprise of finding, for one sentence, another with the same meaning. Translation then is indeterminate.

This does not mean merely that correctness of translation is undetermined by all the possible data. Of course our data are always incomplete; they never determine one translation as conclusively right and all competitors as conclusively wrong. So we might think that the correctness of translation is always evidence-transcendent. There is a fact of the matter here. One is right and the others wrong, although we may never be in a position to tell which.

This is not Quine's conclusion. What could there be, after all, in virtue of which one of the translations is right and others wrong? The only possible answer is the meaning of the original sentence. But that meaning is not determinate enough to be able to adjudicate between rival translations, so as to make it the case that at most one is right (though we may never be able to tell which).

What is more, this does not mean that translation is impossible. We might hold that the meaning of a given sentence is so rich and particular that it could never be captured by another sentence in a different language. All translations, on this approach, would be at best approximations. But Quine's point here is that there is nothing determinate in the meaning of the original sentence for the translations to approximate to. Instead of insisting on the possibility that there be no adequate translation, we should recognize what indeterminacy really means; the different indistinguishably good translations are all as good as translations can hope to be. They represent what correct translation is. So we see that instead of there being no correct translations, there will always be more than one. Two different sentences in one language can both be correct translations of a single sentence in another.

One could try to reject this conclusion on the grounds that for many French sentences there does seem to be a determinately right translation into English. Quine would accept that this is so, but hold that it is only so because in this familiar case there is an agreed general scheme for French – English translation. With such a scheme and within it, there is determinacy of translation. But the choice of a scheme is indeterminate. There will always be more than one equally good candidate.

Quine takes his start not from the familiar case but from what he calls *radical* translation (see Quine, 1960, ch. 2). This is an enterprise, supposedly conducted by a field linguist, of writing a 'translation manual' for a completely unknown language, with no help from bilingual speakers, previously prepared dictionaries or agreed general schemes. (A translation manual is a sort of dictionary that matches sentence with sentence rather than word with word.) The radical translator is faced with the task of writing such a manual on whatever evidence he can glean; roughly, on the evidence of sentences uttered or assented to by the 'natives' and the circumstances of those utterances and assents. He tries to establish a relation between the two, the question being 'In which observable circumstances will the natives assent to "*p*"?'. Translation here must be indeterminate because no amount of evidence will guarantee that the translation we offer will be uniquely correct. We can eventually be sure that it is correct enough, but never that there is no other equally correct but different translation.

The argument so far has been that since meaning is indeterminate at the non-observational level, translation must be too. We shall find reason for disquiet about this argument. In 7.4 I offer arguments which attempt to establish the indeterminacy of translation directly. The indeterminacy of meaning would then follow from the indeterminacy of translation, rather than vice versa. Meanwhile we turn to consider an area in which Quine is not willing to assert indeterminacy, that of observation sentences.

7.2 QUINE AS A FOUNDATIONALIST

We have seen already that verificationism, the adoption of VP[1], is a natural expression of foundationalism. We saw the foundationalist distinction between inferentially and non-inferentially justified beliefs mirrored in the verificationist distinction between strongly and weakly verifiable statements. The foundationalist here insists on an *asymmetry*; he has a two-tier theory, holding that there are two sorts of justification. Non-basic beliefs are justified in terms of the basic and the basic are justified in some other way; the asymmetry lies in the fact that justification is all one way, from non-basic to basic. Verificationism replicates this asymmetry in the theory of meaning.

Quine offers us a theory rich in asymmetries of the same sort. Despite his generally holistic approach to questions of meaning and questions of justification at the non-observational level, he insists on the sort of asymmetry between observational and non-observational that is characteristic of the foundationalist. These asymmetries revolve, as one would expect, around the notion of an observation sentence. This notion, according to Quine (1969, pp. 88 – 9), is

> fundamental in two connections. . . . Its relation. . .to our knowledge of what is true is very much the traditional one: observation sentences are the repository of evidence for scientific hypotheses. Its relation to meaning is fundamental too, since observation sentences are the ones we are in a position to learn to understand first, both as children and as field linguists. . . . They afford the only entry to a language.

Quine's epistemology here is a consequence of his theory of meaning and translation. The field linguist, engaged in radical translation, asks himself under what conditions the natives would assent to a given occasion sentence S, and under what conditions they would dissent. With most sentences, particularly non-observational sentences, no clear answer will emerge because the natives will not all behave in the same way in the same conditions. We might explain this by saying that whether the natives will assent or dissent to S will depend normally not only on their present situation but also on the other beliefs which they bring to that situation. But this would itself be merely an instance of the general fact that with most sentences it is possible for two people to understand them but disagree about their truth. There are sentences, however, which are immune to this sort of problem. These are sentences such that everyone who understands them will agree on their truth value no matter what the circumstances. We can in this special case hope to specify meaning completely in terms of assent/dissent conditions. And this means that for such sentences meaning is determinate and translation is determinate; we can hope to find a sentence in another language with exactly matching assent conditions. And if translation is determinate, meaning here must be atomistic rather than holistic. Each sentence must have a meaning all its own, if that meaning is able to be exactly copied by a sentence in another language. Sentences of this sort are the observation sentences.

It is not just that, as it happens, some sentences are of this special sort. If that was all there was to it, we could be pardoned some uneasiness; we might feel that we haven't been shown much reason for supposing that there are any sentences such that all who understand them will agree on their truth-value no matter what the circumstances. Remember that, for Quine, observation sentences do not report private events such as the occurrence of a sensation. They report the occurrence of certain sensory stimuli, and the stimuli are here thought of as publicly available; the same stimuli can occur to more than one person. (Saying that two sentences can have matching assent/dissent conditions is the same as saying that they can be stimulus-synonymous.) Are there any such sentences? Quine offers as examples of single-word sentences 'Red', 'Rabbit' and 'The tide is out', though he says that taken with maximum strictness only the first of these would qualify (Quine, 1960, p. 44). We can imagine that there might be some argument about this.

What persuades Quine, however, is not that his examples are so convincing but that he knows that there must be some examples, and these look like the best candidates. How does he know that this is how things must be? The answer lies in a sentence quoted above: "observation sentences are the ones we are in a position to learn to understand first, both as children and as field linguists".

It is clearly possible to learn a language from scratch, since we have all done it. But if holism is true and the meaning of each sentence depends on the meanings of others, how did we do it? There seems to be nowhere where we could start, no sentence whose meaning is, as it were, self-contained enough to be learnable as a first step towards learning the rest. But there must be some place to start, something which the learner, whether child or linguist, can get under his belt and use as a firm datum by which to test hypotheses about what further sentences might mean. Our holism must be tempered, then, by respect for the needs of the language-learner. We must be atomists somewhere in the theory of meaning, for otherwise we shall make language-learning (of the radical sort) impossible.

It is in the contrast between holism at the non-observational level and atomism at the level of observation that Quine is revealed as a foundationalist. The asymmetries are there for all to see. Observation sentences, where meaning is firm and translation possible, afford the only entry to a language; this is the semantical asymmetry. Observation sentences can be individually verified and our acceptance of them justified one by one, and constitute the evidence on which the non-observational, that is to say the whole of science, must rest; this is the epistemological asymmetry. For Quine there are data and there is theory, and whatever desirable internal characteristics the theory may have, its justification is achieved, if at all, in the way our verificationalist semantics taught us that it should be; that is, by appeal to the difference that the truth of the theory should make to possible experience and by direct (strong) verification of whether experience does in fact go the way the theory says it should. Quine's position then shows the characteristic features of foundationalism.

7.3 ATOMISM AND HOLISM

Quine's atomism at the observational level is grounded in his adherence to verificationism, as an expression of empiricism in the theory of meaning. And he takes this to show that it is impossible for good empiricists to avoid going along with him. "The sort of meaning that is basic to translation, and to the learning of one's language, is necessarily empirical meaning and nothing more.... Surely one has no choice but to be an empiricist as far as one's theory of linguistic meaning is concerned" (Quine, 1969, p. 81). And this thought furnishes a crucial argument in favour of foundationalism and its asymmetries. This is that empiricism leads to verificationism, and verificationism embodies the foundationalist asymmetries. Therefore one cannot be an empiricist without being a foundationalist.

I do not think that this conclusion is correct. Against it, I shall argue first that what Quine means by verificationism is not the only empirical theory of meaning, and second that a theory which abandons atomism at the observational level in favour of a more complete holism would be generally preferable both for empiricists and for others.

We start with the three principles laid out in 6.2; VP, UP and MP. I said there that UP and MP followed 'naturally' from VP, but this was not the whole truth. VP is about what it is for a sentence to be significant rather than meaningless, while MP is about what it is for a sentence to have one meaning rather than another. We should hope that a theory of the first sort would help us with questions of the second sort, but we could not, I think, require in advance that this be so. For surely it is compatible with VP, as expressed, that two sentences should have the same observational consequences but differ in meaning. But this situation is exactly ruled out by MP. It is clear then that MP goes significantly further than VP; it may follow naturally but it does not follow 'logically'.

The trouble lies in the move from VP to UP. VP leaves it still as an open possibility that some sentences have more to their meaning than just the effect their truth would have on the evidence of our senses. And if there are any such sentences, UP will be false as it stands. There would be sentences whose observational consequences we know but of whose other contribution (whatever that may be) we are ignorant. But if we abandon UP as it stands, we have no means of deriving MP. A truer and weaker version of UP,

UP2: a knows the meaning of $p \rightarrow a$ knows the difference the truth of p would make to the evidence of a's senses,

does not allow us to assert the sort of identity enshrined in MP, because it no longer contains the biconditional 'iff'.

If this is so, Quine is wrong to say that one cannot be an empiricist in one's theory of meaning unless one accepts his brand of verificationism, centred on MP. He derives from MP his holism in the theory of meaning, but insists that we cannot account for language learning as an empirical activity, unless we allow that some sentences have a determinate meaning and are therefore independently (strongly) verifiable.

The attack on Quine therefore has two prongs, the rejection of MP and an attempt to show that we do not need to be atomists in order to account for the possibility of language learning. The first has already been achieved; Quine is wrong to link empiricism with MP. If VP is sufficient for the empiricist, MP is not necessary.

Why is it not possible to suppose that the initial data from which we start to learn the language are less than solid, and that they stand to be revised, reassessed and maybe abandoned in the light of what happens later? Surely all that is required for us to make a start is that there should be sentences whose meaning is more nearly confined to what is immediately available to us, not that there be sentences whose meaning can be completely given in terms of their assent conditions. All that is needed, then, is a difference in degree, not in type. It is true enough that one could not start one's language learning from the laws of physics and logic; much is needed before we can even begin to understand these. But this does not show that the sentences from which we *can* start must differ in type from those, only that their degree of observationality must be much greater. If there is always an element of the meaning of our sentences which is non-observational, then observation alone will not reveal the whole meaning. But this only shows that we will not learn the whole meaning at once, at the beginning. It does not show that we cannot start, but only that our initial moves will need to be reassessed later. We do not need, then, to embrace the semantic asymmetry in order to give an account of language learning. And in that case the epistemological asymmetry which depends on it falls to the ground. We can, if we wish, adopt a more complete holism which includes observation sentences, without failing to meet the demands of empiricism. It remains then to show that this is the right course for us to take.

7.4 THE MERITS OF A MORE COMPLETE HOLISM

We are looking for reasons to out-Quine Quine; to go further in the direction of indeterminacy than Quine was willing to. Would it be sufficient simply to say that Quine's reasons for indeterminacy at the non-observational level seem really to extend to the observational, and that his reason offered for excepting the observational is less than compelling? Perhaps Quine could happily agree that the distinction between centre and periphery in theory is throughout a matter of degree, and that we never suddenly switch from indeterminacy to determinacy.

There is a certain irony in offering this as a compromise, since elsewhere in the philosophy of science Quine insists that there is no firm distinction between observation and theory. If he seems to forget this insistence in the theory of meaning, it is because he is persuaded that language-learning requires determinacy somewhere. If we drop this requirement, we can rest content with ascribing a lower degree of indeterminacy to the observational. This position does seem to have been adopted by Quine in some earlier writing (Quine, 1960, § 10, and Quine, 1953, ch. 2).

Whatever the merits of this compromise, however, it is not one that is entirely happy, given what has been said earlier. There are perhaps three difficulties with it.

The first is that one of the three planks on which Quine's argument for indeterminacy rested was his empiricist theory of meaning MP. We have seen no reason to accept MP, and have taken the view instead that VP, which is weaker, is sufficient for empiricism. Quine's initial route to indeterminacy is therefore not available to us.

The second is that, in insisting that the unit of empirical significance is the whole of science, Quine must be allowing that our entire theory does not suffer from the indeterminacy which affects the meaning of individual sentences. It seems then that if the unit of determinate meaning is the whole of science, there should be available determinacy of translation at this level. But I think that Quine would wish to insist on indeterminacy of translation even here.

The third is that the argument from indeterminacy of meaning to indeterminacy of translation may look less than compelling. Why should the fact that a sentence has not a meaning all its own mean that there will be more than one correct translation of it? Surely we might still hope to find, for a sentence whose meaning is indeterminate, another whose indeterminate meaning matches exactly that of the first. It might be more convincing, therefore, to establish the indeterminacy of translation directly and use that conclusion to buttress previous arguments about indeterminacy of meaning. In this way we can hope to find consistent arguments in favour of a more total holism. Quine himself offers two such arguments, and there is a third well within the Quinean tradition.

First is what he calls the 'argument from above'. This argument attempts to establish indeterminacy of translation directly from the underdetermination of theory by data. We need first to distinguish underdetermination from indeterminacy. We might hold that theory is underdetermined by data in the sense that two rival theories encompass the same data equally well, but insist that one of them is right and the other wrong despite our inability to tell which is which. Indeterminacy comes over and above the underdetermination of theory by data; it holds that given two equally successful theories there is no fact of the matter about which is correct. Quine holds that translation is indeterminate as well as underdetermined, while our total physical theory is only underdetermined. (He adopts the latter position because he wants to make the best possible sense of our feeling that our physical science or something like it is uniquely true, the truth; we don't need to make any such claims for translation.) The argument is that the indeterminacy of translation follows from the underdetermination of physical theory; for the native we are translating has a physical theory which is naturally underdetermined by his evidence, and our translation of his theory, being a theory about what his theory is, is underdetermined too. Quine claims, therefore, that in translation "the same old empirical slack, the old indeterminacy between physical theories, recurs in second intension" (Quine, 1970, p. 179; cf. Quine, 1975b, pp. 302 – 4). But this argument seems less than convincing. Why should a double dose of underdetermination yield indeterminacy, if a single dose does not? Quine seems simply to slur over this question in the sentence quoted, by writing 'indeterminacy' where he should have written 'underdetermination'. I take it then that the 'argument from above' fails, at least as it stands.

A second Quinean argument, which is more compelling, concerns the criteria which we actually use in the construction of translations. If we examine these, we find that there is more than one criterion, and that the different criteria compete with each other. What do we demand from a translation manual? We are going to use it in order to interact with the people we are translating, and in order to understand them and their practices. We find that different criteria operate together, differently weighted according to the general purpose of the translator. One criterion for successful translation is that by and large our translations of the natives' beliefs should show them to be largely true. We take it that a translation which imputes widespread error is to that extent implausible. But another criterion is that our translations should impute to the natives beliefs which we can make sense of them having. These two criteria are sometimes called the principle of charity and the principle of humanity; the latter name is due to Grandy, who argues that the principle of charity will not suffice alone (Grandy, 1973). And these two principles can conflict. Sometimes we have a choice between imputing to the natives a false belief which we can understand them having acquired, and a true belief which we cannot see how they could have acquired. For instance, we might have to choose between saying that they believe there is a spirit in the wire and saying that they believe there is an electrical charge there. Which of these we say will depend on how we balance the two principles of charity and humanity, and that in turn will depend partly on our own purposes and partly on how willing we are to suppose that the natives differ radically in belief from ourselves. If we are willing to suppose this, as many practising anthropologists are (some are keen to suppose it rather than merely willing), we shall probably be able to write a translation manual which appears to show it to be the case. But there will always be another equally good manual which does not, or which at least differs in degree.

There are further criteria which we would reasonably apply to translation manuals, e.g. that the translations they offer be simple (e.g. easily learnable), or that they be effective in enabling us to control the natives. But enough has been said to make the main point, that with multiple and competing criteria we must expect there to be more than one manual meeting those criteria equally well. Each manual satisfies the criteria for good translation, and hence 'gives the meaning' of the native sentence; but each manual offers a different 'home' sentence to do it with. One can see then how indeterminate translation is.

We can distinguish between two sorts of principles governing any intellectual enquiry. First there are principles of evidence. These lay down conditions which, if fulfilled by a theory, are evidence that the theory is true. In science, for instance, we might take it that a theory that provides a convincing explanation of the data is therefore the more likely to be true. Second there are regulative principles which are concerned with the practical use of a theory. In science we might suppose that simplicity is a virtue; a simpler theory will be easier to manipulate and falsify, but it is not for that reason more likely to be true. (There are two views about this; one can hold that simplicity is evidence of truth and hence that the principle of simplicity is not regulative.) The suggestion now is that the principles of charity and humanity are not principles of evidence. No one supposes that our translation is the more likely to be 'correct' the more it attributes true beliefs to the natives. These principles are regulative principles; they derive their force from the (varying) practical purposes of translation. The more we suppose the natives' beliefs to be false, the more difficult our social interaction with them will become.

This argument for indeterminacy of translation urges that once the principles of sound translation have been satisfied, even though they can be variously weighted and hence equally well satisfied by different manuals, we should take it that meaning is what those competing translations preserve. That is to say that the regulative principles of translation are what give content to the notion of meaning. There is no further principle of translation, 'preserve the meaning'. This would be a principle of evidence, if it was different in content from the other, regulative, principles. But it does not differ in content from them; it merely summarises their combined effect. Meaning is then what (and whatever) good translation preserves.

This argument for the indeterminacy of translation offers no scope for a distinction other than one of degree between the observational and the non-observational levels. And it offers us a way of moving from indeterminacy of translation to indeterminacy of meaning. It is one of the reasons we can offer in favour of a more complete holism in the theory of meaning.

The third argument concerns the relation between belief and meaning. In radical translation we have (at least) two tasks: to establish what the native sentences mean and to discover what the native believes. If we already knew the first, we would have little trouble with the second; if we already knew the second, the first would be easy enough too. But we have to do both at once. How then is it possible for us to get started? We have to pretend that we know what they believe in some initial group of circumstances in order to make any reasonable hypotheses about what their sentences mean. And this pretence is clearly lacking in justification. All we can do is to continue switching from side to side, relying on hypotheses on one side as if they were firm in order to test hypotheses on the other, and then relying on those in order to retest the hypotheses which generated them. The suggestion then is that indeterminacy stems from this interplay between belief and meaning. A pleasing example is that of the man who says that he keeps two rhinoceri in the refrigerator, and squeezes the juice of one to drink for breakfast in the morning. Is it that he means by 'rhinoceros' what we mean by 'orange'; or is it that he means the same as we do but has strange beliefs about rhinoceri? There are various things wrong with this question; the purpose of the example here is to show first that there will always be alternative ways of balancing attributions of belief and meaning in our attempts to understand the native, and second to call in question the feeling that there must be a fact of the matter at issue. In the example, what difference could it make to the man concerned which hypothesis is the truth? For him, there doesn't seem to be much difference. But if there is no difference, the question which is the right answer must be indeterminate. The answers differ not because there is a fact of the matter at issue here and now, but because they key differently into a more general account of the person concerned.

The interplay between belief and meaning has the consequence, then, that translation is indeterminate. It also has the consequence that belief is indeterminate; in the example above it was suggested that there is no fact of the matter about what exactly he believes, any more than there is about what he means. Meaning then is indeterminate because of the indeterminacy of translation.

This last argument offers no scope for a distinction between observational and non-observational. If we differ about the presence of redness, this could as well be due to a difference of belief as to a difference in meaning. We have here, then, two arguments suggesting that our holism should become complete. I take it that a holistic theory of meaning would lack the asymmetries characteristic of foundationalism. If the epistemological asymmetry in Quine stems from the semantic asymmetry, holism in the theory of meaning undermines both. In that case we have a general reason for preferring a non-foundationalist theory if we can find one. A holistic theory of meaning should lead to a holistic epistemology. In the next chapter I begin to consider the basis of such an epistemology, the coherence theory of justification.

7.5 VERIFICATIONISM, ANTI-REALISM AND FOUNDATIONALISM

Classical phenomenalism, which is an extreme form of empiricism, is anti-realist. It hopes to dispel the argument from error by showing that all true statements are in principle verifiable (and not just weakly verifiable, if possible). Less extreme forms of empiricism are realist. Quine holds that theory is underdetermined by data, but not indeterminate; this is a realist position. Foundationalism can be an expression of any of these forms of empiricism; as theories of meaning they contain the asymmetries characteristic of foundationalist epistemology. But if a foundationalist leans away from these stronger or weaker forms of verificationism and towards a greater holism in the theory of meaning, there is a certain symptomatic tension in his position. This is the contrast between his holism in the theory of meaning and his atomism in epistemology. And the gap between these two means that this foundationalist now relies entirely, not on support elsewhere in philosophy, but on the two 'internal' arguments from regress (see 4.1). If these arguments can be defused by or rendered inapplicable within a more holistic approach to epistemology, then, it would be pure gain. And I shall argue in the next two chapters that this is in fact the case. My conclusion will be that in the absence of any compelling reason to admit the asymmetries characteristic of foundationalism, we shall do best to adopt a theory without them.

FURTHER READING

See Quine (1960, ch. 2) on radical translation, and Quine (1970) on arguments for the indeterminacy of translation.

Hookway (1978) discusses those arguments constructively.

Dummett (1978, ch. 22) argues that the thesis of the indeterminacy of translation is either true and banal or significant but mistaken.

An important question in Quine's philosophy is to what extent the thesis of the indeterminacy of translation is independent of the thesis of the indeterminacy of sentential meaning (6.3) and thus of the demise of the analytic/synthetic distinction. Dummett (1978, ch. 22) discusses this, as does Hylton (1982).

Davidson (1974) discusses problems associated with the interplay of belief and meaning; see also D. Lewis (1974).

8
Coherence Theories

In the last two chapters we have begun to treat our beliefs as a kind of interrelated theory, and the problem has been how the beliefs are related. There are of course many aspects of this question which we have not examined, but we have found reason to reject one answer to it. This is the view that the relation is crucially asymmetrical; that there is an asymmetrical distinction between evidence and theory under which evidence confirms and disconfirms theory in a way in which theory cannot confirm or disconfirm evidence. Foundationalism offers such a structure in its assertion that the direction of justification is all one-way, and in its claim that there are some comparatively fixed points in the structure, the basic beliefs. The notion of inference from fixed points clearly embodies the relevant asymmetries. The notion of inference itself is asymmetrical. It is possible to infer B from A without being able to infer A from B.

The notion of coherence, on which a more completely holistic theory is based, is intended to be symmetrical. But to know whether that intention is successful we need to know more exactly what coherentists mean by 'coherent'.

All coherentists agree that consistency is a necessary condition for coherence. Bradley added (Bradley, 1914, pp. 202 – 3) that a coherent set should be complete or comprehensive in some sense. (We shall see why soon.) But consistency and completeness were not enough; they did not capture the feeling that a coherent set stuck together or fitted together in a special way. To capture this, classical coherentists use the notion of entailment (p entails q iff, given p, q *must* be true). Brand Blanshard wrote that in a fully coherent system "no proposition would be arbitrary, every proposition would be entailed by the others jointly and even singly, no proposition would stand outside the system" (Blanshard, 1939, vol. 2, pp. 265 – 6). But this account of coherence in terms of mutual entailment is disputed. Ewing suggested that it would be sufficient that each member of a coherent set be entailed by all the rest (Ewing, 1934, p. 229), and that anything further than this would be disastrous. Indeed, can we make sense of the idea of a system within which each member entails all the rest?

Instead of answering this question directly, we can move towards it by considering an objection to any use of the notion of mutual entailment as the central element in a coherent set. That notion, as Blanshard uses it, is symmetrical enough. But entailment as traditionally understood is not a matter of degree. And this is important because coherentists want to give a sense to the notion that as one's belief-set grows, it improves (we hope); it becomes more coherent. And this is not just because it becomes more complete; completeness can hardly be a virtue in itself. And we cannot rely on the point that the relations of entailment only hold between members of a complete set, because this would not really capture the sense in which we aim, in expanding our belief-set, to make it more coherent. Since we are never likely to achieve a complete coherent set, the definition of coherence in terms of entailment has the consequence that nobody's beliefs are actually coherent at all. (Other problems with the appeal to entailment are explored in Rescher, 1973, ch. 2.5.)

So if we are to have a coherence theory of justification, we need to give a good sense to the idea that justification can grow. An alternative account of coherence, offered in Lehrer (1974) and Sellars (1973), defines a coherent set as one which is consistent, complete and mutually explanatory. The idea here will be that, as the set increases in size, we can hope that each member of it is better explained by the rest. Explanations can improve in quality; this accounts for the growth of justification. And the notion of *mutual* explanation is clearly symmetrical, in the required sense.

Two comments could be made on this account of the coherent as the mutually explanatory. First, it seems that the requirement of completeness can be quietly dropped. This is because the need for completeness is already accounted for by the search for a higher degree of mutual explanatoriness. And it is just as well, because there is no really clear notion of completeness available here. We might perhaps suppose that a complete set contains every proposition or its contradictory. But this will be of no help unless we have a clear notion of 'every proposition'. In the same way, we have no clear idea of a perfect explanation, a point from which things cannot be improved. That point is at best one which we approach without limit; there is no content to supposing that we might have reached it. So doubts about completeness make me happy to leave it out of the definition of coherence. (Other reasons will emerge later.)

The second point is that coherence is a property of a set of beliefs, not of the members. The set is coherent to the extent that the members are mutually explanatory and consistent. This will be important in what follows.

It may seem, then, that our account in terms of mutual explanation is an improvement on that which appeals to entailment to tie the coherent set together. But I think that the mutual explanation account restates rather than replaces Blanshard's use of entailment. For Blanshard's understanding of entailment is not the traditional one. Traditionally, 'p entails q' is understood atomistically, as a feature of the individual meanings of p and q; given the meaning of p and that of q, if p is true then q must be, and this independently of considerations elsewhere in the system. This understanding of entailment is the basis of Rescher's complaint that where p entails q, q is a redundant member of the set; and hence that a coherent set is infected with mutual redundancy, contrary to Blanshard's stated intention. And it is the basis of our remark above that entailment is not a matter of degree. But Blanshard does not conceive of entailment in this way, as we would expect of anyone who is a holist in the theory of meaning. For him, entailment only occurs within a system; and since the system determines the meanings of p and of q, it determines the strength of the link between p and q. So as the system grows, that link can become stronger.

There is anyway an obvious intuitive link between entailment, as Blanshard sees it, and explanation. To explain q by appeal to p is to show why q should be true, given p. The explanation works to the extent that it shows that, given p, q must be true. Explanation thus reveals entailment, in Blanshard's sense. And like entailment, explanation should be viewed holistically rather than atomistically. So at the end of the day our two accounts of coherence collapse into each other.

Before we turn to the coherence theory of justification we need first to consider the coherence theory of truth; the two are closely connected.

8.2 THE COHERENCE THEORY OF TRUTH

This theory holds that a proposition is true iff it is a member of a coherent set.

If we are doubtful about the possibility of a fully coherent set, we shall hold as coherentists classically did that truth is a matter of degree. Propositions are true to the extent that there is a coherent set of which they are members. Notice, however, that the theory does not identify truth with coherence. It gives no sense to the notion of a true set. Instead, it defines truth for members of sets. A proposition is true iff it is a member of a coherent set. Propositions cannot be coherent, in the required sense, and sets cannot be called true unless they are members of larger sets.

However, the theory does purport to offer a definition of truth. It does not restrict itself to telling us what circumstances would justify us in taking a proposition to be true. It might do this by claiming that we are justified in believing that *p* is true to the extent that doing so would increase the coherence of our belief-set. The coherentist does make this claim; he does offer a *criterial* account of truth, a theory about what are the criteria for truth. But he also offers an account of what truth itself is, a *definitional* account. The two accounts are supposed to fit together, as we shall see.

Many philosophers who have shown an interest in the coherence theory of truth have disputed the view that the theory offers a definition of truth on the grounds that, taken that way, the theory is manifestly false (e.g. Russell, 1907). It is manifestly false because no matter how tight our account of coherence we shall have to admit that there may be more than one coherent set of propositions. Nothing in the notion of coherence, as defined, gives us any right to say that there is a unique most coherent set. But it is obviously the case that there can be at most one complete set of truths. So truth cannot be defined in terms of coherence alone.

The situation might remind us of Quine's thesis of the underdetermination of theory by evidence. If there is more than one theory equally effective in handling the evidence, what are we to say about the different theories? Can we perhaps say that they are all true, or that all their members are true? It seems that we cannot. If our different coherent sets are all of them verging on complete, if they constitute complete but different descriptions of the world, how can we admit that all the parts of these different descriptions of the world are true? Surely if the descriptions are different, they are competing, and the prize they are competing for is the prize of *truth*. Hence only one of these competing sets can contain nothing but truths, and the coherence theory of truth is wrong.

This objection to the coherence theory of truth is standard. We can call it the plurality objection. It arouses extreme indignation amongst those who call themselves coherentists. Brand Blanshard writes (1939, vol. 2, pp. 275 – 6):

> This objection, like so many other annihilating criticisms, would have more point if anyone had ever held the theory it demolishes. But if intended to represent the coherence theory as responsibly advocated, it is a gross misunderstanding.

Blanshard is arguing that the plurality objection fails to appreciate the empiricist character of his coherentism. For he takes it, as do other coherentists such as Bradley, that there is only one coherent set, and that this set is distinguished from all rivals by being empirically grounded. This is so, according to Bradley, because of the very aim of thought and enquiry, which is to discover the most systematic ordering of our experience (Bradley, 1914, p. 210; cf. p. 203):

> My experience is solid. . .so far as in short it is a system. My object is to have a world as comprehensive and coherent as possible, and, in order to attain this object, I have not only to reflect but perpetually to have recourse to the materials of sense. I must go to this source both to verify the matter which is old and also to increase it by what is new. And in this way I must depend upon the judgements of perception.

What these coherentists are saying is that the enterprise is to start from the data of experience and to construct a set of beliefs around those data which will order the data in the most systematic (coherent) way. To do this we may need to reject *some* of the data, but we cannot reject them all because our very aim is to make sense of what we have as data. So the set of beliefs which we do construct *must* be empirically grounded, and this grounding in the data of experience guarantees that there will be only one set which constitutes 'the most systematic ordering'.

This appeal to the need for an empirical grounding manages to exclude all the more fanciful putatively coherent sets of propositions from our reckoning. Thus, for instance, a perfect expansion of the Sherlock Holmes stories would not have to be counted as a true description of the world, despite its coherence. But unfortunately, even when we have ruled out all such coherent sets, there will be more than one remaining. For nothing in the appeal to the need to order the data of experience can make it the case that there need be one most systematic ordering. There may, for all we can do to prevent it, be more than one equally good way of 'ordering' the data or of fitting them into an explanatory system, particularly when we remember that some of the data will be rejected on the way. This is, after all, just what the underdetermination of theory by evidence amounts to. So the plurality objection still has teeth.

The right defence against the plurality objection is offence. We should ask whether there is any other theory of truth, any other account of what truth is, which fares better. It emerges quickly that none of the standard theories of truth have the desired consequence that there can only be one set of truths. Certainly the traditional opponent of the coherence theory, the correspondence theory, faces the same difficulties. Correspondence theories try to erect an account of truth upon the undeniable remark that for a proposition to be true is for it to fit the facts. But as long as facts and true propositions are kept separate from each other, what is there to prevent there being two distinct sets of propositions which "fit the facts" equally well? We must either admit that the plurality objection is as effective against one theory as it is against another, and abandon the demand that 'the truth' be somehow unique, or admit that though the truth must be unique, it is somehow not part of the role of the theory of truth to show this.

But perhaps the plurality objection still has a point. After all, the coherentist must admit that the competing theories are all true (since they are all equally coherent), while the correspondence theorist can say that one is true and the others false. The correspondence theorist has this advantage because he says that there is something beyond and distinct from the competing theories, the world, which can make it the case that one is true and the rest false. So the coherentist cannot really give a good sense to the notion that the different theories compete or are incompatible, it seems. And this is a weakness not shared by his opponent.

The reply to this comes in two parts. First we can say that for the coherentist each theory is incompatible with every other because one cannot embrace two theories at once, on pain of loss of coherence. So from the point of view of someone with a theory, every other theory is false because it cannot be added to the true theory. And second, it is only from the point of view of the world, a point of view external to any theory, that the correspondence theorist has an advantage. Only those people who hold no theory at all but view all theories from outside can give a sense to the notion of incompatibility between theories beyond that which the coherentist has already given. But there is no such thing as a theory-free, external, viewpoint. So the coherentist can give an account of what it is for two coherent theories to be incompatible, and there is no further account which only the correspondence theorist can give.

This theory holds that a belief is justified to the extent to which the belief-set of which it is a member is coherent. Each belief is to be evaluated by appeal to the role it plays in the belief-set. If the coherence of the set would be increased by abandoning the belief and perhaps by replacing it by its opposite, the belief is not justified. If the set is more coherent with this belief as a member rather than with any alternative, the belief is justified. This notion of justification is relative to individual believers. The full account should be: if a's belief-set is more coherent with the belief that p as a member than without it or with any alternative, a is (or would be) justified in believing that p.

What is the link here between justification and truth? A belief-set with reasonable coherence will make each of its members justified. But that does not mean that they are all true. It may be that the belief-set cannot be further expanded; that after a while the addition of further beliefs, however it may be done, always continues to decrease the coherence of the growing whole. In that case the members of the set are not all true, because they cannot all be members of a genuinely coherent whole. But they are still justified (for a). Equally a belief may be true, since the proposition which is its content is in fact a member of a coherent set, without that meaning that it is justified for a. So a belief can be true without being justified and justified without being true, on the coherence account. Justification can grow, but as it grows it need not be approaching truth. Of course as a belief-set grows and becomes more coherent, we have more and more reason to suppose that its members are true. But they may not be; indeed it is always quite probable that further expansion will require revision somewhere.

Despite the distinction between belief and justification, however, coherentists stress as a virtue of their theory that truth and justification are according to them all of a piece. The coherence of a belief-set goes to make its members justified; the coherence of a set of propositions, believed or not, goes to make its members true. The sense in which, on the theory, truth is one thing and justification another does not detract from the advantage of having a smooth link between justification and truth.

Suppose that, as Ewing (1934), Rescher (1973) and Lehrer (1974) suggest, we adopt a coherence theory of justification but reject the coherence theory of truth. (Perhaps we are impressed by the plurality objection.) We are left with a mystery. Surely our theory ought somehow to show why justification is worth having, why justified beliefs ought to be sought and adopted, and unjustified ones discarded. An obvious way of showing this is to show how or that justified beliefs are more likely to be true. If we take coherence as criterion both of truth and of justification, we have a good chance of being able to do this. The alternative is to suppose that justification is a matter of internal coherence, a question of fit between objects that are all of the same sort, while truth is a matter of the correspondence between propositions and objects of a different sort, facts or states of affairs. But then it would be difficult to find a reason for thinking that where the internal relation of justification is present, the external relation of truth is probably present too. So there is an enormous advantage in having theories of truth and justification that fit each other. The theory of truth ought to fit the epistemology and not be allowed to ride independent of it.

What are the objects which are linked by the relation of mutual explanation in a coherent set? In the coherence theory of truth they are propositions; in the coherence theory of justification they are propositions too. So when we talk of the justification of a's belief that p we are asking whether the proposition p forms, with other propositions which a believes, a promisingly coherent set. If it does, the truth of p is explained by appeal to the truth of those others. (A different approach is taken by Lehrer (1974), where he suggests that what needs to be explained is not the truth of p but rather the fact that a believes that p.) So in this respect also our theory of truth fits our theory of justification.

As well as this, coherentists would say we have more direct reasons to do without the asymmetries of foundationalism. We have seen no compelling reason to adopt those asymmetries yet (but see 8.4 and 9.1), and in the absence of such a reason we should take it that there is only one form of justification, the same for all beliefs. There are no fixed points by appeal to which other beliefs are assessed. Each belief is assessed in the same way, by considering the effect of its presence on the coherence of the whole. So there are no restrictions on what can be appealed to in support of what. The test, as Bradley says, is system and not any one-directional criterion of fitting the evidence.

Equally, in the event of a difficulty there are no antecedent requirements about where revision should be made. We have no independent reason to prefer to retain highly observational beliefs in preference to theoretical ones. The right revision is the one that results in the most coherent new whole, but we cannot tell in advance what sort of revision is most likely to achieve this.

Coherentists would claim that this holistic theory fits our actual practice far better than the more restrictive foundationalist account. In practice there are no taboos on what can be appealed to in support of what and no requirements about which sorts of statements should be retained in preference to others if there is a clash. We don't always preserve the observational at the expense of the theoretical. We do, for instance, suppose that you cannot be right when you say that this curtain looks orange to you, on the grounds that objects with the molecular structure of this curtain just don't look orange. Equally, we do support our observational beliefs by appeal to our theoretical ones (a weak form of foundationalism could perhaps admit this, of course; see 4.3). So there is no theoretical need to accept the asymmetries, and our practice reveals that we don't do so anyway.

In this way coherentism makes a virtue of necessity. In the absence of fixed points and the lack of any clues about where revision should start, we know that at any time our belief-set is merely provisional. Revisions will be called for, and the need to revise may occur anywhere. This is a form of fallibilism (see 4.2). Coherentists welcome it and claim that their approach reveals the strength of fallibilism; fallibilism is not an unfortunate defect but an essential part of the epistemological enterprise, the drive continually to revise in the search for greater coherence.

Further support for the theory comes from its ability to justify the principles of inference we use. Foundationalists suppose that we need not only basic beliefs but also principles of inference to take us from those beliefs to the more sophisticated superstructure. We understand, perhaps, what justifies the basic beliefs; but what justifies the principles of inference? The classic example of this question is our third sceptical argument (1.2) about induction. We shall consider this in chapter 13. But the inductive principle is not the only principle of inference at issue. Further principles might be:

1   If I seem to remember doing an action then (probably) I did the action. (Memory)
2   If others tell me that they observed an event, then (probably) the event did occur. (Testimony of others)
3   If it seems to me that a certain object is before me, then (probably) it is before me. (Perception)

Such principles cannot themselves be justified by appeal to basic beliefs, nor as conclusions of inferences from those beliefs. Foundationalists seem therefore to have to find yet a further form of justification for their principles of inference. Whether they can achieve this or not, coherentists face a much easier task. For them, principles of inference are of course necessary as one of the ways in which the coherent set is bound together. But they can be justified in the now familiar way, by appeal to the increase in coherence which results from the adoption of a principle. Use of a principle can be expected to increase the size of a belief-set, and is justified if the set increases in coherence as it increases in size. And if there are competing principles, as when we consider an alternative to 1 which includes a restriction to certain circumstances, then that alternative is justified whose use most increases the coherence of the whole. (These questions will be examined further in chapters 11 – 13, and doubt will be cast on the answer mooted here.)

Another advantage of coherentism, suggested by Rescher (1973, p. 332), is that it directs attention away from the individual's struggle to construct his own epistemology, which is the classical conception of the epistemological enterprise (see 5.1); instead it gives a sense to the notion of knowledge as a social phenomenon, something that can be shared and which can increase by means of that sharing. This claim seems to depend on the ease with which coherentists can justify the use of principle 2. It is as if coherentists start from the traditional egocentric problem of what each of us is justified in believing. In this respect they don't diverge from the tradition except in failing to insist that the initial data are restricted to basic facts about one's own sensory states. However, the testimony of others can be used more or less immediately to increase the coherence of one's own belief-set, and so one can make an early move away from the egocentric predicament and think of oneself as a collaborator, even as one more likely to learn from others than to contribute to the sum total of knowledge (a sort of epistemological modesty). This falls short of supposing that knowledge is entirely a social phenomenon, as some would wish, but it approximates to that position despite taking the traditional starting point.

Coherentists also suppose that just as their approach provides a possible justification of induction, so it offers a general stance from which the sceptic can be defused, if not rebutted. We shall consider this claim in 9.3, 9.5 and 13.3.

Finally, we saw in chapter 7 a general reason for seeking a more complete holism in the theory of justification, to suit the adoption of a holistic theory of meaning. Coherentism is *the* holistic theory; it provides what is required.

These are the main advantages which coherentists would claim for their theory. We now turn to consider the central attack on coherentism. This is the complaint that coherentism and empiricism are incompatible.

8.4 THE ROLE OF EMPIRICAL DATA

In 8.2 we considered the plurality objection to the coherence theory of truth, and mentioned the standard reply. This is that one coherent set is picked out from the others by being empirically grounded. The enterprise of thought is to start from the data of experience and to construct a set of beliefs around those data which will order them in the most systematic way. But this empiricist approach seems to reveal a difficulty for coherentism as a theory of justification. For it appears to reintroduce a distinction between two sorts of justification. The coherentist should be a *monist* here; he should claim that justification is everywhere of the same sort. But doesn't the notion of empirical *data* introduce a form of pluralism? For the role of a datum seems unable to be captured by a theory whose sole concern is an internal relation between beliefs. A datum stands as such not because of any relation it bears to other beliefs, but because of its source. It has a claim to acceptance because it is part of our input, part of what experience is giving us.

Surely, then, we have to make room for the notion of someone's beliefs being justified, at least in part, by reference to something beyond the beliefs themselves; by reference, in fact, to his experience. But this amounts to abandoning our coherentist monism and resorting to the sort of asymmetry characteristic of foundationalism. Only foundationalism can give to sensory experience the sort of special role it must have in any empiricist account of the justification of experience. Empiricism and coherentism are incompatible.

The first question is why the coherentist should worry about this attack at all. He has been put in the position of maintaining that belief-sets which bear no relation to anyone's experience may have all the defining characteristics of coherence. But he would allow this only if he accepted the distinction between belief and experience; and this distinction is not one on which all interested parties will agree. Provided that we maintain with Kant that it is impossible to draw a suitable distinction between the cognitive and the sensory 'elements' in sensory experience, or maintain that all experience is a form of cognition or judgement (i.e. acquisition of belief) rather than a form of sensation, we can construct a form of coherentism which does not fall foul of the argument. If a coherentist requires for justification that all cognitive elements be interconnected, there is no possibility that beliefs wholly disconnected from sensory experience might yet count as justified, once we take experience to be cognitive.

This defence, however important, is less than complete. For even if we accept that experience is a form of belief, we can still insist on a distinction between sensory beliefs and others (without yet specifying exactly how it is to be drawn), and with that distinction re-express the empiricist's point as the demand that the sensory beliefs support the others. But this is a demand for something beyond mere coherence, for the relevant notion of support is intended to be asymmetrical. It brings an asymmetry into the theory of justification in just the way that the coherentist is so keen to avoid. (And similar notions, for instance that our sensory beliefs are our evidence or our data, have the same effect.) The requirement that the sensory support the non-sensory amounts to the view that justification is one-way, from sensory to non-sensory, and hence to the view that justification takes two forms, first the justification of the non-sensory by the sensory, and second the (somehow different) justification of the sensory. And this is to abandon the essential monistic thesis of coherentism in favour of some form of foundationalism, limited though that form may yet turn out to be.

The coherentist might of course try to escape this attack by claiming that a mere distinction between sensory and non-sensory beliefs does not amount to any invidious asymmetry of the sort which is being foisted upon him. But I think that there is no escape for him this way. First, it is not the distinction itself which creates the asymmetry, but the demand that, so distinguished, the sensory beliefs support the non-sensory beliefs. Second, there seem to be good independent reasons why even a coherentist must ascribe to the sensory beliefs some special role in the epistemology of the individual. Not all these reasons are of equal weight, but I shall mention three.

First, those objects whose justification we are considering are belief-sets, and all the belief-sets with which we are familiar (our own and those of our contemporaries) are as a matter of fact empirically based. We have no cause to concern ourselves, therefore, with non-existent belief-sets which lack empirical grounding. Second, for a set to count as a *belief*-set — for the propositional attitude concerned to be that of belief — it must be thought of as some sort of a response to an impinging environment. It isn't that beliefs which were wholly disconnected from experience would merely be unjustified; they wouldn't be beliefs at all. Third, it seems possible, although the question is to be determined empirically, i.e. by test, that an asymmetrical reliance on the experiential such as is expressed by thinking of our experience as our evidence would actually produce, from the same input, belief-sets with greater coherence, and if this is so there are reasons from within the coherentist approach itself for introducing an asymmetry into the account.

Given that there is to be this asymmetry, can the coherentist cope with it? We might try to do so by distinguishing between two sorts of security that beliefs can have, antecedent and subsequent. *Antecedent security* is security which a belief brings with it, which it has prior to any consideration of how well it fits with others or of the coherence of the set. We could hold that sensory beliefs have a degree of antecedent security in being prima facie reliable or justified; there will be greater degrees of antecedent security up to infallibility. *Subsequent security* is security which a belief acquires as a result of its contribution to the coherence of the set. All justified beliefs, on a coherence account, have a degree of subsequent security.

Coherentists would traditionally claim that no belief has any greater antecedent security than any other. We could call this position pure coherentism; an extreme form of it maintains that no beliefs have any antecedent security at all. But we might be persuaded by the argument above to suppose that sensory beliefs do have an antecedent security that others lack. If this 'weak coherentism' is consistent, it would perhaps meet the demands of empiricism. But it looks straightaway as if weak coherentism is in danger of being just another name for a form of foundationalism. After all, prima facie reliability and such characteristics were mentioned in 4.3 as central to non-classical forms of foundationalism. Is it possible then to be an empiricist and accept an asymmetrical relation between sensory and other beliefs, without thereby becoming a foundationalist? In our discussion of Quine (7.2 – 3) it seemed that the empiricist insistence that our beliefs be grounded in experience should be somehow compatible with complete holism both in epistemology and in theory of meaning. Can we show in greater detail how this is possible?

8.5 COHERENTISM AND EMPIRICISM

The most fruitful coherentist approach can be found in the work of F. H. Bradley. Bradley is an empiricist, in this respect expressing himself as clearly as the most ardent could wish:

> I agree that we depend vitally on the sense-world, that our material comes from it, and that apart from it knowledge could not begin. To this world, I agree, we have forever to return, not only to gain new matter but to confirm and increase the old. (Bradley, 1914, p. 209)

Here we see Bradley ascribing to the 'data of perception' or the 'sense-world' an asymmetrical role in the individual's epistemology. In fact the asymmetry is complex. It is partly genetic; material *comes from* the sense-world, and without that world knowledge could not *begin*. And it has a continuing role, both in our need continually to return to previous 'data of perception' and in our need to make sense of the continuing flow of new sensory life. This complex asymmetry is one which echoes (if I can reverse the temporal order) Quine's arguments for the verification theory of meaning; these were either genetic, as when he writes of the sort of meaning which is basic to the learning of one's language, or continuing, as when he writes of the sort of meaning that is basic to translation (7.2).

Bradley is willing to accept that the sense-world plays a special role in epistemology, but he is unwilling to accept that that special role emerges in the sort of asymmetry which characterises foundationalism (ibid., p. 210):

> In order to begin my construction I take the foundation as absolute... But that my construction continues to rest on the beginnings of my knowledge is a conclusion which does not follow. For it is in another sense that my world rests upon the data of perception.

Bradley holds that experience provides data (genetic asymmetry), but that the question whether something which appears as datum should remain as accepted fact is one which is not even partially determined by its origin as datum. Data stand for acceptance into our world in the same way and by the same criteria as does any other proposition. The test in each case is what he calls 'system', or in other words the question whether the coherence of our world is increased by their admission as accepted fact. In this respect there is no asymmetry; all propositions (in the sense, as it were, of proposals) that are justified receive a justification of exactly the same sort.

Is Bradley's position, accepting one asymmetry but rejecting another, consistent? One might say against it that even if we agree that all propositions, data and the rest, are justified by their contribution to system, there remains a crucial asymmetry which is not genetic. For the system had as a prime aim the need to make sense of the sense-world; even if in carrying out that aim we reject some elements of that world there remains an asymmetry in the purpose of systematisation. This asymmetry is revealed in the demand that by and large items which are taken to be data should be accepted. It is a point against any system that it requires too substantial a rejection of the 'data of perception', whether or not the coherence of the system is thereby increased.

One could of course take the easy way out and argue that this objection is only valid against pure coherentism, which holds that all beliefs have equal antecedent security; it gets no grip on weak coherentism, which accepts that some beliefs have greater antecedent security than others and can thus offer an account of the necessity that by and large items that are taken to be data should survive epistemological scrutiny. But I think that this would be to miss the point. For the question really is whether this sort of antecedent security, if we are forced to admit it, amounts to an asymmetry in the account we give of justification and thus to a two-tier theory of justification such as only the foundationalist can provide. If it does, we have here an argument as effective against weak as against pure coherentism. So there are two separable questions here; does the necessity constitute some form of antecedent security for sensory beliefs, and, if so, does the antecedent security introduce an asymmetry which forces us to admit a two-tier theory of justification?

The antecedent security which sensory beliefs enjoy seems to amount to this, that we are to accept them as true if nothing counts against them. But don't we do this, and do so quite reasonably, for anything we are willing to count as belief? Any belief will remain until there is some reason to reject it. So *all* beliefs have an antecedent security, in this sense. And this does not introduce two forms of justification. There is no asymmetry created by accepting that all beliefs have some degree of antecedent security, provided that the antecedent security they enjoy is everywhere of the same sort.

But perhaps the problem is that different beliefs have different degrees of antecedent security, and that empiricists characteristically hold that sensory beliefs have *more* of it than others do. Can a coherentist make sense of this idea in his own terms? The problem seems to be that if one belief can be more secure than another in this way, this fact is independent of and prior to all considerations of coherence with other beliefs, and so reintroduces an asymmetry for which there can be no coherentist explanation.

The problem then is whether the coherentist *can* be an empiricist, not whether he *should* be one. And the empiricist is here distinguished by an attitude he takes towards his sensory beliefs; he demands more than another might before he is willing to reject them. But if this attitude is extrinsic to those beliefs themselves, and can without damaging distortion be seen as a further belief, it is a belief which the coherentist might share. And if he does share it, the required results will emerge. The removal of a sensory belief will create greater disturbance and require more to justify it, simply because the characteristic empiricist belief is part of the belief-set too. So this coherentist's sensory beliefs will have a greater degree of security, but it will be subsequent, not antecedent, security; for it is to be seen entirely in terms normally available to the coherentist, i.e. in terms of the internal coherence of his belief-set.

If this is right, pure coherentism is stronger than weak coherentism. If the weak coherentist is distinguished by his willingness to admit different degrees of antecedent security, his position is genuinely and unnecessarily weak.

The conclusion then is that coherentism is compatible with empiricism. Whether a coherentist *ought* to be an empiricist is a different question, which we shall meet again in chapter 11. But the coherentist seems to have one promising avenue here. For him it is an empirical question whether at the end of the day a more coherent system will result from the adoption of the empiricist attitude to sensory beliefs; whether this form of empiricist stubbornness will eventually pay off. And this is the sort of way in which the coherentist *should* seek to justify empiricism.

FURTHER READING

'On truth and coherence', ch. 7 of Bradley (1914).
Rescher (1973, ch. 2) introduces distinctions between 'criterial' and

'definitional' theories of truth, and rejects the coherence theory's claim to be definitional. It is not clear whether a criterial theory of truth is recognizably distinct from a definitional theory of justification.

Firth (1964) discusses the question whether a coherentist account of knowledge can give a good sense to the idea of empirical knowledge being based on experience; the defence he offers seems to be a form of weak coherentism.

Sellars (1979) responds to Firth in a way more consistent with pure coherentism.

Ewing (1934, ch. 5) is a sympathetic critic of coherence theories. He agrees with Rescher that the coherence theory of truth should be taken as criterial rather than definitional.

Blanshard (1939, chs 25 – 7) offers the most recent authoritative statement of an unblushingly coherentist position.

The notion of the coherent as the mutually explanatory seems to derive from Sellars (1963, pp. 321 – 58).

The argument of 8.4 – 5 is expanded in Dancy (1984a).

Cornman (1977) suggests that a mixture of foundationalism and coherentism will prove "the most reasonable theory of empirical justification".

9
Coherence, Justification and Knowledge

9.1 THE REGRESS ARGUMENT

What can coherentists say about the regress argument (4.1)? This argument is, after all, supposed to show that the distinction between inferential and non-inferential justification is not optional; it is forced upon us, on pain of infinite regress and a collapse into scepticism. The difficulty here is that, as I expressed it before, the regress argument depended upon a conception of justification which was both non-holistic and linear. (It was linear in the sense that it supposed that A might be justified by B, B by C and so on, either *ad infinitum* or with eventual circularity.) It needs therefore to be rewritten in terms of the holistic conception of justification which is central to coherentism. Can this be done? I cannot in fact see any way of making the regress argument effective against coherentism.

The coherentist account of justification can be written thus: a belief B1 is justified to the extent to which it contributes to the coherence of the belief-set of which it is a member. Suppose that the set contains as members B1 – Bn, and suppose also that the sort of holistic justification we are concerned with can reasonably be called inferential. It may even be inductive, if induction is to be seen generally as inference to the best explanation (as is argued in Harman, 1970). Now, do we face the same sort of danger that unless there is another form of justification, all justification will be conditional (see 4.1)? There seem to be two ways in which this danger might arise.

The first is that B1 is only justified if B2 is (say), and so on. But this does not follow from the coherentist picture. Even if B2 were not justified, there being an alternative B2′ which would make a greater contribution to the coherence of the set B1 – Bn, still B1 can be justified; it is justified, roughly, if no alternative would make the set more coherent. So there seems to be no sense in which the justification of B1, even though it exists by appeal to other members of the set and the role they play in the construction of the set, is conditional upon the *justification* of other members. It is of course conditional upon their presence, but this sort of conditionality does not create a vicious infinite regress.

The second attempt might be to hold that B1 is to count as justified by appeal to its contribution to the coherence of the whole. But its place in the whole could only justify B1 if the whole were itself justified. So the justification of B1 is again only conditional; but this time it is conditional upon the justification of the set of which it is a member. I think there are two ways of making what is effectively the same reply to this. The first is to say that this sort of conditionality does not matter, since the set is, we hope, unconditionally (actually) coherent and hence actually justified; there will then be no danger of a regress forming, since at the first move we find something whose justification is not conditional. I am not entirely happy with this reply, however, since it may be held to admit that there are two forms of justification, that of parts and that of wholes. A safer response is to say that coherentism gives no sense to the notion of the justification of an entire set. A member is justified by its contribution to the coherence of the set; justification is defined in terms of coherence, but justification is one thing and coherence another (cf. remarks at the end of 8.1).

This is not a merely verbal point, a 'conventionalist sulk' or an unreasoned refusal to call something 'justification'. Behind it lies a more substantial account of the practice of seeking justification and of our procedure in what Levi calls 'the enterprise of knowledge' (Levi, 1980). At any point we find ourselves with a large set of beliefs of various sorts, and probably there are tensions within the set if not downright contradictions. The question for us is where to go from here. What we are looking for is that adjustment which will most increase the coherence of the whole. Any belief can be discarded or replaced, but each belief is keyed into others in ways which mean that its rejection will create further disturbance. A belief is accepted as justified if there is no visible alternative that will do better. But there is no sense in which the whole belief-set is up for justification, for retention or replacement. The best, indeed the only thing we can do is to improve its internal coherence, using the broad structure of the set we have to assess the contribution made to it by individual members and new candidates. If this is what the process of justification is, it should hardly be surprising that no sense is given to the question whether the entire set is justified or not.

It seems then that coherentists escape the conclusion that the 'inferentially' justified beliefs are only conditionally justified. They can hold that each belief is (or should be) actually and non-conditionally justified by its contribution to the coherence of the whole. If this is right, we are forced to see the regress argument not so much as an independent argument for foundationalism but as an expression of the foundationalist approach to justification; an expression which exposes the consequences of taking justification to be non-holistic and linear.

There is however a different regress waiting for us. I have suggested that a belief can be justified by the fact that it makes a contribution to the belief-set of which it is a member. But can it really be sufficient for me to be justified in holding a belief, that it does in fact increase the coherence of my belief-set? What if I have no notion that this is the case? Surely I would only be justified in holding this belief if I do somehow take it to contribute in the right way. And even then this may not be enough. Can it really be sufficient that I do take it that the belief contributes in this way? I might be quite unjustified in taking it that this is so; this second belief might be quite gratuitous, or held for entirely irrelevant reasons. Don't we also require that I be justified in taking it that the first belief contributes to the coherence of the whole?

This regress is perhaps easier to see formally. Where q = 'a's belief that p contributes to the coherence of a's belief-set', we seem to be in danger of defining JBap in terms of:

1   q
2   Baq
3   JBaq.

But this constructs a new regress. For each justified belief p there must be a further justified belief q, and so on *ad infinitum*. In our present case, taking r = 'a's belief that q contributes to the coherence of a's belief-set', we have to continue

4   r
5   Bar
6   JBar,

and this move, once made, will have to be repeated *ad infinitum*. This new regress derives from taking an internalist approach to justification. It should remind us of the regress mentioned in 3.5.

To see whether it is a threat to coherentism, we need to be clearer about the contrast between internalism and externalism, and about the supposed advantages of externalism.

For the coherentist who is not vulnerable to the earlier regress argument the internalist regress creates a very similar problem. For the foundationalist, however, things are much worse. It looks very much as if the internalist regress will make the earlier regress quite unstoppable, no matter what subtleties we may invent. Suppose that we do reach some basic beliefs; and suppose that what makes them able to be non-inferentially justified is a certain epistemic property E (which might be anything from infallibility downwards). We are pushed by the internalist to hold that a's basic belief that p can only be justified by appeal to E if a believes that his belief has E; and then we are pushed further to admit that it is also required that he is justified in believing that his belief has E. But once this is allowed, the regress becomes unstoppable. Even the discovery of some non-inferentially justified beliefs will not stop the regress, since they can only be justified in the presence of a further justified belief. So no belief of any sort will ever be more than conditionally justified.

This gives us a very strong incentive to draw in our horns and become externalists by reducing what we require for justification. The externalist has a much easier time in two ways. First, he has no trouble with the standard regress argument. Let us take as an example of an externalist position the following definition of JBap:

JBap = a's belief that p was acquired by a reliable method.

Since inference from justified beliefs is a reliable method of belief acquisition, both inferentially and non-inferentially justified beliefs can be subsumed under this definition. Inferential justification is not particularly the province of the internalist. Now it is going to be easy for the externalist to light upon an externally justified belief, on this account. There is no need to go as far as the basic level, as traditionally conceived. If we suppose that asking one's parents is a reliable method of belief acquisition, as it might conceivably be (at least in certain circumstances), then any belief gained this way will count as non-inferentially justified. The regress argument has really lost most of its teeth here, though its bite will still provide us with the distinction between inferential and non-inferential justification.

Second, the externalist seems to have no trouble with our second sceptical argument, from error (1.2). The main thrust of this argument was that I must be able to point to a difference between this case and other relevantly similar cases where I was wrong, before I can be said to know now. But this demand seems to arise only on an internalist perspective. The externalist is quite happy to suppose that so long as there is in fact a difference between this case and others I can know now even though I am quite unable to point to the difference. If this is right, all that our second sceptical argument does is to express a further general difficulty for internalist accounts of knowledge and of justification.

Given these advantages in externalism, why should anyone be an internalist? The answer is that philosophers are only internalists because they feel they have to be. Before we can feel confident in opting for externalism, then, we need to be sure that we have properly understood what lies behind internalism. And before we can do that, we need to distinguish various degrees of internalism that surface in a rather confused way in current literature.

9.3 DEGREES OF INTERNALISM

Let us suppose that there is at least one clause c in a definition of Kap or JBap which does not start with B$a-$ or with K$a-$. An instance was given above: a's belief that p was acquired by a reliable method. Internalism might be any one of the following claims:

1 there should be no such clause c;
2 for every such clause c there should be a clause Kac;
3 for every such clause c there should be a clause Bac;
4 for every such clause c there should be a clause JBac.

There are different reasons for holding or denying each of these. 1 and 2 are the most extreme. 3 is by far the least demanding, and I shall argue that we should prefer it or at least that we should prefer it to 4. As a way of doing this I offer some comments on each in turn.

1. Taken literally, this would rule out every current definition of knowledge because in each case the first clause violates it. We could restrict the scope of 1 to the analysis of justification; but that might be to miss the point, as do so many compromises. What is the point of 1, then? One point might be that justification, the

assessment of beliefs for inclusion or rejection, is an activity to be carried out by the individual. But the individual cannot distinguish between his beliefs and the truth in any particular case. Hence where there is a clause Bap and a separate clause p one at least is redundant. If this lies behind the assertion of 1, we could reasonably restrict it to the analysis of justification on the grounds that in the determination of what he knows the individual is not in a privileged position. Even this goes against a firm philosophical tradition starting from Plato and emerging strikingly in Descartes. Accepting it for the moment, however, we can perhaps discern another impetus behind 1, so restricted, coming from a controversy in the philosophy of mind. Here there are two views about what determines the nature of a mental state such as belief. The first view (the analogue of internalism) holds that the nature of a belief is determined entirely by its subjective characteristics; thus the believer is uniquely privileged in being able to tell the nature of his own beliefs. Contrary to this is the view (the analogue of externalism) that the nature of certain sorts of belief is determined by something other than their subjective characteristics; crucially it can sometimes be determined by the nature of the surrounding world. This is not the weak view that the nature of the world causes the nature of the belief, but the strong view that the nature of the belief is logically dependent on the nature or existence of some feature of the world. An example will help here. What makes it the case that a belief is a belief about a particular kettle, say? Is the 'about-ness' a subjective internal characteristic of the belief, a characteristic which it could carry with it entirely independent of the existence or nature of any object (the kettle, perhaps)? Or is the 'about-ness', despite being an essential property of the belief, still logically dependent upon the existence and nature of the right object? In the case of such beliefs about particular objects (*de re* beliefs), there is no separable internal residue which we could think of as the 'internal' part of the story, and suppose present even when there was no relevant object. There is no lowest common factor shared by the successful and the unsuccessful '*de re*' belief.

This sort of externalism in the philosophy of mind is disputable, but is likely to have interesting consequences in the theory of perception (to be discussed later in 11.4). If we adopt it, where does it take us in the theory of knowledge and justification? Not very far, I think. What it does is remove from us the desire to suppose that everything relevant to justification should be transparently available to the believer; for if what he believes is dependent not only on his subjective states but on the independent state of the world, there is no point in insisting that every clause in the definition of justification begin with K*a* − or B*a* − . We may have hoped by this to ensure that justification is an activity for the individual, but we hope in vain. Since the procedure cannot achieve what we intend, we may as well not start.

This sort of externalism is only contentious in the theory of justification. In the theory of knowledge, it seems to be patently true, although on one reading this externalist approach to knowledge may lead to a rejection of the belief condition for knowledge, seeing knowledge not as belief plus something but as a separate state of mind. But this takes us far from our present concerns. For the moment, it seems that if there is a debate between internalist and externalist conceptions of knowledge, we have not yet captured it.

2. This version of internalism comes from Armstrong (Armstrong, 1973, pp. 153 − 7) although it is foreshadowed in Plato's *Theaetetus* (209E − 210B). As presented, however, it concerns only the theory of knowledge. There is no suggestion that to be justified one needs to *know*, for instance, that one's method is reliable. What is more, it is not convincing in the theory of knowledge either. It also creates an infinite regress. I suggest that it be quietly forgotten.

3. This is the least demanding theory. It cannot be attacked on the basis of externalism in the philosophy of mind, since that sort of externalism argued only that there was no point in insisting that all clauses begin with B*a* − or K*a* − . And it creates no infinite regress, unless conjoined with 4. (It was the combination of 3 and 4 which constructed the regresses of 3.5 and 9.1). It seems equally applicable to knowledge and to justification, and it offers a good sense of internalism, since it requires that the believer 'internalize' the facts which make his belief justified, or his true belief knowledge. If there is a sense of 'internal' justification in which all that we can ask of a man is that he retain beliefs which, so far as he can tell, meet the conditions for justification, this sort of internalism offers a relevant distinction. Internal justification occurs when all the relevant clauses B*a* − are true; external justification occurs when all the other clauses are true too.

It might seem that this theory is as much externalist as internalist, since it gives a sense to the idea of a belief being, *de facto*, externally justified which is different from the notion of internal justification. But that would be wrong for two reasons. First, according to the theory external justification includes internal justification. We can have the latter without the former, but not vice versa; so no sense is given to the idea that someone can be actually justified in a belief even though he has not grasped some of the facts in virtue of which he is justified. Second, this internalist theory clearly stands in opposition to an externalist theory like Nozick's. There is a sort of sliding scale here, and this theory is somewhere in the middle.

One of the thoughts lying behind this theory is an analogy between epistemology and ethics. When considering our attitude to a moral action, are we satisfied if the action was in fact right, or do we demand more? Surely we demand also that the agent should have believed the action to be right. Otherwise the action has no moral properties at all; it is just fortunate, rather than deserving of moral approval. Similarly in epistemology the internalist might urge that external justification must at least start from and include the internal.

I take it then that this weakest theory is a recognizable form of internalism and does satisfy some at least of the thoughts from which different sorts of internalism spring.

4. This more demanding theory is the one which leads to the regress. We can pursue the analogy with ethics to show how it seems none the less attractive and even required. We have already suggested that an action cannot be right unless its agent believes it to be right. But don't we have to add something to this? What if the agent's belief is entirely coincidental? It might be that his reasons for thinking it right, if he has any, were just irrelevant; he may, for instance, have thought the action right because it was done on a Tuesday. We may feel, then, that we need to add the requirement that the agent's belief that the action is right be justified. And this takes us to the present more extreme form of internalism. In epistemology the same thoughts are present. If we require the agent to believe that his first belief was, e.g., acquired by a reliable method, we must surely require that this belief be not entirely coincidental, that he have some good reason for it and so that it be justified.

Although there is some force in this train of thought, it is mistaken. What in fact is driving us from theory 3 to theory 4, as at the end of the previous paragraph, is the thought that justification and knowledge must somehow not depend on coincidence or luck. This was just the point of the Gettier counter-examples (2.2); nothing in the tripartite definition excluded knowledge by luck. The insistence that every clause $Ba-$ be matched by one $JBa-$ is an attempt to solve Gettier's problem and rule out knowledge by luck. The insistence that every clause $JBa-$ be matched by one $BaJBa-$ is our internalist theory 3. Put the two together and a vicious regress results, as we saw in 3.5. The solution therefore must be to find another answer to the problem of knowledge by luck; if we achieve this we have no need to add theory 4 to theory 3. The vicious regress is not a consequence of internalism alone, but of internalism added to something quite independent.

Our conclusion so far is that there is a form of internalism which is not vulnerable to the internalist regress of 9.1. Although externalism offers advantages against the sceptic, internalism is still an available option.

9.4 INTERNALISM AND COHERENTISM

Do coherentists have a free choice between internalism and externalism? It seems that they do. The relations between members of one's belief-set that make the set coherent are surely able to exist whether one believes that they do or not. So if we can persuade ourselves that internalism is unnecessary, the advantages of externalism are available to the coherentist.

There is a small doubt about this comforting conclusion. For it seems obvious that the conditions demanded by the most extreme forms of internalism would, where present, go to increase the coherence of their belief-set.

Coherentists think in terms of an increase of justification as the belief-set becomes more coherent. And it seems that the coherence of the set would always be increased by the addition of the belief that the relevant relations of mutual explanatoriness exist. This is to say that if those relations do exist, one would always be justified in believing that they do. This, however, shows only that justification is increased by the move from externalist to internalist perspective, not that it is never present without the internalist addition. Even the most extreme externalist can agree that there is a gain in the internalization of the relevant facts; and the coherentist is in a peculiarly good position to show that this is so.

If we have a free choice, which should we choose? The main attempts to argue for either position (Goldman, 1980, for externalism, and Bonjour, 1980, for internalism) suffer from an insecure grasp of the contrast between the two positions and a tendency to rely on the analogy between ethics and epistemology, which I also used in distinguishing between different forms of internalism (cf. also Pollock, 1979, pp. 108 – 11). But use of this analogy is unlikely to be effective, for two reasons. First, it is easy enough to dispute the strength of the analogy. Second, the relation between 'subjective' and 'objective' rightness in ethics (the analogue of internal and external justification) is not yet well understood and remains hotly contested.

So the present position seems to be that there are no decisive arguments on either side. My own view is that internalism has the greater intuitive support. This means that I cannot be happy in relying entirely on the possibility of externalism as a response to the sceptical argument from error; there would be an instability inherent in such a position. We still need to find a strategy which avoids the argument from error and is available to the internalist.

9.5 COHERENTISM, REALISM AND SCEPTICISM

Does coherentism itself provide such a strategy? The argument from error was expressed in realist terms; like the first sceptical argument, it seemed to depend upon real but unrecognizable (evidence-transcendent) differences. If this is right, and if coherentism turned out to be incompatible with the sort of realism required, a coherentist would have a perspective from which the argument from error is no longer a threat.

So the question now is whether coherentism is a form of anti-realism. To answer this question we need to provide a philosophical map of forms of anti-realism. There are four degrees of anti-realism, ranging from extreme solipsism, through idealism and phenomenalism, to what I shall call pure anti-realism.

The solipsist (as here defined) holds that all conceivable propositions concern his own experiences. The most extreme solipsist will only conceive of his own present experiences; more relaxed solipsists will take of their own present and past experiences, present and future experiences, or past present and future experiences.

The idealist holds that all conceivable propositions concern his own experiences or those of others; and again there are the variations to do with time, the choice of present, present and past, past present and future etc.

The phenomenalist holds that all conceivable propositions concern either actual experiences of his own or of others, or experiences that he or others might have or would have had in different circumstances. So the phenomenalist talks about actual and possible experience, while the idealist restricts himself to the actual. And again, there are versions of different strengths, according to the temporal distinctions between past present and future actual and possible experiences.

The pure anti-realist holds that some conceivable propositions concern matters other than the actual or possible experiences of himself and others, but that we still cannot understand such propositions as able to be true *unrecognizably*. So the pure anti-realist, like other anti-realists, denies the possibility of evidence-transcendent truth, but admits that some truths concern things such as material objects which are not to be thought of as reducible to experience. For an anti-realist can admit that there is a material world so long as he insists that it has no evidence-transcendent properties.

There are different strengths of pure anti-realism too, depending on what is meant by 'unrecognizably'; we need to ask 'unrecognizably by whom and when?'. Answers can vary; the strictest would be 'unrecognizably by me now'. Weaker forms would include 'unrecognizably by someone at some time or other', and the weakest form would be 'unrecognizably by a being with greater cognitive powers than ours, such as God'.

Just as there are different strengths of anti-realism, there are different strengths of realism. The realist who holds that we *can* conceive of propositions as able to be unrecognizably true must answer the same questions about what this unrecognizability amounts to. But we shall not pursue this complication.

We can now return to the question whether coherentism is a form of anti-realism. What sort of affinities are there between forms of anti-realism and coherentism? A classical position in philosophy is a combination of idealism and coherentism, both as theory of justification and as theory of truth. This combination is found in Bradley and Blanshard. And we can see why an idealist is likely to be a coherentist. The idealist holds that there is nothing other than experience and belief; he might even, as was suggested in the last chapter, say simply that there is nothing other than belief, sensory and non-sensory. And if so, there is nothing external to the belief-set which could discriminate true beliefs from false ones. Truth must be an internal characteristic, a relation between elements which are all of the same type rather than an external relation between experience or belief and something else. And coherentism conceives of truth as just such an internal characteristic. So an idealist should perhaps be a coherentist.

But there seems to be no reason yet why the coherentist should be an idealist; the link between the two is all one-way. We can conceive of truth as an internal relation in the coherentist way without adding the idealist view that the propositions so related are only concerned with experience.

We might however feel that, if not an idealist, the coherentist should adopt pure anti-realism. This would be because the coherence theories of truth and of justification are here combined. If we accepted only the coherence theory of justification, marrying it to a correspondence theory of truth, it would be easy to see that truth remains evidence-transcendent. For justification, no matter how great, remains on this view an internal relation; and it would always be possible that that internal relation be present, but that truth, the external relation between the coherent set and the world, be absent. This mixed view is then a form of realism (for an example of which see Ewing, 1934, p. 250). But we argued in 8.2 that it is an unattractive combination, because it was hard to see how, on that combination, a justified belief should be more likely to be true.

The more consistent combination of coherentism in theory of truth and in theory of justification bids fair to establish the impossibility of evidence-transcendent truth and so to commit us to anti-realism. For as justification grows, it grows towards truth. There seems to be no gap left between 'best possible justification' and truth. But this is just the anti-realist result needed to defeat the argument from error.

If this is right, then, coherentism is revealed as a form of anti-realism, and as the basis for an epistemology immune to our sceptical arguments. But if, on the other hand, a realist can consistently adopt coherentism, we lose this comforting result. And some forms of coherentism do seem to be compatible with realism. The question crucially turns on the attitude we take to the idealized notion of a fully coherent set of propositions and on the exact sense we give to the doctrine of degrees of truth. Coherentists differ about this doctrine, and it is in that difference that the distinction emerges between those who are realists and those who are not.

The realists will claim that there is no such thing as the set of all true propositions. At any time, or timelessly, there is, for each set, a larger and more coherent set. But if truth for propositions is defined in terms of coherence of sets, there can be no such thing as a proposition which is at the limit of truth. Nor can we say that propositions are approximately true, or that they get nearer and nearer to being true, considered as members of larger and larger sets. For to suppose this is to suppose that there is a conceivable state which cannot be improved on, which is called 'being true' and which we are gradually approaching. But there is no such state; it recedes as fast as we approach it. All propositions then are less than perfectly true, because the notion of perfect truth is an unattainable ideal.

With this approach there now seems to be room for the coherentist to be a realist. Truth, having attained the status of an ideal, lies beyond any possible belief-set. For any such set, no matter how large, there remains the possibility that it is false. There is no such thing as a point at which one could say, or as it were conceive, that one has now got to a point where the possibility of falsehood no longer exists. And this is not because of the shortness of human life or the fallibility of the human cognitive system. Rather it is a relation between the finitude of any possible belief-set and the infinitude of the ideal fully coherent set. On this account of the coherence theory of truth, truth is evidence-transcendent in a very strong sense.

This conclusion is contentious and important. We shall argue in 11.1 and 11.6 that anti-realism is committed to an unsound theory of perception. If all coherentists were anti-realists (idealists, say), this conclusion would destroy coherentism. So it is important that there should be a form of coherentism which is compatible with realism. Fortunately it seems that there is.

Whether this is right or not, we should beware of taking it as completely obvious that anti-realism does constitute a position invulnerable to scepticism, particularly to the argument from error. It is true that both the first two sceptical arguments of chapter 1 do appeal to the unverifiable hypothesis that we are now brains in a vat being fed our current experiences. But the argument from error, although it is presented as depending on the belief that truth is evidence-transcendent, can in fact work on the much more mundane point that we humans are *never* in so good a position that there is no room for error, no possibility, given the evidence, that our present belief is false. Even if there is no gap between the existence of the best possible evidence for p and the truth of p, there is always a gap for us between the evidence we have and the truth of p. How then can we tell whether we are in a situation in which p is true rather than one in which it is false? No matter how strong our antipathy to the existence of unverifiable differences, this sceptical question still has a bite.

The conclusion of this chapter is that coherentism is not vulnerable to any regress argument, but does not itself provide a response to scepticism. That response has still to be found.

FURTHER READING

The distinction between internalism and externalism has only recently become the focus of explicit attention. Goldman (1980) and Bonjour (1980) debate relative merits, but do not seem to agree on what internalism is. Pollock (1979) supports a form of internalism, as does Kvanvig (1984).

Classic statements of idealism and phenomenalism are Berkeley's *Principles of Human Knowledge* (Berkeley, 1954 or any other reputable edition) and Mill (1867, pp. 244 – 57).

By contrast, Dummett (1978, ch. 10) introduces pure anti-realism.

Kant's attempts to combine idealism and realism are discussed in Stroud (1984, ch. 4) with special reference to Kant's success against the sceptic.

Externalism in the philosophy of mind is discussed by the contributors to Woodfield (1982), without much reference to its effect on epistemology.

Part III
FORMS OF
KNOWLEDGE

10
Theories of Perception

10.1 IS THERE ROOM FOR A PHILOSOPHY OF PERCEPTION?

There are two general questions to be faced before we enter the murky territory of the philosophy of perception. The first is what philosophers could hope to add to the studies of perception undertaken by psychologists and neurophysiologists. The second is how an epistemologist can pay due respect to the results of those studies without getting involved in some form of vicious circularity.

In answer to the first we should perhaps say that philosophers concern themselves with very general questions about perception. These questions are ones on which psychologists do and should have views; their views here should be sensitive to their more specific results, and hence philosophers should not expect to avoid some knowledge of those results. But the more general questions can be discussed in their own right, as I hope the next two chapters will show.

The second question is raised by our answer to the first. If an epistemologist must accept as relevant the sorts of results that psychologists and neurophysiologists produce, how can he avoid the charge that his approach is circular? The circularity lies in the attempt to construct a general account of justified belief which assumes in advance that the beliefs of professional psychologists, for example, are justified. To answer *this* question we need an account of what philosophy is and of its relation to the sciences, for the claim that philosophers study more general questions increases rather than decreases the difficulty about circularity. We shall return to this matter in chapter 15.

10.2 THEORIES OF PERCEPTION

There are three main families of theories of perception: direct realism, indirect realism and phenomenalism. In this chapter we will be doing a bit of philosophical geography and picking out the main members of each family and the sorts of considerations used in their favour and against them. To avoid clutter, I have avoided attributing positions to their main protagonists until the references at the end of the chapter, where there is also a map of the positions to which it may be helpful to refer.

First, for an initial grasp of the differences between the three families we need to get a preliminary view of what is meant by realism in this context, and what the contrast is between the direct and the indirect.

Realism in the theory of perception (which we shall call perceptual realism) can be initially but vaguely characterized as the view that the objects we perceive are able to and commonly do exist and retain some at least of the properties we perceive them as having, even when they are unperceived. This is to say that the existence of the objects we perceive and at least part of their nature is independent of the existence of any perceiver. This sort of realism looks different from that discussed in 1.4 and 9.5, which we shall call metaphysical realism. We shall eventually have to decide how the two sorts of realism are related (11.6), but by then our account of perceptual realism will have been improved.

The contrast between the direct and the indirect is notoriously slippery and difficult to pin down firmly, as we shall see. It is sadly common for philosophers to inveigh against loose use of this contrast in their opponents and then to do little better themselves. Our initial definition of direct perception may be vague, but it is not so vague as to be useless. We shall take it that a perceiver P directly perceives an object O if P perceives O without perceiving any intermediary I. P would be perceiving an intermediary I if, as things are, it is only in virtue of perceiving I that P perceives O. P's relation to the intermediary I, if there is one, need not for these purposes be exactly the same as P's relation to O, and commonly will not be. The way in which P is aware of I need only be analogous to the way in which P is aware of O. So examples of indirect perception might be one's perception of oneself in a mirror and one's perception of an actor on the television. There is in both cases a more immediate object of awareness, in perceiving which one is said to perceive oneself and the actor; the intermediary object, of which one is here directly aware, perhaps, is the reflection in one case and the image in the other.

Indirect perception has been defined here in terms of analogous sorts of awareness. There will be sorts of awareness which are not perceptual, e.g. the awareness of pain, perhaps, or of the position of one's own limbs. So when we speak of perception as awareness we must remember the existence of non-perceptual awareness.

Now the dispute between the direct realist and the indirect realist concerns the question whether we are ever directly aware of the existence and nature of physical objects. Both, as realists, agree that the physical objects we see and touch are able to exist and retain some of their properties when unperceived. But the indirect realist asserts that we are never directly aware of physical objects; we are only indirectly aware of them, in virtue of a direct awareness of an intermediary object (variously described as an idea, sense-datum, percept or appearance). The direct realist denies this claim.

Phenomenalism is a form of anti-realism; the phenomenalist denies the existence of a physical world lying behind and able to come apart from the world of experience. For him, the only possible object of awareness is experience and complexes of experiences; there is no reality apart from experience. If this is so, the only objects of awareness are direct objects; there is nothing left over for us to perceive indirectly. The phenomenalist, then, can be seen as agreeing with the direct realist about the directness of perception and the absence of intermediaries, but as agreeing with the indirect realist that the direct objects of perception are not physical objects. This description is preliminary: it will be revised and, I fear, complicated in 10.6.

We also need to say more about the notion of directness as defined. That notion is vague, mainly because we have given no precise sense to the notion of an intermediary; we have only spoken sketchily about perceiving one thing 'in virtue of' perceiving another, and about the need that the two sorts of perception be 'analogous'. These terms can and should be sharpened if we are to be sure that we have a really clear grasp on the distinction between direct and indirect realism. Meanwhile the present vagueness of the distinction is not an argument in favour of either side.

Our definition of directness, though unsatisfactory, is not entirely spineless. There are two crucial notions which tend to be either invalidly inferred from it or even simply confused with it. The first is that of infallibility. We may wonder how it is possible to be mistaken about the existence or nature of something of which we are directly aware. If the object is directly present to me in the most intimate sense available, there seems to be no room for me to be wrong about it. But this is just an error. In the defined sense of 'direct', we can be mistaken about an object even when directly perceiving it.

And we can see that it is an error by considering the argument in 4.2 to the effect that our knowledge of our own sensory states is fallible. Whether that argument was successful or not does not matter here. What does matter is that, even if successful, it raised no doubt about the directness of our awareness of our own sensory states. There was no temptation to conclude from our fallibility here that our awareness is only indirect, and that there is some other more direct object than our own sensory states. So direct awareness need not be infallible.

It is worth stressing this point because of the resistance it can arouse. If we start from a notion of direct perception, we tend to think of a directly perceived object as standing nakedly open to inspection, in such a way that perceptual error about its nature is impossible, and maybe also that there cannot be facts about it which we have failed to notice; that we are not only infallible here but omniscient. On this model of directness, it is easy to see that there is no such thing as direct perception of the physical world, and the indirect realist wins the argument by default. But on the model we are considering, starting from the notion of indirect perception as defined, the direct perceiver need not be either infallible or omniscient, and an interesting debate is generated between two possible theories.

The second mistake is to suppose it obvious that an object of which we are directly aware must exist and have the qualities we attribute to it at the moment at which we are aware of it. This is a thought about time; the awareness and its object must exist at the same time. In the above expression of that thought there is still a hint of the desire for infallibility. But forgetting that as irrelevant, we can still ask whether the object of direct awareness must not at least exist at the moment of awareness. Surely the direct object is presented to us; it is directly present to us. But how can it be now present to us if it is now non-existent? At best the non-existent must be thought of as absent (temporally and geographically), and so not present.

There is an unfortunate ambiguity in the notion of the 'present' here, and I suggest that the argument above trades on it. In one sense of 'present', the present is contrasted with the absent (temporally or geographically). In another sense, the present is that which is presented, that of which we are directly aware. So long as we do not trade on this ambiguity, I see no argument to force us from one sense to the other. In the sense defined, I suggest that an object such as a distant star can have ceased to exist by the moment at which we are directly aware of it.

This suggestion may seem counter-intuitive. If you find it so, you will be confirmed (I expect) in this when you notice that if it is right there will be available a sense in which memory can be direct awareness of the past. I mention this now so as not to be accused of cheating later. It does not yet mean that memory *is* direct awareness of the past; only that we cannot argue that memory must be a form of indirect awareness just because its object is past.

10.3 DIRECT REALISM

Direct realism holds that in sense-perception we are directly aware of the existence and nature of the surrounding physical world. All direct realists agree about this, the directness side of things. They differ, however, in the degree of realism they are willing to espouse. The realist, in our present sense, holds that physical objects are able to exist and retain some at least of the properties which we perceive them as having, even when unperceived. The crucial phrase is 'some at least', and the question is which, exactly. We shall distinguish two types of direct realism, the naïve and the scientific; in the nature of the case, however, there must be many possible intermediate positions.

The naïve direct realist holds that unperceived objects are able to retain properties of all the types we perceive them as having. By this he means that an unperceived object may still have not only a shape and size but also be hot or cold, have a colour, a taste and a smell, be rough or smooth and make a noise or keep silent. The naïveté of this position lies in the word 'all'. The position becomes less naïve as 'all' retreats to 'nearly all' and then to 'most' and so on, but it is simplest for us to view it in the starkest and most extreme case.

Opposed to the naïve form of direct realism is scientific direct realism. This scientific version takes it that science has shown that physical objects do not retain when unperceived all of the properties we perceive them as having; for some of those properties are dependent for their existence upon the existence of a perceiver. Thus colour, taste, sound and smell, heat and roughness are not independent properties of the object which it can retain unperceived. The object only has them in relation to the perceiver. The scientific direct realist accepts the directness of our perception of the world, but restricts his realism to a special group of properties.

The distinction made her is a close relative of Locke's distinction between primary and secondary qualities (see J. Locke, 1961, Bk 2 ch. 8). Locke held that the 'primary' qualities of shape, size, molecular texture and motion have a different status from that of the 'secondary' qualities such as colour, heat, smell, taste etc. (we could call these the 'sensory' properties). According to Locke, an object which we perceive as coloured does not retain when unperceived any quality of the sort we perceive it as having. There is a sense in which it remains coloured, of course; for its primary properties, which it does retain, remain such that in suitable conditions it will look coloured to the perceiver. An object retains the 'primary quality ground' for the secondary qualities it appears as having, then. But colour-as-we-see-it, heat-as-we-feel-it and taste-as-we-taste-it are not properties which the object can be said to retain when unperceived; and for that reason we cannot suppose that those properties are independent properties of the object when it is perceived. Colour-as-we-see-it is really more a property of our way of being aware of the physical world than a property of that world itself.

Locke provided a miscellany of arguments for this position. He suggested variously that experimental evidence forces it upon us, and that the naïve alternative is inconceivable. A weaker argument than the appeal to the inconceivability of any alternative is an analogue of Ockham's razor. This razor is the general principle that we should not multiply entities further than necessary; we should not, for instance, admit the existence of numbers or of other putative sorts of entities unless we have literally no alternative. The analogue of this argument in our present case is that we should not admit the existence of a sort of property if we can avoid it. Parsimony is always the right attitude in metaphysics, perhaps. And now the appeal to science can come in. For we can say that the sorts of explanation that contemporary physics offers give us no need to suppose that the secondary qualities are independent properties of physical objects. This can be maintained in two ways. First, we need to appeal to the primary qualities of microscopic objects to explain the primary qualities of macroscopic objects, but we don't need to ascribe secondary qualities to the microscopic objects in order to explain the secondary qualities of the macroscopic ones. For the shape and size of an ordinary object are explained by appeal to the shapes and sizes of its component parts, but the colour and heat of an ordinary object are not explained by appeal to the colour and heat of the parts; we don't need, in our explanation, to think of those parts as having colour or heat at all. Second, our explanation of the perceptual event of an object's looking square is a causal explanation which requires us to attribute to the cause some shape or other (normally at least). But our explanation of an object's looking blue, so far as we can explain this at the moment, requires no similar property, no colour in the object; the explanation relies only on relations between primary properties of object, eye, brain and local conditions. Parsimony then demands that we abandon the idea of there being in the object anything like colours-as-we-see-them. The world, so far as it exists independent of perceivers, is a world of primary qualities alone.

This appeal to the authority of physics is obviously impressive. It does not make it impossible for the direct realist to maintain his position, for Ockham's razor is only a methodological principle, not a necessary truth. But it does raise an obstacle. I think that the naïve form of direct realism is nevertheless more attractive than the scientific form. What then can be the reasons for this preference?

There are two points that can be made against the scientific form. The first is a general disquiet about the operation of the primary/secondary quality distinction, which was first raised by Berkeley (Berkeley, 1954, *Principles* §§ 8, 14 − 15; see also the first of his *Three Dialogues*). The question is whether our experience of the world, an experience in which primary and secondary qualities appear intermingled and of similar status, is such that we can conceive of the sort of separation that the scientific view calls for, and can suppose that we understand what it is like for there to be a spatial world with primary qualities but no secondary ones. The question, then, is about the intelligibility of the scientific conception of the world. We cannot imagine what it would be like to perceive such a world as it really is. It would be impossible to see the objects of that world and to distinguish them one from another without perceiving them as coloured. What persuades us, then, that we can conceive of what such a world is like even though we cannot conceive of what it would look like? There seems to be some danger here of crediting ourselves with powers of which we cannot make good sense.

This first point is a general disquiet about the primary/secondary quality distinction. The second point is that even if this distinction is sound, it is not obvious that it is available to the direct realist. For there may be an incompatibility of approach here. If there is, it is difficult to pin down. An initial suggestion is that for a direct realist our awareness of colour and heat can hardly be of a different order from our awareness of shape and size. Both sorts of properties are presented with equal directness; the colour of the object is as much part of it as its shape and size are. A second version might be that it is not clear what account of colour perception the scientific direct realist can give. There is a danger that the account will be a form of indirect realism; for surely colour is directly perceived if anything is, and so if physical objects are not themselves coloured we shall have to find some other probably intermediate object which *is* coloured. But if we admit an intermediate object to bear the sensory properties, we might as well abandon direct realism altogether.

These remarks are less than clear, but they express a difficulty with scientific direct realism which argues in favour of the naïve form as being more consistent. The naïve form, however, has its problems too. But we shall see that most of them are problems for the scientific form as well.

The first problem is the inclination to protest that we cannot conceive of colours-as-we-see-them continuing to exist unperceived. This remark, if true, is as much a criticism of the scientific form as of the naïve form; for the scientific form holds that this is conceivable, but that science has given us reason to believe that though conceivable it is not true. But is this protest justified? (And if it is justified, what will prevent it from being equally effective in the case of shape-as-we-see-it and size-as-we-see-it, as Berkeley argued that it is?) It cannot be a straightforward appeal to intuition, for intuition, so far as it goes, seems to me to be here all on the side of the naïve realist. What argument lies behind it?

The first argument is that perceived colour alters according to the condition, not only of the object, but of the surrounding circumstances (crucially, the light) and of the perceiver. Therefore there can be no such thing as the real colour of the object; any choice among the different perceived colours must be arbitrary and probably depend upon human purposes. But if real colour is defined relative to human purposes have we not abandoned our claim that objects retain a colour unperceived? The answer is no. The *real* colour need not be the one which continues unperceived; we could instead, and better, define the real colour as that which is perceived in normal conditions. This leaves it possible for objects to retain a colour unperceived, which may or may not be their real colour. In maintaining that they retain a colour unperceived, the naïve realist is not committed to saying which one they retain. Anyway the argument from the changes in perceived colour caused by changes in the observer is invalid. The suggestion that some colour continues unperceived is compatible with the view that we perceive physical objects directly as coloured and with the view that the colour of an object can alter according to its surroundings (e.g. neon light, twilight).

The second argument is that objects lose their colour in the dark Therefore, it may be said, colour can only be said to exist in conditions suitable for perception; this is what makes it hard to say that colour can exist unperceived. But, first, the naïve realist need not admit that objects lose their colour in the dark; he can say instead that they retain a colour which, because of contingently unfavourable conditions, we cannot see. And even if he does admit that colour ceases in the dark, he can still escape. For the fact that colour can only exist in the presence of suitable light does nothing to show that colour cannot exist unperceived, so long as we admit that suitable light can be present unperceived.

The second and more worrying group of problems for naïve direct realism concerns the possibility of perceptual error and hallucination. There is a right and a wrong way to express this difficulty. The wrong way is to say, as was very commonly said, that naïve realism is simply refuted by the existence of perceptual error; for we cannot be directly perceiving something if the way we see it to be is not the way it is. This is the old mistake of supposing that directness entails infallibility, and there is no reason for any sort of direct realist to worry about it. However, the bald statement that directness of perception is compatible with perceptual error seems insufficient, and the reason for this is that perceptual error needs an explanation, and it is not obvious how the direct realist can provide one. So the right way to put the point is to say that direct realism is unlikely to be able to provide an explanation of perceptual error without collapsing into indirect realism. This was a move made against scientific direct realism and its account of colours; it now occurs more generally as a difficulty for any direct realist.

I take this difficulty seriously. But before considering it (in 11.3), we need to look at indirect realism to see how and why it claims to do better. Anyway, it is hard to understand the claims of direct realism until one sees what is maintained by the opposition.

10.4 INDIRECT REALISM

Indirect realism holds that in perception we are indirectly aware of the physical objects around us in virtue of a direct awareness of internal, non-physical objects.

This is the most straightforward form of indirect realism, and it is the one with which this section is concerned. There are further forms of indirect realism which will be mentioned (only to be rejected) in chapter 11. They include the suggestion that we are never *aware* of physical objects, but infer their presence from the nature of the internal objects of which we are (directly) aware.

For the moment, however, we shall concentrate on arguments in favour of the theory stated. The tradition contains an enormous wealth of argumentation designed to force us to admit the presence of the internal direct object. I offer here four attempts.

The first is an appeal to introspection. Surely each of us knows from our own case that when we are aware of an external object our perceptual state has its own nature. Two people, aware of the same object, will be in different perceptual states. And the difference between those states can be described as a difference in *content*. The different states have different perceptual content. And what can the content of our awareness be other than an object of awareness? We are aware of that content, and it is only in virtue of our awareness of that content that we are able to be (indirectly) aware of the material object thus presented to us. So the content of our perceptual state is the direct object of awareness, our intermediary object.

The second argument is known as the time-lag argument. When we perceive an object such as a star, it is quite possible that the star has ceased to exist by the time that we perceive it. The star therefore can only be an indirect object of perception, because it is not present to us at the moment of perception. If it is an indirect object there must also be a direct object; and if there is one in this case, there must be one in all cases. For there is always a time-lag, even if only very short, between an object's being so and our perceiving that it is so. And if so, though the object may continue, the state of the object which is presented to us is not in existence at the moment of perception, and cannot therefore constitute the content of awareness, which must be present at that moment.

This argument clearly relies to a great extent on the second confusion pointed out in 10.2, that of supposing that the direct object of perception must be present at the moment of perception. If it adds anything to that confusion, it adds considerations like those of the first argument. Awareness must have a content; the content must exist at the moment of awareness, and must be an internal direct object. Since this just *is* the first argument, the time-lag argument seems to add nothing new.

The third argument is the notorious argument from illusion. This has appeared in many guises; there is a sense indeed in which the previous argument could be called an argument from illusion (or even two senses, one not very complimentary). But the central form of the argument from illusion is based on the fact that genuine perceptual experiences are qualitatively indistinguishable to the perceiver at the relevant time from illusory experiences. The word 'illusion' should be taken very carefully here. The argument takes its strongest form when we concentrate not so much on illusion, when an object appears to us to be different from the way it actually is, but rather on hallucination, when we take there to be an object in front of us which does not in fact exist at all. The direct realist seems to be forced to say that in normal cases perception is a relation between perceiver and (external) object, but that there are abnormal cases of hallucination which, although indistinguishable to the perceiver in their general nature, are of a completely different type, being not a relation between perceiver and object but a non-relational state of the perceiver. The phenomenal similarity between the two cases (i.e. the fact that the person concerned cannot tell them apart) is a reason for avoiding any analysis of them that makes them radically different in nature. So the indirect realist concludes that the best analysis is to suppose that both states have an internal object, but only one has an external indirect object. Since the existence and nature of the indirect object is not intrinsic to the nature of the perceptual state of the perceiver, the phenomenal similarities between the states do not prevent us from saying that one is graced by an external object and one is not.

This argument is not conclusive. It is possible to suppose that the two states do differ so fundamentally despite their phenomenal similarities, but the argument from illusion acts as a reminder that there is at best something awkward about this, and that it would be much more attractive to avoid it. I agree that direct realism is committed to the awkward distinction, but think that for all its awkwardness it may still be preferable to indirect realism (see 11.2 for reasons).

The final argument for indirect realism is an argument based on the achievements of neurophysiology. This argument stresses the enormous complexity of the causal processes involved in perception, the details of which we are only beginning to glimpse. Given that complexity, it asks, how can we claim that we perceive the external object directly? There are many states or processes of the brain intermediate between the external object and the perception; surely then the object is separated from us, and can only be perceived indirectly by means of the effects which it has on our retinal surfaces etc.

This argument is a mistake. We can easily agree on the importance of recent neurophysiological discovery, but not so easily on its relevance to the point at issue. For what is the sense in which the brain processes occur as intermediaries between us and the external object? The sense in which this is so is causal; their occurrence is causally necessary for the perception to occur. But, crucially, we are not aware of their occurrence in any sense even distantly analogous to the sense in which we are aware of external objects. So the neurophysiological processes do not function as intermediary direct objects of perception. This argument, then, is not an argument for indirect realism at all.

What we are left with as a result of all these arguments is the point made by the first that the content of awareness should be taken to be an internal object, and the perhaps not critical awkwardness in direct realism exposed by the argument from illusion. Neither point is conclusive. The second point can wait until we examine in more detail the success, or lack of it, with which the direct realist can deal with the phenomenon of perceptual error (11.3). The first contains more assertion than argument; its success must depend upon an examination of the difficulties in taking contents of awareness as objects. These difficulties are explored in 11.2.

10.5 NAÏVE AND SCIENTIFIC FORMS OF INDIRECT REALISM

We can distinguish between naïve and scientific forms of indirect realism. The naïve form holds, in a familiar way, that the indirect object of awareness has properties of, by and large, all the types that the direct object has. Thus the indirect object, the physical object, has colour, smell, tastes etc., as well as shape and size. Scientific indirect realism, which is much the commoner view, holds that the indirect object has only the primary properties, and that the secondary (sensory) properties only belong to the direct object.

There is, as Locke would say, nothing like them in the (indirect) object.

There are problems for both options. The scientific form involves the sort of separation of primary from secondary properties which we earlier saw to be questionable. But the way in which that separation functions within indirect realism is different from the way it functions within direct realism, and may be thought to be less objectionable. After all, one of the objections to it in 10.3 was that it was incompatible with the general thrust of direct realism, and was likely to lead to a sort of indirect realism in the account of colours and the other sensory properties. The question whether we can conceive of a world of objects which have only primary qualities was raised but not answered. The matter is contentious. So the scientific form of indirect realism is a possible option, for all that we have said so far.

The naïve form, however, is grossly implausible. It involves the grotesque suggestion that as well as the visible colours belonging to the direct objects of awareness, there are other colours, not visible in the same sense, belonging to the indirect objects. But we cannot accept the suggestion that there are two sorts of colour, one visible and the other invisible; or, since this is an overstatement of the position, that there are two ways of being aware of colour, one direct and one essentially indirect. We are strongly tempted to say that colour is something of which we can only be directly aware, at least in normal cases. And I think this temptation should not be resisted.

In these two sections I have offered a map of four types of realism in the theory of perception. I have argued that the naïve form of direct realism is stronger than the scientific form, and that the scientific form of indirect realism is stronger than the naïve form. We have found no conclusive arguments in favour of either of the surviving theories, nor generally in favour of direct rather than indirect realism (nor vice versa). I offer here the preliminary suggestion that direct realism is supported by an enormously strong intuition that the physical world in some sense lies open for direct inspection; for an inspection which is not by proxy. On the other hand, the pronouncements of physics favour the sort of distinction between primary and secondary qualities which seems to fit better within an indirect realism.

10.6 PHENOMENALISM AND IDEALISM

The account given of phenomenalism in 10.2 was preliminary; it needs complication if we are properly to understand the relation between phenomenalism and perceptual realism.

In 9.5 we distinguished between idealism and phenomenalism as forms of anti-realism. The initial contrast between the two can be seen most clearly in the work of Bishop Berkeley (Berkeley, 1954, *Principles of Human Knowledge*). His idealism was what might be called metaphysical; he claimed that physical objects just are collections of actual ideas. For him an object cannot exist unperceived; the *esse* of a physical object is *percipi* (for it to exist is for it to be perceived). Objects can perhaps reappear after a gap in perception, but they cannot continue unperceived during the gap. The danger that most objects are on this account very gappy, and the consequent problems about reidentification after a gap, were met by Berkeley's claim that God is a permanent perceiver of all possible ideas. By this claim Berkeley ensures that physical objects have a continuous existence analogous to the sort of existence which the realist would claim for them; it is no more than analogous because for the realist objects are continuous and independent, while for Berkeleian idealism they are continuous and dependent.

There are traces also in Berkeley of the more flexible view that physical objects exist so long as it is *possible* to perceive them, even though they be not actually perceived (cf. Berkeley, 1954, §§ 3, 58). One way of expressing this view is to say that according to it objects are collections of actual and possible ideas; but this is a bit odd, because one is not sure what a possible idea is, and whether it can be collected into a bundle with actual ones. However we express the view, it clearly implies that physical objects can exist unperceived, so long as they are still able to be perceived. This is a phenomenalist conclusion.

Phenomenalism is more flexible and (therefore) more plausible than idealism, for it seems to give a more natural sense to the idea that physical objects can continue to exist unperceived; and for this reason it yields a better theory of perception. Unlike idealism, phenomenalism can offer something by way of explanation for the occurrence of perceptual events. The phenomenalist can say that what explains the fact that I see my car in the garage whenever I open the door is that the car is there all the time, waiting to be seen. (We shall consider in 11.1 whether this explanation is as effective as it looks.) And for this reason phenomenalism is thought of as the main form of perceptual anti-realism. Idealism is left out of account, despite the fact that it may in the end be the more consistent theory and that Berkeley may have been right in preferring it.

There is a distinction between types of phenomenalism, which is relevant to the way we conceive the relation between phenomenalism and realism. This is the distinction between eliminative and reductive phenomenalism. And the same distinction can be drawn between types of idealism, where it can be most easily understood.

The crucial question here is whether the idealist admits or denies the existence of physical or material objects. The eliminative idealist holds that there is no such thing as a material object; there is nothing but experience (idea, sensation). The reductive idealist holds that there are indeed material objects, but they are nothing other than complexes of experience. Berkeley was of the latter type, though he complicated the question by distinguishing between what philosophers (scientists) meant by 'material object', which he said was incomprehensible, and what ordinary people meant by it, which he said was true.

The distinction between eliminative and reductive phenomenalism means that our original account of perceptual realism needs amendment. We said that the perceptual realist holds that material objects (are able to) exist and retain most of their properties when unperceived. The eliminative phenomenalist denies this, certainly. But the reductive phenomenalist can and does assert it. We need therefore a new and better ground for the distinction between perceptual realism and its opponents. This can be found when we consider what account the rival theories give of the nature of the world when not experienced.

All agree, perhaps, that during the intervals between experience there remains the possibility of experience. A consequence of the permanent existence of a physical object is that if someone were to be at the right place at the right time they would have an experience of such and such a sort (or, better, the world would seem to them to be in such and such a way). But the realist is distinguished by wanting to say that as well as the permanent possibility of experience there is a permanent ground for that possibility, something distinct from it and supporting it; and this something is a material world. This proposition is denied by all phenomenalists, and it is in that denial that the weakness of phenomenalism can now be exposed.

FURTHER READING

Ayer (1969, chs 1 – 2) gives a classic account of the argument from illusion, but draws from it the idiosyncratic conclusion that indirect realism is not a substantial theory about the nature of perception but a recommendation for a new philosophical language (in keeping with his views about the nature of philosophy).

Strawson (1979) supports naïve direct realism, but strangely maintains it to be compatible with some form of scientific realism.

Cornman (1975, introduction) gives a helpful analysis of the critical notion of direct perception; his ch. 6 defends naïve realism against most objections. My discussion is much indebted to Cornman's.

Jackson (1977, ch. 1) discusses the distinction between mediate and immediate objects of perception.

In my view the books by Cornman and Jackson are the best available on the philosophy of perception.

I have tried to ensure that my terminology in this chapter is reasonably representative. The various theories can be mapped as follows:

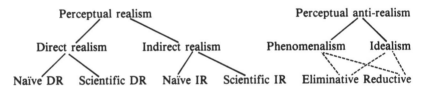

Direct realism is often simply called naïve realism, but this obscures an important distinction. Indirect realism is often called representative realism, or the representative theory of perception.

The theories are discussed as follows in this chapter and the next:
Naïve direct realism is tentatively preferred to scientific direct realism in 10.3.
Naïve indirect realism is rejected in 10.5.
Idealism is rejected in 10.6.
Phenomenalism is rejected in 11.1.
Scientific indirect realism is rejected in 11.2.
Direct realism is examined in greater detail in 11.3 – 5.
Scientific direct realism is hesitatingly preferred to naïve direct realism in 11.6.

Philosophers who may be currently considered as champions of the different theories are:

Naïve direct realism: Strawson (1979), Armstrong (1961 – but cf. Armstrong, 1968, chs 10 – 11, esp. p. 227), Cornman (1975).

Scientific direct realism: Sellars (1963, ch. 3).
Naïve indirect realism: Mackie (1976, ch. 2) (an examination of Locke's views).
Scientific indirect realism: J. Locke (1961), Jackson (1977).
Phenomenalism: Ayer (1969, ch. 5), C. I. Lewis (1946, ch. 7).

For the period 1900 – 50 most philosophers were indirect realists. Now the pendulum has swung in favour of direct realism; Jackson (1977) is an exception to the rule.

The suggestion that Sellars is what I have called a scientific direct realist is contentious; Cornman thinks of Sellars as an indirect realist (Cornman, 1975, pp. 271 – 2). The matter turns on whether sensa, which Sellars thinks of as explanatory theoretical constructs, are thought of also as intermediate objects of perception.

Although Cornman rejects a theory which he calls naïve direct realism, his 'compatible common sense realism' seems to be a version of what I have been calling naïve direct realism, because it is a form of direct realism which rejects the primary/secondary quality distinction.

11
Perception:
the Choice of a Theory

11.1 PHENOMENALISM AND THE EXPLANATION OF EXPERIENCE

Suppose that on some occasion it seems to you as if there is a wall in front of you, and you are right; there is a wall and you can see it. What explanation can be given of the fact that it seems to you as if you are in front of a wall? How are we to explain the occurrence of a perceptual experience?

The realist has an answer which appeals very strongly, and the question is whether the appeal can or should be resisted. The explanation springs from the continuous existence of a material object with certain properties, and the new event of a perceiver coming into contact (if only visual) with it. There was a wall there all the time, and this explains why when you arrived and opened your eyes you seemed to see a wall.

The phenomenalist's parallel answer is that there is indeed something continuous here, which explains the occurrence of this perceptual experience now; but it is not quite the realist's wall. There is a continuing or permanent possibility of experience, which is triggered by the occurrence of suitable conditions (which the realist would call your arriving on the scene with your eyes open). So the phenomenalist explains your seeming to see a wall by appeal to the permanently true subjunctive conditional, that if suitable conditions were to occur you would seem to see a wall.

The problem is that this subjunctive conditional seems itself to need an explanation. How does it come about that the subjunctive conditional is true? Now the realist need not deny its truth, nor even its relevance in the explanation. But he can provide an explanation of its truth on the same lines as before; it is true because there is a continuous physical object acting as *ground* for the permanent possibility of sensation. You would seem to see a wall if you opened your eyes, because (among other things) there is a wall there all the time. What can the phenomenalist appeal to, to ground the subjunctive conditional?

The standard phenomenalist reply to this is to appeal to regularities in actual past experience. The subjunctive conditional is grounded in regular conjunctions of experiences of being in a certain place and experiences of a wall; you would seem to see a wall in these circumstances because regularly in the past you (and others) have done so. We can in suitable cases infer a subjunctive conditional from a statement of such regularity in experience, and this is just because the regularity goes to make the subjunctive conditional true.

But this reliance upon past regularities to ground the subjunctive conditional seems to provide the wrong sort of explanation for the perceptual experience we started off with. We can be helped to see this by an example. Suppose that there is an arch supporting our wall. What explains the ability of the arch to support the wall? An answer which appealed to regular success of similar arches in supporting similar walls would be an answer of the wrong sort. It might silence us, or satisfy us, but it ought not to. For our demand for an explanation for the ability of this arch to support this wall should not be satisfied by a gesture towards other similar cases. We know that the arch *does* support the wall; what we want to know is why. Appeal to past regularities seems not to tell us why, but only that the arch will or does support the wall; this information may be interesting, but it is not what we were after. What we want to know is what there is about *this* arch which makes it able to support *this* wall, and remarks about other arches seem not to be directly to the point, and indeed to make the problem worse. For if there is a problem or mystery about *this* arch, talk about other arches will just make the mystery more mysterious, not less.

Similarly, when we ask for an explanation of a perceptual experience, we are asking for an account in terms of *this* situation; we want to know what there is about this situation which grounds its ability to cause certain perceptual experiences. The phenomenalist reply in terms of previous regularities is not what we are after, though it is all he can provide. Only the realist is able to provide an answer, in terms of the unobserved but continuing properties of the object we see. So the realist can offer a contemporaneous and relevant ground for the subjunctive conditional about experience; he grounds it in the permanent nature of a distinct sort of thing, a physical object. But the phenomenalist cannot in the end provide a relevant explanation of perceptual experience.

What is the relation between this criticism of phenomenalism and that which we considered in 6.3? We argued there that the meaning of a statement about a material object was not equivalent to the meaning of any collection of subjunctive conditionals about experience. And what we have provided here is a new reason for thinking that to be true. For it is only if the two are not equivalent in meaning that one could serve as a ground for the other. If they were equivalent, there would be no explanatory potential in the move from one to the other. But a statement about a material object can explain and ground the truth of a subjunctive conditional about experience.

What reply would a phenomenalist be likely to make to this argument? The proper response is to query the assumptions underlying the argument. We can distinguish between dispositional and categorical properties of objects. The dispositional properties are the abilities which the object has to operate in certain ways under certain conditions. The categorical properties are not dispositions to act in certain ways (which is not yet to say what they are). We might feel that we know that if an object has a dispositional property, it must also have a categorical property. For a dispositional property needs a ground which is non-dispositional. For instance, sharpness is a dispositional property. But a knife that is sharp must be so in virtue of the non-dispositional arrangement of its molecules; this arrangement is a categorical property which grounds the knife's disposition to cut easily, and maybe also others such as the disposition to look grey in a certain light.

We might feel that dispositions cannot exist without a ground; that if an object is disposed to behave in a certain way or to have certain effects, this is only because it has certain categorical properties, an intrinsic nature which grounds and explains its ability so to behave. And this feeling is simply all that was expressed in the argument that subjunctive conditionals about experience need the sort of grounding which only a realist can countenance. For only a realist can provide a suitable, i.e. non-dispositional, ground. But the feeling can be questioned, despite the fact that for some people it is so strong that they dignify it by calling it a conceptual necessity or a rational requirement. We can show how questionable it is by showing that the sort of explanation which contemporary physics offers is in general dispositional; the basic properties of matter are currently thought of as dispositions, and if basic presumably as ungrounded dispositions. For instance, physicists think of electric charge as a basic property, though they suppose there to be some link between this basic property and a disposition to behave in a certain way. But what is the difference between the basic property and the disposition? It is not that one supports or grounds the other; rather they are indistinguishable. So if we can accept basic dispositional properties in physics, we can surely accept them in philosophical psychology. And so, contrary to the argument, subjunctive conditionals about experience do not need a categorical grounding of the sort which only a realist could countenance.

In reply we might distinguish three stages. First there are what we could call 'subjective dispositions'; these are an object's dispositions to appear in a certain way to a perceiver. Next there are 'objective dispositions'; these are dispositions to act in certain ways, definable without reference to a perceiver. Finally there are categorical states of the object, which ground but are not themselves dispositions to act in certain ways. The phenomenalist reply above claims that subjective dispositions can be explained without recall to any third stage of categorical property, such as only the realist can provide. The answer to this is that the fact that physics takes some dispositional properties as basic in no way reconciles us to the idea that the subjective dispositions we are concerned with could be basic. Whatever the basic properties are, the disposition to appear red could not be among them. Therefore, though we may be prepared on some occasions to admit the existence of ungrounded objective dispositions, we should not accept the possibility of a phenomenalist account of objective dispositions. I think then that the phenomenalist move, though it does much to improve the standard of the argument, does not succeed in showing how to explain a perceptual experience in phenomenalist terms.

11.2 INDIRECT REALISM: DOUBLE AWARENESS AND A DOUBLE OBJECT

If phenomenalism is rejected, our choice is between the two forms of realism. The remainder of this chapter argues in favour of direct realism. I try to show that we cannot make good sense of the role of the 'internal' direct object of awareness, and take this to be sufficient argument against indirect realism. I then try to defend direct realism against objections.

In chapter 10 I gave the main arguments for indirect realism and its claim that we are only indirectly aware of the physical world. Indirect realists claim that we are more directly aware of something else. The question is what, and what role these more direct objects can play.

There have been various answers to the first question. The internal objects have been called percepts, sensa, sensibilia, sense-data, appearances, ideas and more besides. The question, however, is not the name we should give them, but what the objects so named are supposed to be like. We could, after all, say that we have shown that there must be an internal direct object; let us call this object a 'sensum' and now examine our arguments in greater detail in order to discover what they can tell us about what these sensa are like. What sense do the arguments give to the word 'internal', for instance?

The argument from illusion, as I expressed it in 10.4, leads us to suppose that hallucination is a state of the perceiver which is directed towards an object; but that, because it is hallucination, the existence and nature of that object are not logically dependent on any facts about the perceiver's surroundings, nor upon the physical states of the perceiver's body or organs. The conclusion is that we can ask even in the normal case for a characterization of how it is with the perceiver, a characterization which does not entail anything about the perceiver's body or about the surrounding world. That characterization includes an account of an object, and the object is 'internal' merely in the sense that its nature is dependent entirely upon the content of the perceiver's awareness, which itself is independent or can at least be characterized independently of any implications for the physical world. So we know at least that a sensum cannot be the surface of a physical object, as was once suggested. But the arguments of 10.4 tell us very little else about the internal direct object of awareness. All we know is that it is an object bearing the properties that form the content of awareness, described without implication for the nature of the physical world. But I think that even from this minimal description we shall be able to find difficulties for indirect realism, to which I now turn.

The Sceptical Objection

A classic complaint against the indirect realist's picture is that it immediately leads us to a very general scepticism about the possibility of any knowledge of the 'external' world. If everything we directly perceive is an 'internal' object, how could we be in a position to form any justified beliefs about a physical external world? For all we know, since we never perceive it directly, there is no such thing as a physical world at all. Berkeley argued that we cannot infer the existence of an external world. It is logically possible even given our awareness of internal direct objects, that there be no external world, and so an inference from the internal to the external cannot be deductive. If the inference were inductive, however, it would rely upon establishing previous successful correlations between statements about internal direct objects and external indirect ones. But *ex hypothesi* we cannot establish such correlations, for to do so we would have to be aware of the external objects independently. Indirect realism holds, however, that we are only ever aware of them indirectly; our awareness of them is dependent on our awareness of a sensum.

This argument has had an enormous effect, and has been a main impetus towards phenomenalism. For if you are convinced of the existence of sensa, and overwhelmed by sceptical doubts about anything else, you will very probably be tempted by the radical solution of simply doing without the anything else, and constructing a world entirely out of sensa and groups of sensa. For all its hoary past, however, there is a growing conviction that the argument is misconceived. If the argument makes crucial use of the idea that we cannot establish the required correlations because we cannot observe external objects, it is mistaken. Indirect realism does not have the consequence that external objects are unobservable; it purports simply to tell us something about what it is to observe them. And if the point is that indirect realism is vulnerable to the sceptical argument from error, the answer is that the argument from error is a menace to any theory of perception including direct realism and phenomenalism; for on any theory there will remain the possibility that things may not be the way they seem.

So the sceptical objection appears ineffective against indirect realism as we have characterized it. If the indirect realist had held that physical objects are unobservable and that we infer their presence and nature from our knowledge of the internal objects which we do perceive, the sceptical objection might have had some role to play. (The importance of this point will emerge in the next sub-section.) But against an indirect realist who maintains that there are two analogous forms of awareness, direct and indirect, the sceptical argument seems powerless.

We turn then to consider whether we can make sense of the notion of the two analogous forms of awareness and their respective objects.

The Direct and the Indirect

Locke's theory of perception is a classic instance of indirect realism, as we have characterized that position. Locke held that in perception there is a double awareness, each with its own object. The internal object, which he called the idea, is *perceived* and the external object, the material thing, is *seen*. In perceiving an idea, then, in favourable cases we are seeing a material thing. So there is a double awareness, one for the internal and one for the external object.

A natural objection to the notion of a double awareness is that to the perceiver there only seems to be *one* sort of awareness and *one* sort of object (we can argue later about whether it is 'internal' or not). What can be said to help us accept the claim that to see an object is to be in two distinguishable but analogous states of awareness?

The answer is that we are in fact quite familiar with the idea that we are aware of one thing in virtue of being (analogously) aware of another. It is in virtue of our awareness of the reflections in a mirror that we are aware of the presence of the objects reflected, and the sense in which we are aware of the reflection is analogous to the sense in which we thereby see the objects. Similarly, we are aware of the image of a television screen in virtue of our awareness of the parts that construct it, and we are aware of the events portrayed (we see them on the screen) in virtue of our awareness of the images which the screen carries. And again, we are aware of (we see) a cow in virtue of our awareness of the presented surface of the cow. So there are familiar instances in which, given suitable circumstances, to be aware of one thing is to be aware, in not quite the same way, of another. There need not then *seem* to be two forms of awareness for us to be justified in saying that there are two forms of awareness going on.

These examples of double awareness are all different from each other in various ways, and this makes it uncertain whether any of them can serve as suitable models for the sort of double awareness which according to the indirect realist is present in every case of perception. In which of the examples, if any, are the two objects of awareness related in a way analogous to that in which the 'internal' sensum is supposed to be related to the external object?

The cases of the dots and the image and of the surface and the cow are cases where the direct objects of awareness go to constitute or are parts of the indirect object. This is not what we are looking for; sensa are not part of the external objects, according to the indirect realist. Only the phenomenalist would want to say that the sensa of which we are directly aware go to constitute the material objects we see, and this shows that here at least we do not have the examples the indirect realist is looking for.

More promising, perhaps, are the examples of the reflection in the mirror and the objects reflected, and of the image on the screen and the events thus portrayed. In these examples the relation between direct and indirect objects seems to be twofold; the indirect objects *cause* the direct, and they *resemble* them. This seems much more what we were looking for, since the indirect realist is likely to claim, as Locke did, that both these relations hold between external object and sensum.

Is it true, however, that our internal direct objects (if we have any) resemble the external objects which cause them? Our scientific indirect realist will want to restrict the claim that sensa resemble material objects to the primary qualities, for he denies that colour-as-we-see-it resembles in any way the quality of colour as it exists in the object (its primary quality ground). But it is very difficult to suppose that sensa can resemble material objects in respect of the crucial primary qualities of shape and size. We give no sense to the question how large a sensum is, or how large a given part of one is. And the feel of a square object is not itself square, nor can it be thought to share the relevant properties of a square object. Even when we consider visual sensa, we cannot suppose that they can share the shapes of the objects they represent to us. At best we can say that a sensum can resemble a picture of the object, but then the resemblance is not between sensum and object, but between sensum and picture. The sort of three-dimensional shape we attribute to objects is not one which our sensa can share. Our sensa can only resemble the way such objects *look*, not the way they are; but this is no help, since our sensa just *are* the way such objects look.

If resemblance is not at issue, can we fall back on the causal relation between direct and indirect objects in our examples to show that they are relevantly similar to the indirect realist's notion of a double awareness? The trouble is that the causal relation is quite insufficient to sustain the analogy on its own. Our awareness in those examples is thought of as double; we are aware both of the image and of the events portrayed. But this is not just because the events portrayed are among the main causes of the images. There are many events which are among the main causes of things of which we are aware, without our being said to be *aware* analogously of those other events. In most cases we are no more analogously aware of them than we are aware of someone by seeing only their shadow. We know that they are there, but this knowledge, even if it be called awareness, is not relevantly similar to our awareness of the shadow. We *see* the shadow and do not see the person. So the removal of resemblance as a ground for the analogy is in the end sufficient to destroy the analogy, since what is left cannot sustain it alone.

The difficulties we have been finding in the indirect realist's notion of a double awareness are not conclusive, and do not refute indirect realism. But they do give us a reason to look for a theory which does not create those difficulties. One such, evidently, is direct realism; but before returning to that theory we should consider briefly the merits (or lack of them) of a further alternative.

This alternative, which we shall call inferential realism, accepts that there are problems in the notion of a double awareness, and escapes them by abandoning one of them. But it differs from direct realism in abandoning not the direct internal object or sensum, but rather the indirect external object. This theory, then, maintains that we are not aware of material objects in any sense analogous to that in which we are aware of sensa. Instead our knowledge of material objects is *inferential*. (A good example of inferential realism is Russell (1926), and more recently Ayer (1976).) Sensa are held to be the only objects of perceptual awareness, and from our knowledge of our own sensa we infer the presence and nature of the material objects which cause them.

One complaint about this approach is that it leaves the material world invisible. We started out trying to explain what it is to see, e.g., a material object, and we end up by announcing that such things cannot be seen at all. This is a highly implausible consequence, at best, but it is not fatal. The inferential realist presumably thinks that one can swallow this medicine because one has to. But we can pursue the point. For it seems that the sceptical objection which was held inconclusive against indirect realism could be effective against inferential realism. What grounds do we have for supposing that there are such things as material objects, if they are invisible, etc.?

The standard answer to this attack is to point to generations of physicists whose practice is to infer from the observable to the unobservable. Doesn't this show that inference from the observable to the unobservable is not ruled out in principle? But this analogy is insufficient. The physicist infers from observation of normal fully-fledged material objects or events to a more arcane world. The difference between his practice and that of the inferential realist is not that the world to which the inferential realist infers is arcane, but that the objects from which he infers do not seem to have sufficient properties to sustain the inference.

Support for this comes from the argument in chapter 5 against the possibility of a private language. If we cannot institute a primary language for the description of sensory experience, i.e. sensa, we cannot hope to sustain the inferential realist's belief that our knowledge of material objects is all inferred from our primary awareness of our sensa.

So we are left pondering the merits of direct realism. The position is that direct realism has enormous intuitive plausibility, but seems likely to have difficulty in dealing with the explanation of perceptual error. Indirect realism has less plausibility, and the arguments in favour of it are inconclusive. The problems we have found in making sense of the idea of a double awareness and a double object seem therefore sufficient to persuade us to take a more searching look at direct realism.

11.3 DIRECT REALISM AND THE EXPLANATION OF PERCEPTUAL ERROR

At the end of 10.3 I suggested that the direct realist needs to do more than bleakly claim that his theory allows the possibility of perceptual error. It is true that direct awareness does not entail infallibility. The danger is, however, that in attempting an *explanation* of perceptual error direct realism will eventually collapse into indirect realism.

The attraction of indirect realism in this area is easy to see. For the indirect realist perceptual error is a mismatch between two objects; a mismatch, for instance, between a square blue sensum and an oblong green box. But for the direct realist there is only one object, so it looks hard for him to talk of a mismatch. What could the mismatch be between?

The argument from illusion urges us to admit that in the case of extreme hallucination there is no external object present at all. But if this is so, what account shall we give of how it is with the hallucinator? The hallucinator has a perceptual experience; he is in some perceptual state. And this perceptual state must be able to be given an independent characterization, one which has no implications whatever for the nature of the surrounding physical world. And the hallucinator's perceptual state, existing here without suitable object, can be replicated in a non-hallucinating perceiver.

In an ordinary case, too, there can be an independent description of the perceiver's side of the story which says nothing about the surrounding world. These independent descriptions describe a perceptual state. But, on the direct realist account, the perceptual state has no internal object and is not an intermediary between perceiver and external object. It seems, then, that if there is to be an account of perceptual error in terms of a mismatch, it must be a mismatch between perceptual state and object. What must a perceptual state be like if it can 'fail to fit' the world?

Direct realists need not allow themselves to be driven in this way by the argument from illusion. Someone who took an extreme externalist position in the philosophy of mind (see 9.3) will hold that there is in perception no such thing as a perceptual state whose nature is logically independent of the existence of the object it seems to be a perception of. There is no residue of that state, common to perceptual and hallucinatory states, and describable without reference to its object. But most direct realists are internalists in this respect and admit the existence of the perceptual state as an object-less residue.

What sense then can be given to the notion of a misfit between perceptual state and world? What are these 'perceptual states' like? What account can we give of them which does not turn them into new objects of awareness? The direct realist might try to appeal here to an analogy with the so-called Adverbial Theory of Sensation. (This theory derives from Chisholm; see Chisholm (1977) p. 30, and Cornman (1975) pp. 73 – 77.) Suppose that we are worried by the expression 'I have a pain', perhaps asking whether it can be true when I am not aware of the pain. The adverbial theory attempts to avoid thinking of the pain as an *object* of awareness by rewriting that expression adverbially, thus: 'I sense painfully'. Part of the sense of doing this is to suggest that the expression 'it hurts' is more revealing than the expression 'I have a pain'.

The analogy could be used to suggest that we should analyse the *content* of a visual or other experience as a *way* of being aware. Instead of talking of experiencing a sensum with a property P we should talk of sensing P – ly or of sensing in a P way. And even if this does amount to the ascription of special sorts of properties to our states of awareness, this is not incompatible with direct realism. For the state of awareness which has those properties is not an *object* of awareness, intermediate between us and the physical world. (This is why Sellars, who holds the adverbial theory, is unlikely to be an indirect realist.)

But even if the direct realist thinks of a perceptual state, or of a content of awareness, as a way of being aware rather than as an object of awareness, how is this going to help him provide an account of perceptual error? He clearly has to suppose that there can be mismatch between perceptual state and world, but taking that state to be a *way* of being aware of the world does not yet yield a clear understanding of the purported mismatch between way and world. We all know that the world may not be the way we take it to be. But this fact does not provide an answer to the question. Rather it *is* the question. How can we make good sense of this fact?

To make progress here we need to introduce a new question about perception, which has already made brief and unheralded appearances in 4.2 and 8.4. One can see perception as a complex form of sensation; one can see it as essentially a form of belief; or one can see it as a combination of belief and sensation. So there are three types of theory:

1 a 'pure sensation' theory,
2 a 'mixed' theory,
3 a 'pure belief' theory.

The first sort of theory need not hold that the perceptual sensations are objects of awareness; it could be an adverbial theory. But it is likely to see only a difference of degree between 'perceptual' sensation and other simpler sensations such as pain. Even if we ignore the question whether there are any visual sensations, e.g., other than those caused by bright lights, strobes etc., we can still feel unhappy about drawing too strong an analogy between 'visual sensation' and a sensation like pain. For even given the view that perception involves the occurrence of some characteristic form of sensation, it seems that *that* sort of sensation cannot occur without a belief, or at least the tendency to form a belief, about the nature of the object causing the sensation. So pure sensation is not cognitive enough to stand as a model for perception. Perception is not the occurrence of sensation about which one may or may not be led or tempted to form a belief. To perceive is to (be tempted to) believe.

But this should not lead us to a 'pure belief' theory of perception either. There are philosophers (e.g. Armstrong (1961) ch. 9) who hold that the characteristic 'sensory' elements of perception are in-essential to the process, and analyse perception simply as a tendency to acquire beliefs about the surrounding world. And there is an interesting, recently discovered phenomenon which might be taken to support their position. This is called blind-sight. It occurs when people who seem to themselves to be blind in the sense, perhaps, that they experience no visual sensations (obviously this description is tendentious) still are able to answer with extraordinary accuracy some simple questions about the shape and location of surrounding objects. They do not know they are accurate; they commonly take themselves to be guessing.

This phenomenon could be held to count as pure non-sensory perception, and to show that the occurrence of visual sensation, although normal, is inessential to perception itself. But the problem is that the subject of our enquiry into perception is not this etiolated though interesting form of awareness, but our own characteristically rich way of being aware of our surroundings. Blind-sight cannot be used to show that the characteristic differences between the senses, and the difference between seeing that something is true and merely coming to believe that it is true, are somehow not important to *our* way of finding things out. Whatever blind-sight is, it is not seeing.

So we seem to have to opt for a mixed theory of perception, under which perception is some sort of combination of 'sensation' and belief. The question is what sort of combination this could be. What we have so far is that perception is to be thought of as cognitive, but that we cannot for that reason ignore the characteristic ways in which things look to someone whose eyes are open, sound to someone whose ears are open, etc. We have a choice here. We can either see the two elements of a mixed theory as separable, or as in the end identical. If we see them as separable, we suppose that the tendency to believe that things are the way they appear to be is somehow extractable from the whole, leaving merely the appearance behind. If we see them as in the end identical, we suppose that for the world to appear to us in that characteristic way just *is* for us to acquire a tendency to believe. This tendency to believe is not something that could occur in the absence of that characteristic way of appearing, and so is not something we could share with the blind-sighted.

It seems to me that the latter alternative is far more plausible. Instead of taking perception to be a combination of two separable elements, sensory and cognitive, we should take perception to be a characteristic *form* of belief (or of a tendency to believe), one not shareable by those who lack the relevant sensory input, and one where the tendency to believe is not separable from the occurrence of that input.

But now, so long as we opt either for a mixed theory or for a pure belief theory of perception, we can offer an answer to the original question about perceptual error and its explanation in terms of a mismatch between perceptual state and world. This mismatch is now seen as an instance of the mismatch between belief and world that occurs when a belief is false. There may be problems in giving an account of false belief, but they are problems we are going to have to face anyway. So this account of perceptual error, which is available to the direct realist, adds no new problems, but merely turns two problems into one.

11.4 A CAUSAL ELEMENT

We have allowed that a person who sees, hears or feels an object is in a perceptual state which can be described without implications for the surrounding world, because that perceptual state can occur in someone, perhaps under hallucination, no matter what their surroundings may be. Not everyone who is in that perceptual state, therefore, can be said to be seeing (hearing, feeling) the objects that surround them. What more is needed, beyond the occurrence of the perceptual state, for the person concerned to *see*?

It would not be sufficient to say that someone sees his surroundings iff he is in a suitable (visual) perceptual state and the world is as in that state he believes it to be. Suppose that I am sitting facing a blank white wall, with my brain wired to a computer which is causing various perceptual states in me, and that among the perceptual states I experience is one of a blank white expanse. Would we say that at that moment I am seeing my surroundings, and at other times not? We would not, and our reluctance here shows how to improve the account of which perceptual states are seeings. Not only must the world be as in that state I believe it to be, but the way the world is must be a *cause* of my believing it to be that way. This causal thought is known as the causal theory of perception. So a suitably caused perceptual state is a seeing (hearing, feeling).

There is something obviously right about this causal suggestion. I want to make two comments on it.

First, the suggestion as we have it at present cannot be quite right; the causal relation between world and perceptual state will have to be specified in greater detail. The example of the benevolent scientist reveals the need for this change. For suppose that the computer controlling my perceptual states is controlled by a benevolent scientist who causes my states to be the states I would have had if I were seeing; that is, he ensures that my perceptual states are not misleading (false). In this case, my perceptual states are caused indirectly by the way the world is, but we would not say that in such a situation I am *seeing* my surroundings. And our reason seems to be that the link between world and perceptual state is not reliable, since it depends upon the will of a potentially capricious experimenter.

In this case there is a causal link between world and perceptual state, but it is not a suitable one. How are we to rule out unsuitable causal links? One way of doing this might be to rely on the (future) results of neurophysiology. What we are to do here is to provide a list of examples which we are willing to count as genuine cases of seeing (hearing, feeling) one's surroundings, and to say that all perceptual states caused in relevantly similar ways to those involved in the specified cases are to count as cases of seeing. This should rule out unsuitable causal routes. The idea is that as philosophers and/or ordinary mortals, we cannot have any idea about what such ways are like; and so we leave the investigation of this to the neurophysiologists. For the moment, however, we help ourselves to their results in advance by a sort of promissory note. (This approach is taken in Grice, 1961.)

However, there is a difficulty here, which lies in the phrase "states caused in relevantly similar ways to those involved in the specified cases". For supposing that the promissory note is cashed and we know the causal history of my present belief in sufficient detail, do we therefore also know which other causal ways are relevantly similar and which not? Not necessarily, it seems; and so the spelling out of the causal clause cannot be abandoned entirely to the neurophysiologists. If they found an apparently perceptual belief that was caused in a completely new way, who would decide whether the way was relevantly similar to previous more well-trodden ways? Neurophysiologists have no special right to make this decision. And we would decide it, not by considering the degree of similarity between different causal histories, but by considering directly whether we wanted to treat this belief as perceptual. We would be deciding whether to increase the store of crucial examples or paradigm cases. Appeal to neurophysiology seems therefore unlikely to resolve all our problems. Nor can we simply say that suitably caused perceptual states are seeings; to do this would simply be to avoid answering the question. So the causal requirement raises difficulties which we cannot at the moment see how to solve. (Strawson attempts to resolve these problems in Strawson, 1974, ch. 4.) And this leads to the second comment I want to make on the causal theory of perception.

The need for a causal element was shown by allowing that the difference between someone seeing his surroundings and someone hallucinating is not an 'internal' difference. As far as they are concerned they may be in identical perceptual states. The difference lies entirely in the fit and in the causal relations between these perceptual states and the 'external' world. And this approach raises all the traditional questions like what 'internal' evidence we have that we are now seeing rather than hallucinating, and what exactly needs to be added to the internal perceptual state to make it a seeing. But all these questions and difficulties could be avoided if we denied the assumption on which they are based, that there is a residual common core to the two sorts of situation. The existence of this common core is what the argument from illusion is trying to establish. But an externalist in the philosophy of mind (see 9.3) wants to deny the existence of any such thing, and say rather that though we may not be able to tell whether we are seeing or hallucinating, that does not mean that the two situations share an internal common core. Rather, the two situations are different despite being (sometimes) indistinguishable. The fact that we cannot always tell the difference does not mean that they are 'internally' identical. An externalist wants to say that seeing is a sort of state of mind only available when there is a suitable external object. Whether one is in that sort of state depends therefore on the existence of a suitable object. But the object is not separable from the state in such a way that we can ask whether it is or not causing that state in the right way. There is no question of the object causing *that* state in the wrong way. There is another sort of state which may be caused in the wrong way, but that is another matter. (McDowell (1982) shows the importance of this externalist position.)

So the attraction of externalism in the philosophy of mind, for our purposes, lies in its intransigent response to the argument from illusion and the resulting ease with which it can handle the otherwise awkward question about the causal relation required between perceptual state and object. But this sort of externalism is as yet not well worked out; its internalist rival is very much the received approach.

11.5 PERCEPTION, CAUSATION AND JUSTIFICATION

In 11.2 we argued that a perceptual state (if there are such things despite externalist protests) is not so much a complex sort of sensation but rather a characteristic form of belief. And now as epistemologists we should ask why we are justified in relying on beliefs of that characteristic form.

There are two questions here which it is important to distinguish. The first is under what conditions will a perceptual belief count as justified. Our answer to this question is coherentist; a perceptual belief is justified iff the set of which it is a member is more coherent with it than without it. But there is a second question which we began to approach in 8.5, in the discussion of antecedent and subsequent security. This is the question whether (and if so why) perceptual beliefs have a certain degree of antecedent security; whether they are, *qua* perceptual, going to be that much harder to dislodge. We might say that perceptual beliefs are normally justified, or that to see how things are around you is normally to know how they are. If this is true, it would perhaps follow that every perceptual belief has as such a good start, a better chance of proving eventually justified. But if it is true, why is it true?

We might start by suggesting, with Nozick, that our perceptual beliefs are normally knowledge because perceptual beliefs normally track the truth. But this answer is defective in two ways. First, the question really was why such beliefs normally track the truth. Second, this Nozickian answer seems, as we would expect, to be externalist – externalist in the old sense of the internalism/externalism contrast of 9.1 – 2. The fact in virtue of which my perceptual beliefs are to count as knowledge (a fact about tracking) is not one of which I as believer need to be aware. But since we have seen no reason yet, other than that of laziness, for being externalists, we cannot rest content with any externalist answer.

A second attempt to answer our question takes the line that it is a conceptual necessity that our perceptual beliefs be largely or normally true. (This suggestion is made in Hamlyn (1970) pp. 177 – 83, and Shoemaker (1963) pp. 229 – 39.) Now if this is true, an appeal to it must be externalist, since most people (including most philosophers) do not believe it. But the arguments for it are not conclusive. They are two. The first is an appeal to the canons for correct translation (see 7.4). It is suggested that we would never be right to translate a foreign word as 'see' or 'perceive' if most of what we were thereby taking to be perceptual claims come out false (by our lights). Therefore we can only understand as perceptual some process whose results are normally true. But this argument is far too strong, and makes invalid use of the maxim that translation should preserve truth wherever possible. We could in the same way prove that we cannot understand the natives as having moral beliefs unless the moral beliefs we attributed to them normally came out as true (by our lights). A better argument is that the perceptual reports of others form a large proportion of our criteria for statements about how the world is. It is impossible, therefore, for the world to be generally different from the way people see it to be. There is a general difficulty about the use of this argument here, since the argument is at least coloured by anti-realist thoughts, while we are trying to work within a direct realist approach. But, apart from that, the argument seems to exaggerate the role of agreement. It may be that we have no hope of constructing a theory of how the world is by ourselves, without the presence of others; but it does not follow that the role of others is restricted to or crucially defined in terms of a need for agreement. And without the need for agreement there is no hope for the idea that our perceptual beliefs *must* be (normally) true.

A third answer comes from the discussion of 8.5, and is one particularly congenial to the coherentist. We suggested there that a more stubborn adherence to perceptual beliefs, one which demands a bit extra in the way of counter-evidence before it will reject them, leads and is expected to lead to greater coherence in the belief-set. This is rather like the coherentist justification of various principles of inference considered in 8.3. But there are problems for this approach.

We might admit that for anyone who does hold this implicit belief, there will be a sense in which his perceptual beliefs are (normally, defeasibly) justified. And we might admit that as a matter of fact, all of us do implicitly hold this belief. But what if there were someone who didn't? What we are trying to show, without departing from internalism, is that everyone has an internalist reason for taking perceptual beliefs to be justified *qua* perceptual; the reason must not therefore rely on the existence of a belief which someone might not have. We are trying to show, somehow, that even if people don't take perceptual beliefs to be justified, they ought to.

Is it true that increased reliance on perceptual belief yields increased coherence? If it is true, then we can argue that everyone ought to believe it, because of the increased coherence that results from the addition of that belief. There is a way of arguing from truth to justification, then, within the constraints of internalism and coherentism. But what tells us that the crucial proposition is true? Without a reason to believe it true, we have no reason to suppose there will be increased coherence in a belief-set which includes it.

And this turns the argument above on its head. In the absence, therefore, of reason to believe it true, this answer to our original question depends on an unsupported hypothesis. Maybe a way can be found to bolster the coherentist answer to our problem; this would be congenial to the programme of this book. But if not we will have to resort to a different sort of answer.

A fourth answer relies on the causal element introduced in the previous section. One difference between perceptual beliefs and others is that we think of perception as some sort of response to the world, and of the world as confronting us and open to our inspection. In a successful case, the main reason why we see the world in a certain way is that that is the way the world is. A perceptual belief that p, then, can have as a main cause the fact that p. This distinguishes perceptual beliefs from others. I cannot perceive that all men are mortal, nor that $e = mc^2$; these facts cannot be the main causes of my belief, even if they do function causally in some way.

This does not mean that all perceptual beliefs do have as main causes the relevant facts. If that were so, perceptual error would be impossible. The point is that in each case this can be so, not that it is so in all cases.

This causal difference between perceptual beliefs and others does not itself mean that perceptual beliefs are more likely to be true; the causal point is not a statistical point. But we can use a new notion of directness, carefully, to say that perception is a peculiarly direct rapport with the world (where successful). This notion of directness is different from the one we have been using so far, but it is still not a weak substitute for infallibility. All we can say is that a perceptual belief is our securest form of contact with a world directly presented to us.

This amounts to saying that a true (i.e. successful) perceptual belief is normally knowledge. If there is any knowledge of the world around us, perception is knowledge. But how can we use this to show what grounds the justification of perceptual beliefs? We have abandoned the attempt to prove directly that perceptual beliefs are very likely or more likely to be true. Instead we are relying on a belief which someone who takes himself to be perceiving always has and is right to have: namely that his perceptual state, if successful, constitutes a peculiarly direct form of contact with the world.

We might use this to show the justification of perceptual belief by appealing to a suggestion made in 3.2. There we mentioned a possible link between justification and knowledge, using the following schema:

A belief is justified iff in circumstances C it would be knowledge.

And we gave the following instance of this schema, which was the only immediately obvious one:

JBap ≡ (p □→ Kap).

And we can now see a special case of this approach in our account of perception. The very reasons why justification accrues to perceptual beliefs are reasons why if true they will be knowledge.

11.6 DIRECT REALISM AND COHERENTISM

In this final section I argue that a pure anti-realist such as Dummett is committed to phenomenalism in the theory of perception, which we have already shown to be unsatisfactory (11.1); that a coherentist should be a direct rather than an indirect realist; and that scientific direct realism may eventually prove stronger than its naïve alternative.

What is meant by perceptual realism, and what is the relation between that form of realism and the metaphysical realism considered in 1.4 and again in 9.5? The perceptual realist holds that objects are able to exist and retain (some of) their properties unperceived. Metaphysical realism holds that there are at least some propositions which are either true or false but whose truth value is left undetermined even when all possible evidence is in. Can one consistently adopt one realism without the other?

In 9.5 we distinguished various forms of metaphysical anti-realism, from solipsism to what we called pure anti-realism. The solipsist, idealist and phenomenalist must clearly adopt a perceptual anti-realism. What about the pure anti-realist? It might seem that he can be a perceptual realist, so long as his realism is direct rather than indirect. For perceptual realism is the view that the possibility of perceptual experience has as ground something independent of and distinct from that possibility, namely the continuously existing material world. If we can conceive what it is like for there to be such a ground, but not what it would be like for it to exist unrecognizably, we have married perceptual realism with pure anti-realism. But our perceptual realism here must be direct, because an indirect realist will find it hard to avoid saying that the material world which is the indirect object of perception is something independent of and so able to exist beyond the reach of possible experience.

I think, however, that there is an unfortunate tension in this amalgam of perceptual realism and pure anti-realism, which eventually destroys it. The most consistent pure anti-realist will not allow that we can conceive of a state of affairs which is sometimes recognizable and sometimes unrecognizable; for consistency we should be saying that we cannot conceive of what it is like for something to be unrecognizably true on *any* occasion, because our understanding of truth for that sentence is so closely linked to what we take as evidence for it that we cannot separate them and suppose the truth to be present and the evidence not (or vice versa). But surely the direct realist, in supposing that there is an *independent* and distinct ground for the possibility of experience, is supposing that that ground could be unrecognizably present, or apparently present but in fact absent. The concept of independence here includes that of independent variability. And this is inconsistent with pure anti-realism, which seems therefore committed to a position in the philosophy of perception which we have already rejected, namely phenomenalism.

I argued in 9.5 that the coherentist could still be a realist of the strongest form; and such a coherentist is likely to be a realist in the theory of perception. If so, what sort of realist should he be? I want to suggest that direct realism is both compatible with and congenial to the spirit of coherentism, while indirect realism reopens the gap between justification and truth in an unacceptable way.

The central question is the sense we give to the coherentist idea that justification and truth are not properties of radically different types; or that justification as it grows tends towards truth (though it may never get there). The realist who thinks that the properties of physical objects are both directly observable and able to continue unobserved supposes that the very same state of affairs that he observes can be present unobserved. This is the direct realist; the indirect realist holds, however, that the object of which we are directly aware cannot be conceived of as able to continue unperceived. The continuing world whose nature is what makes our states of awareness *true* is thus distinct from any conception of that by appeal to which our perceptual beliefs are *justified*. Truth is presumably a relation between indirect and direct object, while justification is a relation between direct objects of awareness; a perceptual belief is justified if it fits other beliefs well. But this creates a distinction between truth and justification that is of the wrong sort, as far as the coherentist is concerned.

The sort of scepticism which arises when we think that behind the apparent world there may, for all we know, lie a completely different real world, or even no real world at all, is one to which indirect realism has historically been very prone. Indirect realists have tended to accept that this is a possibility and argue that none the less we can have knowledge about the real world in virtue of our awareness of the apparent world. For a direct realist, however, although there is a distinction between the way the world is and the way we perceive it to be, this distinction is far less radical; this is because the nature of the real world is just of a piece with the nature of the qualities we perceive it as having. The properties which in perception we take the world to have are properties which it is possible that the world does have and which it can retain when unperceived.

For these two reasons, then, I think that the coherentist can only consistently adopt a form of direct realism in the theory of perception. But this is of course no hardship, since direct realism is already the most plausible theory, on independent grounds.

Which form of direct realism is the one he should prefer? I gave arguments in 10.3 which tended to show that naïve direct realism was more consistent than its scientific rival. But those arguments may now seem less effective. They were two: first, a doubt about the distinction between primary and secondary qualities, and, second, the fear that use of that distinction will cause the scientific direct realist to collapse into indirect realism in his account of colour perception. But the discussion of perceptual error in 11.3 seems to dispel that fear. And if this is so, we have reopened the possibility that the coherentist should yield to the primary/secondary quality distinction and opt for scientific direct realism.

FURTHER READING

Grice (1961) on the causal element in theories of perception and its relation to scepticism.

Cornman (1975, ch. 7) examines indirect realism (classing Sellars as an indirect realist) and rejects it.

Jackson (1977, ch. 6) replies to objections to indirect realism.

McDowell (1982) argues in favour of the externalist response to the argument from illusion.

Snowdon (1981) uses an externalist approach to query the need for a full causal theory of perception. The effects of externalism in epistemology are briefly alluded to at the beginning of Sellars (1973).

Strawson (1974, ch. 4) continues Grice's work on the causal theory.

Weiskrantz (1980) gives an introductory account of the phenomenon of blind-sight.

Rock (1984) is a clear introduction to the psychology of perception, accessible to philosophers.

On the choice between a 'mixed' theory and a 'pure belief' theory of perception, see Peacocke (1983, ch. 1). Sellars (1963, pp. 155 – 6) protests against the assimilation of sensation to thought.

12
Memory

12.1 THEORIES OF MEMORY

We might think that to perceive is to be aware of the nature of ones's present surroundings, and similarly to remember is to be aware of the nature of one's past. The similarities and differences between memory and perception will be a constant theme of this chapter; the similarities will appear far greater than the differences. But we already know that the contrast in the first sentence is misconceived; the surroundings whose nature we are aware of in perception need not be temporally present, and we shall find reason to doubt whether memory is restricted to an awareness of one's past.

The extent of the similarity between memory and perception is witnessed by the existence of analogues, in the theory of memory, for each of the three families of theories of perception. We can distinguish again between direct realism, indirect realism and phenomenalism. This already makes it tempting to think of memory as perception of the past; the temptation ought not necessarily to be resisted, though there may also be other forms of memory which cannot be thought of as perceptual.

In considering the claims of the three theories we shall often find repetitions of arguments already deployed in the theory of perception. This means that we shall be able to go along a bit faster; it also offers a new context within which the strength of those arguments can be reassessed.

As a preliminary, we need to say what is meant by realism in this new area. Our account should and can match the account given in 10.6 (which was an improvement on the initial version of 10.2). Realism about memory is the view that the occurrence of actual memories and the availability or possibility of other memories than those we actually have, have as a ground something entirely different from those memories, something whose nature explains their possibility. That something is of course the past, the previous history of the world. In memory we remain aware or recover awareness of something which is independent of our awareness of it, for the way the past was is not dependent upon our ability now to remember it.

12.2 INDIRECT REALISM

The indirect realist holds that to remember is to be indirectly aware of the past. When we remember, there is a direct object of awareness functioning as intermediary; this is the memory image. The memory image is our internal direct object.

Arguments for indirect realism about memory tend to resemble arguments for indirect realism in perception. There is the urge to turn the content of awareness into a second object; there is the time-lag argument, which is especially tempting in the theory of memory; and there is a version of the argument from illusion. We have already seen that these arguments are inconclusive, and the additional temptingness of the time-lag argument here does not turn inconclusive arguments into conclusive ones. No argument compels us to admit the existence of an intermediate direct object of memory.

This dismissal of indirect realism is too quick, especially when we remember that indirect realists have been in the majority in the recent history of philosophy. We can supplement it, however, with the following points.

First, the problems for indirect realism in the theory of perception really arose when we tried to give an account of the double awareness and the double object. These problems seem to occur in just the same form in the case of memory. If the image is an intermediate direct object, how does it function as such?

Second, the intermediacy between the remembering mind and the past event is double. Since the arguments for indirect realism are the same in the case of memory as in the case of perception, the indirect realist is likely to discover two direct objects of awareness between the remembering mind and the original object. First there is the original direct object, intermediate between the perceiver at that time and the thing perceived. Then there is a second direct object now present to the remembering mind and somehow related to (probably resembling) the previous direct object which is now beyond the reach of awareness since it has ceased to exist (by the time-lag argument). We cannot suppose that the previous direct object recurs after a gap in which it is dormant, for two reasons. First, it is not obvious that such things as memory images can return to existence after a gap. We ought rather to suppose that a new image is created resembling the previous one; otherwise we shall be tempted to say that the recurring image is somehow 'stored' during gaps between our awareness of it, and thus begin to think of the memory as a sort of storehouse of unused images, a most unattractive conception. Second, even if an image can in principle return to existence after a gap, memory images often differ so greatly from original images (taking these to be our original direct objects) that it is hard to see them as survivors of those images. We have both the gap and the dissimilarities, then, to count against the identity of the differing images over time. But the double intermediacy between mind and indirect object accentuates all the problems about the relation between direct and indirect object in the case of perception. For instance, we considered in 11.2 the objection that the existence of a distinct object of awareness intermediate between us and the world will make it impossible for us to know how that world is. Anyone impressed by that objection will find it even more telling in the case of memory.

The third question commonly raised in objection to indirect realism here concerns our ability to distinguish between memory and imagination. The indirect realist conceives of both of these as producers of images. But we take some of these images to be memory-images and others to be mere products of the imagination. What criterion do we use to tell them apart?

This question has often been presented as the demand for an infallible criterion. The thought is that without an infallible criterion distinguishing memory from imagination we shall in a given case be unable to say whether we are remembering these things or merely imagining them; and if we cannot say that, we surely cannot say that someone who remembers the past has knowledge of the past. How can memory give us knowledge of the past, if we can't tell for sure whether we are remembering or imagining?

This worry about sceptical dangers is real but misplaced. The dangers of this sort of sceptical argument from error are real, but we must not suppose that the way to remove them is by the discovery of an infallible criterion. There are no infallible criteria, and no theory should be impugned for failing to provide one. The sceptical argument from error still needs to be dealt with; but we need to deal with it generally rather than just here, and we should not take the attempt to deal with it as the search for infallible criteria.

Our question then is how we do in fact distinguish between the images that are memory-images and those that are not. There are two classic answers to this question. The first is Hume's (Hume, 1967, Bk 1 pt 1.3). Hume suggested that memory-images are in general more vivid, forceful and lively than others. It is not entirely clear what Hume meant by this. There is, after all, a sense in which the products of the imagination are generally more vivid than those images that are the fading traces of the past. But perhaps Hume would not deny this. A more profitable way to understand Hume is to remember that he also distinguishes belief from imagination by the same criterion. The contents of our beliefs are more lively and forceful than the contents of our imagination. And by this he means that our beliefs affect our actions in a way that our imagination does not. If this is right, Hume is suggesting that memory is a form of belief. Our ability to tell memory from imagination is an instance of a more general ability to tell what we do believe from what we don't.

Before going on to assess this answer, let us consider an alternative. Russell suggested (Russell, 1921, ch. 9) that our criterion here is a feeling of familiarity which standardly accompanies memory-images and not those of the imagination. This feeling can be very strong (and even misplaced as in the sense of *déjà vu*) or very weak. But it is generally present, and constitutes the criterion we are seeking.

The trouble with Russell's answer is not so much that the presence or absence of this feeling is not a totally reliable mark (which we should expect, there being no totally reliable marks). Rather the problem is to distinguish the feeling of familiarity from the belief that the present image somehow represents the past. Russell claims that feeling and belief are distinct (*ibid*. p. 169), the belief being always based on the presence of the feeling. The reply is that there is no feeling of familiarity in such a case other than the belief which the feeling is supposed to ground. The so-called feeling just *is* the belief which it is supposed to ground.

This makes it appear that Russell's answer is no answer. If the question was what criterion we use to distinguish between memory and imagination, the answer cannot be that we believe in one case and not in the other. The belief cannot be the criterion, since it is just for that belief that we are seeking a criterion. Hence the belief appears as criterionless.

The same result emerges in Hume's case. Agreeing that memory is a form of belief attached to a present image, we can find no criterion by which we ascribe belief in one case and not in the other. The ascription of belief is again criterionless.

It seems therefore that the question which images are memory-images cannot be answered; but it is a question which the indirect realist can reasonably be expected to answer. We shall see that the question can be answered by the direct realist, but that is because the question will have changed. The direct realist's question is not about images, but about beliefs. Which beliefs are memory-beliefs?

The main obstacle to our accepting indirect realism in the theory of memory is that we seem to have two alternatives: either adopt indirect realism both for perception and for memory, or adopt direct realism in both cases. A mixed theory, direct in one case and indirect in the other, would not be attractive because the arguments accepted in one case seem to spill over so effectively into the other. Having argued for direct realism in the theory of perception, it is unlikely that we can consistently accept indirect realism for memory.

12.3 DIRECT REALISM

The direct realist holds that in memory as in perception, our awareness of the past is direct. There is no intermediary 'internal' object in virtue of our awareness of which we are indirectly aware of other things. Memory-images, if and when they occur, do not function in the way the indirect realist suggests. Memory-images are not as prevalent as philosophers have tended to think, and even when there is an image the image is not an object of awareness, but (part of) the way in which we are aware of the past event.

So the direct realist plays down the role of the image or internal object in memory as in perception. Is this reasonable? Isn't the direct realist in danger of missing what is really characteristic of memory?

To answer these questions we need to investigate what have been called the different forms of memory to see how they are related and what role imagery plays in each form.

One form of memory, of which so far we have said little or nothing but which is still perhaps the most common, is *factual memory*. Factual memory is factual knowledge, knowledge that *p*, which has been acquired in the past; that knowledge may have been lost (forgotten) and recovered, or never lost but simply retained. Most of our knowledge is factual memory, it seems. But some is not; our knowledge of what we are now perceiving is not factual memory, even though it might be impossible for us to have that knowledge if we were entirely deprived of factual memory.

The facts with which factual memory are concerned need not be concerned with the past. I can remember that I shall be in London next weekend, or that there is more than one variety of woodpecker. So here is an important sense in which memory is not solely concerned with the past, let alone with one's own past.

Factual memory does not depend in any way upon the occurrence of suitable images or other 'internal' direct objects. We can see that this is so because so much of our factual memory is 'unimaginable' in a special way; it concerns facts for which there cannot be relevant images. Mathematical knowledge is largely factual memory, for instance. One cannot have an image of 2 + 2 being equal to 4.

It looks then as if factual memory, despite its prevalence, is quite unlike memory as conceived by the indirect realist. It is not concerned with the past, particularly, and the occurrence of images is neither required nor even especially relevant. But this surely just shows that there is another form of memory which the indirect realist *was* talking about. And this looks obvious anyway. Factual memory is concerned with the retention or recovery of any sort of knowledge. And if this is all there is to memory, we could hardly hope to draw interesting parallels between memory and perception. What is more, nothing in the notion of factual memory gives good sense to the idea that only some of the events or objects of the past are things which I can remember. But surely we do think that, in some sense, our memory is restricted to our own past history. This is not to say that we can only remember what we knew before, but to say that we can only remember events and objects of which we were once aware. And if there is a sense in which this last is right, there is room here for analogies between perception and memory and for debates between direct and indirect realists about, for instance, the role and function of imagery.

A not very good way of drawing attention to the distinction between factual memory and what we might now call *perceptual* memory is by appeal to language. Doesn't language offer a distinction between remembering that you did it and remembering doing it, and cannot we suppose that for the second, but not for the first, it is required that you be able to recall the event 'with the same consciousness you had of it at first'? In similar vein we might distinguish between remembering that it looked like this and remembering how it looked, or remembering that the game was drawn and remembering the drawn game. But the linguistic distinctions do not perfectly match the distinction between perceptual and factual memory, if only because perceptual memory can without error be described in terms of remembering-that.

And of course we should be careful not to assume too much about the relation between perceptual and factual memory. For all we know so far, perceptual memory may just be a type of factual memory. Suppose that we offer as initial definitions the following:

a factually remembers that *p* iff *a*'s present knowledge that *p* is grounded in *a*'s previous knowledge that *p*.

a perceptually remembers that *p* iff *a*'s present knowledge that *p* is grounded in *a*'s previously perceiving that *p*.

If we add to these the thought that perception itself can be a form of knowledge (see 11.5), we have the result that perceptual memory is a special sort of factual memory. There would then still be a distinction between the two, but no contrast. (Martin and Deutscher (1966) offer reasons for thinking the above definitions too tight.)

We now need to consider what the direct realist has to say about perceptual memory, that ability to see again, 'in the mind's eye', what one saw before or to re-experience one's feelings or to relive one's actions. This ability is grounded in one's own previous experience (perceptions) and therefore an account of it is bound to depend upon the account of perception given earlier. We have already seen the indirect realist's account; perceptual memory is the awareness of a present image resembling a previous image which represented an object. The direct realist, having rejected the earlier intermediary, is not likely to admit the later one. What extra difficulties are there in this position?

A problem may seem to lie in the possibility that our awareness can alter through time, and can even improve. I seem to be able to decide by appeal to my recollection of a lecture that a colleague was present, even though there is a sense in which at the time I was not aware of her presence. The question is why this phenomenon is thought to constitute an objection to direct realism. Why should the direct realist be committed to saying that our awareness of the object cannot change through time? Or, if not that, why should he be committed to saying that it can only deteriorate? The possibility of improvement is surely an argument for rather than against direct realism, for it supposes that our present awareness of the object is not limited by the nature of some previous experience or image, but can be improved. How can this be possible if we are not directly aware of the object even if at a temporal distance?

If direct realism survives objections of this type, how should it stand in relation to the distinction between sensory, mixed and pure belief theories (of memory now rather than of perception)?

In the case of factual memory, a pure belief approach seems obviously correct. But there is anyway no analogy between factual memory and perception. The analogies seem to be between perception and perceptual memory, that ability to relive one's past. Should we therefore adopt a mixed theory for perceptual memory and keep our analogy intact?

Many philosophers are less resistant to a pure belief theory of memory in general than they are to pure belief theories of perception. The reason is that in perception *appearance* is central, while in memory there need be no way in which the past appears or reappears to the rememberer. But this is just to say that in factual memory appearances are irrelevant, which is admitted. There remains the obstinate phenomenon of perceptual memory, where appearances do count. And given the distinctive nature of perceptual memory, the best course seems to be to preserve the analogy between perception and memory and adopt a mixed theory in both areas. We should suppose that perceptual memory is a distinctive form of belief about one's past. On this account perceptual memory, as belief, is a form of factual memory; but it is a distinctive form. Both are belief, but though someone could have factual memory without perceptual memory, nothing could have perceptual memory without factual memory.

12.4 PHENOMENALISM

We can distinguish as before between reductive and eliminative phenomenalism. Eliminative phenomenalism holds that there is no such thing as the past; there is nothing but the present occurrence of experiences of a certain sort. Reductive phenomenalism holds that there is indeed such a thing as the past, but it is nothing other than a complex of present experiences of that sort. For an event to be past is for us to have or to be able to have a present memory-experience; the past consists in the availability of memory-experiences. (For a view of this sort, see Ayer (1946) pp. 101 – 2.)

Such a theory suffers from defects like those of its counterpart in the theory of perception. What explains the occurrence of a memory-experience? Normally we would answer this question by appeal to the previous occurrence of some perceived event, which is now remembered. But this explanation is ruled out for the phenomenalist. It does nothing but explain the occurrence of a memory-experience by appeal to the availability of that experience. And that seems in the end to be no explanation at all. Nor can the phenomenalist appeal here to previous regularities in the occurrences of memory-experiences. This is not because such regularities lie in the past; there is a phenomenalist version of what it is for them to be past, in terms of the availability of present memory-experiences of them. The appeal to previous regularities is consistent with phenomenalism, then; but it is unsuccessful. It fails because, as in the case of perception, the previous regularities do not provide the sort of explanation we want. They reassure us that the memory-experience was predictable, but they do not tell us why the experience was this way rather than another way.

Phenomenalism in the theory of memory is therefore defective. But there is something to be learnt from the contrast between phenomenalism and realism here. For the phenomenalist, factual memory can only exist if there is perceptual memory. Factual memory requires the existence of past knowledge; but phenomenalists take the fact that there was a time at which I knew that p to consist in the availability of experiences of having known that p; the occurrence of such experiences is what is involved in perceptual memory. For the realist, however, the reverse seems true. Perceptual memory is impossible if there is no factual memory. This is because the realist takes perceptual memory to be a species of factual memory. Given this relation, we can say that if there was no such thing as present knowledge grounded in past knowledge (factual memory), there could be no such thing as present knowledge grounded in past perception (perceptual memory). The tightness of the link here is revealed by the recognition that in favourable cases to perceive that p is to know that p.

The importance of this contrast emerges when we now turn to consider sceptical questions about memory and knowledge. How can a memory-belief ever be knowledge?

12.5 RUSSELL'S HYPOTHESIS

The sceptical difficulties are perhaps best raised by Russell's hypothesis that the world was created five minutes ago exactly as it then was, with a population that "remembered" a wholly unreal past (Russell, 1921, pp. 159 – 60). Nothing that is happening now or will happen can prove that the world was not so created, as Russell says. More importantly, it seems that nothing that is happening or will happen could even count as evidence that it was not so created. If, therefore, we could have no evidence against Russell's hypothesis, surely we cannot know that hypothesis to be false. And if that is so, how can we know anything else about the past? If we knew anything else about the past, say that there have been two World Wars in this century, we would know that the world was not created five minutes ago; we do not know the latter and so we do not know the former.

There are two comments to be made about this argument, before we consider three possible answers to it. First, the argument is merely an instance of the argument from error (1.2), by which we showed earlier that we do not know we are not brains in vats. The core of the argument is the point that where there are two hypotheses which are completely indistinguishable to us, we cannot claim to know which is true, nor even to have any justification for a belief about the matter. The present case is just like that. There is no possibility of finding any evidence which tells in favour of Russell's hypothesis rather than the more traditional picture, or vice versa. Second, it should be clear that the first aim of this sceptical argument is not perceptual memory but factual memory. If the argument is correct, then whether or not there are such things as memory-experiences there will be no instances of present knowledge grounded in past knowledge.

The first possible answer to the sceptical argument is Nozick's. It is modelled on his answer, which we considered in chapter 3, to sceptical difficulties with brains in vats. Nozick would want to resolve it by saying that the principle of inference PC^k on which it relies is false, and so we can know more normal facts about the past even though we cannot know that Russell's hypothesis is false. We suggested, however, in chapter 3 that even if PC^k is false, Nozick's move will not succeed. There is another way of arguing via the principle of universalizability that if we do not know Russell's hypothesis to be false we shall not be able to know more mundane facts about the past. And surely this fits our intuitions. Nozick may want us to say that I can know what I had for lunch today although I cannot know that the world existed more than five minutes ago. But our intuition is strong that we ought not to be able to say this.

Phenomenalism, if sound, would provide a better answer. It holds that the existence of the past is nothing other than the availability of memory-experiences. If this were true, there could not be a situation in which memory-experiences were available, but none of the past events which those memories seem to portray had ever happened. We can put the point, as in 1.5, by saying that it is not as if there are two situations, one in which there are memory-experiences but no past and the other in which there are both memory-experiences and a past to ground those experiences. We must not say, weakly, that there is a difference which we could not tell and which could make no difference to us. Rather, the facts that we could not tell it and that it could make no difference to us show that there is no difference to tell. The availability of the memory-experiences is just what it is for those events to have happened. If this is so, Russell's hypothesis fails to provide any grounds for a sceptical conclusion. This is an instance of the comparative ease with which an anti-realist can reject sceptical arguments.

So the past, as conceived by phenomenalism, is something with which we are directly in touch, on the occurrence of memory-experiences. And there are no past events that lie beyond the reach of memory. There are no facts of the matter about the past other than those for which memory-experiences are available. There may be sentences about the past which purport to express facts about the past but which lie beyond the reach of memory, but those sentences are neither true nor false. They would only be true or false if there were available memory-experiences of the events they describe having happened or not having happened. There are no such available experiences, and so the sentences concerned are neither true nor false.

This conception of the past conflicts dramatically with the realist conception. Realists take it that there are ways in which the world was but which lie beyond the reach of available memory-experience. The past is richer than the possibility of memory-experience. A realist may, but perhaps need not, express his position by saying that every sentence about the past is in fact either true or false, whether or not relevant memory-experiences are available. This is a way of holding that the Law of Excluded Middle, which holds that every proposition is either true or false, is valid for sentences about the past. The phenomenalist seems to have to deny the Law of Excluded Middle, and say that some sentences describe events which neither happened nor failed to happen. So the past, conceived realistically, extends beyond the boundaries to which the phenomenalist would want to limit it.

Once we take the realist line that it is one thing for an event to have happened and another for memory-experiences of it to be available (whether these are thought of as the occurrence of images or of beliefs of a certain sort), we face the usual sceptical argument. The argument from error takes its start from the point that no matter how consistent our memory-experiences may be, there is always the possibility that they are false. We have as yet seen no satisfactory response to the argument from error. Its attack on our claim to know about the past should be expected, and deflected if possible by some general move in epistemology rather than by a special move in the theory of memory. Phenomenalism had the merit of providing such a move.

Another such general move was considered in 1.4. This is the 'transcendental' argument. Faced with the sceptical trend of Russell's hypothesis, we attempt first to maximize its effect. We say, for instance, that if Russell's hypothesis were true, factual memory would be impossible. And not only would there then be no possibility of retaining knowledge gained in the past, but there would be no possibility of gaining new knowledge now. For how could I see that this is a fire if I cannot remember what a fire is? This last move is of dubious validity, as expressed. But we can let that pass; the point is that we attempt to maximize the effects of the sceptical move by every means we can lay our hands on, and then point out that if we are to lose all this, we can hardly see ourselves as rational at all. For how can we be able to take one thing as a reason for another in the absence of the sort of information that factual memory provides? So the effects of the sceptical argument are enormous; so enormous that the argument must be rejected.

I have not expressed this argument in quite the same way as in 1.4. But the main response to it is the same. Sceptical considerations are not weakened by our recognition of the extent of their consequences. We may be the more inclined to doubt the validity of those considerations, but the sheer extent of their consequences is not an independent argument that the considerations are flawed. We cannot avoid an attempt to diagnose the error we need to find in the sceptic's argument in the way that transcendental arguments attempt to do. Our three responses to the classic sceptical argument about factual memory have all failed, then. Where does this leave us? We still need a way of dealing with the argument from error, and we have not yet found one. I shall make my own suggestion in 15.5.

12.6 PERCEPTUAL MEMORY AND JUSTIFICATION

As in 11.5, there are two questions we can ask about perceptual memory and justification. On the account given here, perceptual memory is analysed as a special sort of belief. Our first question is therefore under what conditions such a belief is justified. To this we give the now familiar coherentist answer (cf. Brandt, 1955). Any belief is justified by the effects of its retention or rejection on the system as a whole.

The second question is what justifies our increased willingness to retain a belief just because it is a belief of this special sort. Why is the fact that a belief is of this sort some reason for retaining it?

We cannot here simply reiterate our answer in the case of perception. There we argued that in perception our contact with the world was so direct that in successful cases it must count as knowledge. But the causal routes involved in perceptual memory are nothing like so direct. We cannot say that the original, distant, event can be the main cause for the present perceptual memory. Too much else seems to be necessary, particularly as the temporal distance increases. We need to find some other way of supposing that reliance on perceptual memory as such is justified.

We are taking it that factual memory is possible, and that factual memory, in suitable cases, is knowledge. Given that, perhaps we can use it to answer our present question. Perceptual memory is present belief caused by past perception. We already have the result that in favourable cases perception is knowledge. So in favourable cases, perceptual memory is present belief caused by past perceptual knowledge. Someone therefore who takes himself to have perceptual memory must be taking himself to have a belief grounded in previous knowledge. And in that case he is surely justified in ascribing to that belief an extra degree of resilience.

FURTHER READING

D. Locke (1971) is an excellent brief survey of philosophical theories about memory.

Russell (1921, ch. 9) shows Russell struggling unhappily with the problems of indirect realism.

Brandt (1955) rejects the coherentist theory of justification, but still feels able to offer an account of the justification of memory-beliefs with a distinctly coherentist flavour.

Dummett (1978, ch. 21) is an attempt to make the best sense of the dispute between realist and anti-realist about the past.

Martin and Deutscher (1966) attempt a general account of memory, stressing the need for a causal connection between past perception and present 'representation'.

13
Induction

In preceding chapters we have considered our ability to gather knowledge about our surroundings, and our ability to retain or recover such knowledge later. In the present chapter we consider our ability (or lack of it) to move beyond that knowledge; to construct new knowledge on the basis of the old. We can extend our knowledge by reasoning; by seeing that things we already know provide reasons in favour of other beliefs. Where those reasons are strong enough, we can hope that in believing as they suggest, we have acquired new knowledge. A true belief, based on previous knowledge which provides sufficient inferential justification for that belief, will be knowledge, we may hope.

There are two styles of reasoning, deductive and inductive. Deductive reasoning occurs where we take our inferential justification to be conclusive, in the special sense that it is impossible, on pain of self-contradiction, for the beliefs which are our reasons to be true and the conclusion that we draw from them to be false. When we are right in taking this to be so, our deductive reasoning is valid; otherwise it is invalid.

Inductive reasoning occurs when we take our reasons to be sufficient to justify our conclusion, without being conclusive in the sense above, or when we think we have some but not yet sufficient reason for the conclusion, hoping perhaps that further reasons may yet be found so that the sum total of reasons will be sufficient. This can be most clearly expressed in terms of probability. A successful inductive argument is one which makes its conclusion probable, or more probable than any equally detailed alternative; the (relative) probability it gives its conclusion may not be sufficient yet to justify our believing it, because there may be stronger reasons on the other side, or because the degree of probability gained is not large enough to justify more than an increased willingness to look further. But we suppose it possible that with further reasons we shall eventually be justified in accepting the conclusion.

Inductive reasoning is employed in almost every branch of human enquiry. We can ask whether what we know about the present provides inductive justification for beliefs about the past, as a detective might in a criminal investigation. Or we can ask whether our beliefs about the past justify certain beliefs about the future, as someone might who is considering an offer of marriage (though I do not recommend the approach in this instance). Induction, therefore, is not specially concerned with knowledge of the future. But we might be tempted by the reverse. Can knowledge of the future be gained other than inductively?

There are two ways in which we might hope to gain knowledge of future events other than by inductive reasoning. The first is by supposing that we sometimes know what will happen because we have a non-inferential knowledge of our own intentions. This raises complex issues which we shall do best to avoid for present purposes, merely noting that it is not obvious that this sort of knowledge of the future is entirely independent of inductive support. We may have non-inferential knowledge of our intentions, perhaps, but doesn't our resulting knowledge of the future depend upon a general knowledge that in certain areas our intentions are normally implemented?

The second way in which we might hope for non-inductive knowledge of the future is by supposing that in certain cases we can see what will happen. This suggestion may be made in extreme cases, as when we think of fortune-tellers observing future events in a crystal ball; or in more ordinary cases, as when we talk of seeing that the crash will happen or that the ball will go out. But there is a powerful argument that we can never observe the future in either sort of case.

There needs to be a strong argument, for some of the things that have been said in earlier chapters do seem to make room for the idea that, at least in a limited way, observation of the future is possible. Perceptual belief may be a matter of degree; some beliefs are more perceptual than others, some very perceptual, some less so, and perhaps none purely perceptual. This makes room for us to say, for example, that one can see that a climb is difficult or a cliff dangerous; we have not forced ourselves into a position in which we have to say that such things can only be known by inductive reasoning from what can more properly be said to be seen. Perhaps there is here sufficient latitude for us to avoid ruling out talk of seeing what will happen, which is in fact quite common; for instance, talk of seeing that the ball will go out.

The crucial argument driving us to rule out perception of the future completely is an argument about the direction of causation. We suggested earlier that perceptual beliefs differ from others in that the facts which are their contents are able to be the main cause of the belief in favourable cases. But if there is to be perception of the future, the things that are the contents of the beliefs must lie in the future. But can something that is still entirely in the future be any part of the cause of a present event? Can the future cause the present? Even if we allow that a cause need not precede its effect but can be simultaneous with it, there are arguments that the present cannot be an effect of an event which has not yet happened.

The classic sort of example is that of someone who invariably wakes up five minutes before his alarm clock goes off, no matter what time he sets it for. What prevents us from saying that the cause of his waking is the fact that his alarm clock would go off five minutes later? To say this we have to say that the effect (the waking) can be over before the cause has even started. And this is supposed to be impossible. Suppose that one day he has set his alarm clock for eight o'clock and wakes at five to eight, but the alarm clock fails to go off at eight for some mechanical reason. On that occasion we have to look elsewhere for the cause of his waking, and we are likely to choose an earlier event such as his setting the alarm for eight. But if it is the earlier setting of the clock that caused the later waking in this case, mustn't we in equity say that this is the cause in every case? The ringing of the alarm which occurs (normally) five minutes after the man wakes can then be seen as a separate effect of a common cause, rather than as a later cause of an earlier effect.

This argument can be generalized. It is no reply to say that there might be someone who just didn't wake up when his alarm clock was defective and was going to fail to ring. This is because the structure of any example seems to require that the effect be over before the cause starts, or at least that there be a gap between the beginning of the effect and the beginning of the cause during which someone could intervene to prevent the occurrence of the cause. It is not necessary that anyone should ever intervene; it is enough that invervention be possible. For the possibility of intervention is incompatible with the thought that the waking is caused by the later ringing of the alarm. This is because of what it is for one event to be an effect of another. B is only an effect of A if the occurrence of A is necessary for the occurrence of B. To see this, take a particular morning on which our man wakes up. In supposing this to be the effect of the impending ring, we suppose that if it were not going to ring, he would not have woken up. But the mere fact that we can intervene shows that this conditional is false. Because he has woken up and it might not ring, we know that he would have woken up whether it was going to ring or not. And to know this is to know that his waking is caused by something other than the impending ring.

By this 'bilking' argument, then, the causal order can never be the reverse of the temporal order (see Flew, 1954). And this shows, because of the way that perception requires a causal relation between belief and fact, that we cannot perceive the future. If we are impressed by the argument, then, we shall insist that one cannot really see that it will rain or that the ball will go out. Rather one sees the present weather conditions and trajectory, and reasons inductively to the future rain and the future path of the ball.

13.2 TWO CONCEPTIONS OF THE FUTURE

As before, realists and anti-realists offer competing accounts of the future. The anti-realist in this area takes it that our understanding of future-tense sentences is gained entirely in circumstances which we learn to take as evidence for the truth of those sentences, and that realist suggestions that we can subsequently come to an understanding of what it is for such sentences to be true in the absence of the sort of evidence concerned are fanciful. There are not, in our original understanding of such sentences, two distinct elements to be separated in this way. The sentence is assessed as true or false according to present and past evidence. If, then, there is no evidence either in favour of or against the sentence, it is neither true nor false. Most sentences about the future are in this category. Therefore most sentences about the future lack a truth value.

There is something very appealing about this position. The future has not happened yet, we feel, and hence there is nothing for future-tense sentences to describe and nothing about the future which can make such sentences now true or now false. The openness of the future is not an epistemological defect, there being an enormous number of facts about the future which we can have no hope of knowing (yet). It is a metaphysical necessity; and this distinguishes the future from the past. The past is complete, and its nature makes

past-tense statements determinately (though perhaps not deter-
minably) true or false. We cannot say the same about the future.

If we find this sort of contrast between past and future compelling
we are tempted by anti-realism about the future and by realism about
the past. A more complete anti-realism would reject the contrast,
and say much the same about our conception of the past as about
that of the future. Leaving aside the argument about the past, we
should consider one argument in favour of some form of anti-realism
about the future. This is the claim that a realist about the future
cannot allow that we have free will.

There are arguments against the possibility of free will that are
independent of the present controversy. The causal determinist
argues that every event and every action is caused by other events,
and therefore that in no case is it true that we were able to act
otherwise than we did. For what it is for one event to cause another
is (or includes) that given the first event and the attendant circumstances, the second could not have been otherwise than it was. A
free action is one which could in the circumstances have been
otherwise than it was. So if all actions are caused, no action is free.

This determinist argument is disputed by the compatibilist, who
holds that an action can be both caused and free. The argument
we are concerned with, however, is that of the fatalist, not the
determinist. The fatalist supposes somehow that it is already fixed
what will happen tomorrow, but not for causal reasons. His reasons
are those of the realist, who takes every future-tense sentence to
have a truth value. A fatalist might reason as follows: either I shall
die of cancer caused by smoking or I shall not. If I shall, then there
is no point in giving up smoking. If I shall not, there is no point
in giving up smoking. So there is no point in giving up smoking.
This reasoning starts from the realist assumption that every statement about the future has a truth value; either true or false.

With less caricature, we can present the fatalist argument against
free will as follows. It is already true either that I shall go to that
restaurant this Friday or that I shall not. If it is already true that
I shall go, how can I be said to have the option of not going, and
vice versa? It looks as if the matter is already fixed, and nothing
I could do could change it. Whatever the truth is is unavoidable,
and the rest is impossible.

There is sufficient weight in this argument, despite its appearance
of verbal trickery, to have persuaded Aristotle to abandon realism
about the future (see Aristotle, 1962, ch. 9). Such a move reaps the
usual advantages against the sceptic. For the anti-realist holds that

what it is for a statement about the future to be true is not to be separated from what it is for us to have the best possible evidence that it is true. Therefore there is no possibility that we have the relevant evidence but that the statement is false. The realist complaint that it is always possible, even given the evidence, that the statement be false is dismissed as inconceivable. So anti-realism about the future is very attractive. The difficulty is how to adopt it without adopting a general anti-realism. We have, after all, already argued against anti-realism in the theory of perception.

There is however a more severe sceptical argument in this area, which attacks in general the very notion of evidence that the anti-realist is relying on here. This is Hume's question about induction in general. In considering it we move away from exclusive consideration of knowledge of the future to a more general interest in our knowledge of the unobserved.

13.3 HUME AND HIS CRITICS

Hume's questions about inductive reasoning have already been raised in 1.2; they have lain⁕dormant for a long time, and are now reawakened. We shall not repeat them, but begin immediately to consider possible answers to Hume.

Is the Circularity Vicious?

Hume complains that the only plausible attempt to justify our use of inductive inference involves a vicious circle, because it appeals to experience to justify appeals to experience. But some philosophers have been tempted to maintain that, though there is something like a circle in an inductive justification of induction, it is not vicious (e.g. Black, 1954, ch. 11, and 1958). The suggestion is that an argument such as:

Inductive reasoning has proved reliable in the past. Therefore inductive reasoning is (generally) reliable.

has as its conclusion a statement that the principle of inference which takes us from the premise to that conclusion is reliable. But this is no form of circularity; there is a crucial difference between principle of inference and statement. There would be a circularity if the argument really required as a premise the proposition which also stands as conclusion. But it doesn't require this. There are only two reasons for thinking it does, both of which are mistaken. First, we might say that the argument is inconclusive otherwise. To make it conclusive, add the relevant statement to the premises; but then the argument is blatantly circular. The reply to this is that the argument is a perfectly sound instance of inductive reasoning as it stands. There is no need to add further premises in order to make it deductively valid, and hence conclusive. In general, it can be no complaint against inductive arguments that they are not deductive; the justification of induction is not the attempt to show all inductive arguments to be covertly deductive.

Second, we might think that generally a statement of the principle of inference on which an argument relies should, for full explicitness, be inserted as a premise. But this suggestion leads to infinite regress. For the resulting argument will depend upon some principle of inference, which will therefore need to be inserted; and the resulting argument will depend upon a further principle, etc., etc.

The argument is therefore held not to be covertly circular, because in no sense is the conclusion needed as one of the premises. An argument can therefore establish the reliability of its own principle of inference, when, as above, its conclusion asserts that reliability. We can justify induction inductively.

This is ingenious, but unsuccessful. To see why, we should try to look at it in Hume's way. Does the argument above give me reasons to accept its conclusion? I can only take it as doing so if I already accept, on independent grounds, the principle of inference on which it relies. Hence the argument could never give me a reason to accept its conclusion if I did not have sufficient reason to do so already.

Appeals to Analyticity

Hume's question is how we can have any reason for supposing that past and present observation provides us with evidence from which we can infer inductively. In the absence of such a reason, he insists, there can be no such thing as evidence, no such thing as having inductive reasons for belief.

A classic response is to hold that it is not possible to question whether past and present observations constitute evidence or provide reasons for further belief (see Edwards (1949) and Strawson (1952) ch. 9.2). The statement that observation does constitute evidence is true because of what we mean by 'evidence'. Someone who doubted whether the observed orbit of a planet were evidence about its future orbit would show by this that he didn't understand the meaning of the word 'evidence'. There is no possibility that we might somehow be wrong about what 'evidence' means, and hence no possibility that observations should fail to provide evidence about the unobserved.

This is called the analytic justification of induction, because it amounts to holding that the statement 'the observed past is evidence for the future' is analytic; it is true solely in virtue of the meanings of the words in it. As such, of course, it is not directly available to those who, with Quine, reject the notion of analyticity and the traditional contrast between analytic and synthetic. But there is a further argument against the analytic justification, which can appeal to Quineans and to others alike; it is due to Urmson (1953).

This further argument starts from the remark that to call something evidence is in part to evaluate it, to see it as a reliable guide, which we are justified in following. Now terms that are used for evaluation in this way have a peculiar characteristic (though maybe this characteristic is present less noticeably in other cases), one which can be most easily seen in the case of the most general term of approval, 'good'. We learn the use of this term by appeal to such examples as our mentors (parents, scout-masters) offer us. But we are not thereby restricted to approving of only or all the things they approve of. However this may be, our understanding of the term 'good' can cast off entirely all reliance on the original examples. We can come to approve of a radically or even completely different set of objects or none at all, without thereby showing that we have forgotten what we were taught. And the same is true with the word 'evidence'. Our understanding of that word, gained no doubt in ordinary circumstances, is such that we can without abusing it come to take different sorts of things as evidence, or even to wonder whether anything is really evidence for anything else. And this is of course just what Hume did. It appears then, that the analytic justification does not succeed in ruling out Hume's question as incoherent.

It may be objected that we have missed the force of the analytic justification. It is possible that the analytic justification is intended as an anti-realist answer to a realist question; and that we have only rebutted it in realist terms, thus missing the point. Hume perhaps supposes that there are matters of fact about the unobserved past and future, about which our accumulated experience is normally taken to be inconclusive but relevant evidence. He then points out that experience can give us no reason for supposing that we can cross the gap between observed and unobserved. The anti-realist reply is to insist that there is no gap between the facts of the matter and those propositions which we take to be relevant evidence. Our understanding of what it is for propositions about the unobserved to be true is tied indissolubly to the sorts of consideration which we take to be relevant evidence. The reason why it is an analytic truth that the observed past is evidence for the future, then, is the general claim that our concepts of truth and evidence go together. For a proposition about the future to be true is just for there to be evidence available that it is true; to understand what it is for a statement to be true is just to know what to count as evidence that it is true. Therefore we cannot suppose that we are wrong in taking observations to be relevant evidence; that they are relevant evidence is determined, not so much by the meaning of the word 'evidence', but by the meaning of the propositions for which they count as evidence.

This anti-realist version of the analytic justification of induction seems more formidable. To make a proper response to it we need to approach the matter from a different direction.

13.4 GOODMAN'S NEW RIDDLE OF INDUCTION

Hume posed his question in terms of a practice of inferring from observed regularities to the probable continuance of those regularities. He argued that this practice could not be justified, if justification requires reasons for thinking such inductive reasoning to be reliable. But he did not therefore conclude that inductive *practice* is irrational. He suggested that human nature is such that we acquire a habit of expectation after observing a sufficient regularity in nature. We have no reason to reason inductively, but we cannot help it. Given that we understand what it is to be rational not by reference to what we ought to do (and commonly fail to do) but by reference to what we do do, inductive inference is rational practice but not one grounded in reason.

Nelson Goodman argues that Hume's solution really raises even larger and harder questions of a similar type (Goodman, 1973). Hume's answer is that observed regular patterns create in us a habit of expectation. We so often observe objects falling when released that we naturally expect the next one to do so. And correct inductive inference is defined in terms of inference to events similar to those observed. The most reliable inference is supposed to be the one whose conclusion suggests that the world will go on in the way most similar to its course up to now. But Goodman claims convincingly that this appeal to similarities conceals an assumption which it is hard to justify.

Suppose that up to now all observed emeralds have proved to be green; canons of inductive inference, as understood above, enjoin us to infer that the next emerald will be green and, with less probability, that all emeralds are green. But we can interrupt this cosy story by supposing there to be another predicate 'grue', with the following sense: an object is grue at a time t iff it is green and t is before 1 January AD 2000, or is blue and t is after 1 January AD 2000. Given this predicate, all our evidence that future emeralds will be green is equally evidence that they will be blue. For the emeralds we have observed are no more green than they are grue. It is as true that they are green as that they are grue, and so we are as justified in concluding that emeralds will be blue after t as that they will be green.

What this means is that correct inductive inference cannot be characterized in terms of inference to the continuation of previously observed similarities. We are inclined to suppose that one of the inferences about the emeralds is correct, and the other not (and of course there are infinitely many more such inferences, using predicates such as 'gred', 'grellow' and worse). But we have not yet provided any reason for preferring one to another. Nor have we any workable account of what a correct inductive inference is, by appeal to which we could hope to show that the use of such inferences is justified.

The natural response is to protest that there is something deeply suspicious about artificial predicates like 'grue'. But there is no agreement on what is wrong with them. (In a way the new riddle is simply the question what is wrong with them.) The mere fact that they are artificial is no complaint; it merely shows that we don't use them, not that we ought not to.

One common answer is to suppose that no 'sound' predicate could contain a reference to a particular point in time (or space). 'Grue' is defined in terms of greenness before t, and is therefore unsound. But there are two things wrong with this. First, it is equally true that 'green' is defined in terms of grueness before t; an object is green at t iff it is grue at t and t is before 1 January AD 2000, or bleen and t is after 1 January AD 2000 ('bleen' is defined as grue is, except that 'blue' and 'green' are reversed). So each predicate appears unsound, on this criterion, from the point of view of someone using the other. Second, even if such predicates were to be called 'unsound', we have not yet been told what it is about such predicates that makes inferences concerning them unreliable.

Instead of pursuing further attempts to solve Goodman's new riddle, we end by relating it to previous concerns. First, the anti-realist answer to Hume above offers nothing that will solve Goodman's riddle. The anti-realist appeals to the 'fact' that we do use past observations as evidence for future cases, or that our understanding of what it is for something unobserved to be true is linked to what we take as evidence that it is true. Our understanding of what it is for something to be green in the future is linked to what we take as evidence that it will be green; given the meaning of the relevant statement, then, there is no chance that we are wrong in what we take to be evidence for it. But these remarks do not discriminate between 'grue' and 'green'. The only hope that they would do so rests upon the thought that we have been using the predicate 'green' and not the predicate 'grue'. But this thought is of dubious usefulness, for two reasons. First, it is not clear what difference it makes which predicate we have used; we are not going to be able to show the other one to be somehow invalid on that account. Second, and more important, what about our previous practice makes it the case that we have been using 'green' rather than 'grue'?

It is true that we have been using the *word* 'green'. But what shows that we have not been thinking in terms of grueness all along? What shows that we won't suddenly begin to call blue objects 'green' on 1 January AD 2000? Until we can say which concept we have been using, we cannot hope to argue in favour of one on the grounds that it is the one we use.

This is important because an attractive reason for discounting concepts like grueness is that they cannot be acquired from examples (see Small (1961) for this suggestion). Greenness is a concept we can learn from examples, as we know because we have done it. But this argument collapses when we confront the possibility that we have been using the concept of grueness all along. If we have, we must have acquired it from our experience of grue objects.

The question we have now reached, and the attempt to answer it by appeal to examples, should remind us forcibly of Wittgenstein's rule-following considerations (5.5 – 7). Goodman's question is and should be similar to Wittgenstein's, for Goodman is asking what justifies one way of going on rather than another; this was exactly the question Wittgenstein was considering.

13.5 COHERENTISM AND INDUCTION

The position now is that we have two forms of inductive scepticism to deal with, Hume's and Goodman's. Anti-realism provided some sort of answer to Hume, as we saw, but completely failed to cope with Goodman's new riddle. We now consider the claims of coherentism.

Coherentists make large claims for the ability of coherentism to provide a perspective within which inductive scepticism collapses. Ewing held that "the coherence principle provides the only rational justification for induction" (Ewing, 1934, p. 247); Blanshard agrees (Blanshard, 1939, vol. 2, pp. 504 – 5). There are two constraints within which these claims should be assessed. The first is our present preference for internalism; externalist answers are insufficient. The second is that the answer should be as effective against Goodman as against Hume.

Suppose that we have a succinct statement of an inductive principle of inference, IPI. An externalist move would be to say that the adoption or use of IPI results in increased coherence in one's belief-set; this justifies our use of IPI. An internalist would add to this that we believe that the adoption or use of IPI results in increased coherence, and that so long as this belief is true we are justified in the use of IPI. Internalism does not have to show that this true belief is justified, as we agreed in considering the degrees of internalism in 9.3; to do so would lead to regress, and also here take us straight back into Hume's arms.

But still we have the question whether it is true that the adoption of IPI always results in increased coherence. It is no use trying to show this by appeal to the past; this would involve a well-worn circularity. The question whether the use of IPI leads to an increase in coherence cannot be entirely empirical, therefore. We need a reason in advance, a conceptual link between inductive inference and a increase in explanatory coherence.

Coherentists can provide such a reason. They do this by maintaining that the guiding principle of inductive inference just is "inference to the best of competing explanations" (Harman, 1970, p. 89). For instance, a detective inferring the guilt of one suspect from the evidence is reaching that hypothesis which provides the best explanation of all the evidence. So it is no accident that induction leads to an increase in explanatory coherence. And because both truth and justification are seen in terms of coherence, we can say that the use of induction must take us nearer the truth. What better justification of induction could we hope for?

And there is more to it than this. We have not yet explained Ewing's claim that coherentism is the *only* successful position in this area. To see the basis for this claim, we need to retrace Hume's steps.

How can we know or be justified in any belief about what will happen next? We see the brick hurtling towards the window; our natural belief about the future is reached by inductive inference. What justifies this inference? There is no necessary connection linking the two events of this brick's flight and the destruction of the window. There is no contradiction involved in supposing that one happens and the other doesn't, which there would be if they were connected by logical necessity; and there is no other comprehensible notion of necessity than that of logical necessity. That being so, these two events are conjoined but not connected. Our inference from one to the other must therefore derive from experience of similar conjunctions in the past. And this sort of inference cannot be justified empirically without circularity (see 1.2).

Coherentists such as Ewing and Blanshard stop this train by denying a crucial step. They hold that there is another comprehensible notion of necessity, natural necessity, which links the individual events together; and maintain that anyone who denies this is doomed to inductive scepticism, so that their view offers the only hope.

The sort of natural necessity they are talking about is basic to the possibility of explanation; without it explanation is impossible. For to explain something is to see why, in the circumstances, it had to happen. Philosophers in Hume's tradition, for example Hempel (1942), take explanation to occur when we are satisfied that the relevant event is or was going to happen. But this is not enough. Unless we can see *why* it is going to happen, we have no explanation. And to see why, we need more than knowledge that in previous similar cases this sort of thing happened. That sort of knowledge may enable us to make bleak predictions, but does not help us to an explanation; for explanation we need understanding (cf. 11.1). Hume's argument is that since there is no such thing as a necessary relation between events, we are reduced to the sort of explanation he can offer. But the reply is that if explanation is possible at all, there must be necessary relations between events. In the simple example of the brick and the window, it isn't just that the window will break; it has got to, or is bound to. Our inductive knowledge that it will break is knowledge by inference. The passage of the brick *entails* the breaking of the window; for, given the brick, the window must break. And we know this because it would be far harder to explain the window's not breaking than it would be to explain its breaking. (There are in fact links of mutual explanation.)

Ewing and Blanshard claim to escape Hume's argument by denying his atomism, the view that individual events are conjoined but never connected. It is the atomism that creates inductive scepticism rather than the nature of the case.

But this still leaves us with Goodman. Goodman points out that as well as our own inductive practice there are infinitely many others, each enshrined in its own language; and there seems to be nothing to choose between the languages. Each Goodmanic practice is equally inductive. So if one is justified, all are. Let us suppose for the moment that the previous argument about Hume leaves us with the conclusion that our inductive practice is justified. Why should the fact that other practices would also be justified disturb us? After all, the fact that many other belief-sets would be as justified as our own does not disturb us; justification can be shared. The plurality objection (8.2) only gets its bite when we consider claims to truth rather than justification. So isn't the sort of plurality Goodman points to equally acceptable?

Goodman needs to show that since other practices are possible, ours is not justified. If ours is justified, they are too. And the crucial point is that for each belief which we are justified in holding, there will be another practice, as well grounded as our own, which recommends the opposite belief. For instance, use of the predicate 'grue' leads us to conclude that emeralds are not green but blue after 1 January AD 2000. This means that the two practices are not just different but competing. They compete; nothing justifies the adoption of one rather than the other; so nothing justifies the belief that emeralds will stay green ra. her than the belief that they will not.

At this point we should turn for help to the analogy with Wittgenstein. What we have found is that there is no internal feature of our practice which can render it more justified than any competitor. And there is no external feature that will do this either; the only relevant feature was that our practice is the one we use, and the others are not. This doesn't help much. But we should not despair. The conclusion of Wittgenstein's thoughts about rule-following was that a practice does not need an independent external ground to justify it (5.6). The reason why we look for an external ground is that we think that such questions are external questions; they ask about our practice from a point of view which purports to be outside it. But they are not. Just as questions about the justification of some part of our use of language, for example about our use of ethical terms, are questions asked within our linguistic practice; so questions asked about induction, which is an all-pervading form of life which seems almost to constitute rational behaviour for us, are still questions which we are asking and setting within our scheme of things. Admittedly they cannot be justified from outside that scheme. But this should not disconcert us. If we insist that questions about justification can only be asked from within our practice, we shall be less ashamed of the answers we are so tempted to give to them.

If this Wittgensteinian answer to Goodman is effective, we learn that Goodman's move beyond Hume was a move from an answerable question which the coherentist can answer to an unanswerable question which nobody can answer, in the sense in which it was intended, but which guarantees its own unanswerability and thus rules itself out of court. If we can put Goodman to one side, Ewing was right to claim that coherentism is the only position from which induction can be shown to be rational practice.

FURTHER READING

Hume (1955, ch. 4.2) and Goodman (1973, chs. 3 – 4) are two classic arguments.

Responses to Goodman include Barker and Achinstein (1960), Small (1961) and Quine (1969, ch. 5).

Swinburne (1974) is a good collection of responses to Hume, including those of Edwards, Russell and Black; the introduction is a helpful survey.

The 'bilking' argument against backward causation is in Flew (1954). Dummett (1978, ch. 18) shows greater inventiveness.

Cahn (1967) is a helpful discussion of Aristotelian and other attempts to come to terms with fatalism.

A good expression of determinism is Van Inwagen (1975). Hume's compatibilism is in Hume (1955, chs. 7 – 8).

There is an argument about whether Hume's question about induction should be seen as bleakly sceptical, rather than as an attempt to reduce an incorrect theory of rationality to absurdity. For this, see Stroud (1977, ch.1).

Harré and Madden (1975, chs. 3 – 4) dispute Hume's conclusions. The coherentist response to Hume is given in Ewing (1934, ch. 4.3) and Blanshard (1939, vol. 2, pp. 504 – 11).

14
A Priori Knowledge

14.1 FOUNDATIONALISM AND A PRIORI KNOWLEDGE

Up to now we have been concerned almost exclusively with empirical knowledge, knowledge that can only be acquired by appeal to experience. In this chapter we consider the nature, extent and subject matter of another supposed form of knowledge, *a priori* knowledge.

Foundationalists distinguish between inferential and non-inferential justification; our non-basic beliefs are justified inferentially by appeal to basic beliefs which are themselves justified in some other way, non-inferentially. What, however, justifies the principles of inference on which any inferential justification must rely? Such principles are not themselves justifiable by appeal to basic beliefs, nor as conclusions of inferences from those beliefs. There must, then, be a third form of justification for the principles of inference if the foundationalist programme is to succeed (cf. 8.3).

Foundationalism, as we have seen (4.1), is a form of empiricism, and in its distinction between basic and non-basic beliefs it means to copy the distinction between those beliefs which are presented to us in experience and those which we derive by inference from experience. If principles of inference are justified in neither of these two ways, we must claim that we know them a priori, i.e. without appeal to experience. (This claim is made in Russell, 1926, p. 226.) Foundationalism, then, offers us one empiricist reason for asserting that there must be some knowledge which is not empirical. But there are other reasons too.

14.2 EMPIRICISM, THE A PRIORI AND THE ANALYTIC

Traditional empiricism, in an extreme form, maintained a distinction between ideas and propositions. Ideas are the component parts of propositions; propositions are complexes of ideas, so combined as to be able to be either true or false. (Ideas alone cannot properly be called either true or false.) Extreme empiricism held that all our ideas are derived from experience, and that no proposition or combination of ideas can be known to be true without appeal to experience.

The first of these tenets will not be disputed here, if only because to do so would involve accepting the distinction between ideas and propositions; we shall shortly find reason to be unhappy with that distinction. John Locke attempted to establish it in the only way he could think of, by running through all the crucial ideas one by one and showing how they could each be derived from experience. He had mixed success in an uphill struggle. Difficult cases include the ideas of identity, equality, perfection, God, power and cause.

The second tenet was no sooner stated than abandoned, because it conflicted with the highly plausible claim that many propositions can be known to be true with no further use of experience than that required for us to get the relevant ideas (or concepts) in the first place. This claim is plausible because of the number of examples which support it. 'Red is a colour'; '2 + 3 = 5'; 'a brother is a male sibling'; and (a more complicated example of Locke's) 'where there is no property there is no injustice'. We do not need experience to verify these truths; anyone who can understand them (who has the relevant ideas) is already in a position to know their truth without empirical investigation.

This, however, need not and did not disturb the empiricists. They accepted that we have knowledge which is not gained by appeal to experience, but argued that this could be explained on empiricist principles. They did this by saying that the propositions concerned had a peculiar status. They all express relations between our ideas or concepts, our knowledge of which is *conceptual knowledge*, knowledge about our concepts rather than substantial knowledge about the real, non-conceptual world. Locke agreed that these conceptual truths (which he called verbal truth or trifling propositions) could be known by the exercise of reason rather than by experience, but held that this was compatible with and explained by his concept-empiricism. The ideas whose interrelations we can know in this way are all empirical (see J. Locke, 1961, Bk. 4 ch. 8).

The empiricist who admits that there is a priori knowledge must, then, provide an explanation of this in his own terms. Locke held that propositions which are knowable a priori are trivial propositions expressing the relations between our ideas. Twentieth-century empiricists such as Ayer have maintained that a proposition can only be known a priori if it is *analytic*, i.e. true in virtue of the meanings of the words in it, rather than in virtue of the way the world is. On this account, all a priori knowledge is of analytic truths; synthetic truths can only be known empirically. So the admission of a priori knowledge was felt to make no dent in the empiricist programme because such knowledge was not substantial knowledge about the world. Empiricism became the less extreme claim that all substantial truth is empirical; only analytic truths can be known a priori.

This result does not fit well with the foundationalist's tendency to say that our knowledge of principles of inference is a priori, for such principles are hardly analytic. They are not true in virtue of the meanings of words alone, as we saw in the case of induction (13.3). They seem to be synthetic. How then can the empiricist say that we know them a priori? But we are not here defending empiricist doctrine; our task at the moment is explanation.

14.3 CAN SYNTHETIC TRUTHS BE KNOWN A PRIORI?

Are there any truths which cannot be convincingly called trivial or analytic, but of which our knowledge is a priori if anything? We have already seen one potential example of the synthetic a priori, namely our a priori knowledge of synthetic principles of inference. There are other examples.

One such is that of colour exclusion. We know that no object is red all over and green all over in the same respect and at the same time. And we know this without any need to check it by appeal to experience, because we know in advance that it is not possible to have an experience as of an object red all over and green all over at the same time.

We might object to this by pointing out that it is surely a fact of experience that being red excludes being green. It may in some sense be something which we need no further experience to verify, once we know what it is to be red and what it is to be green. But the fact that one colour excludes another is not a substantial fact about the world, and so our knowledge that this is so is not the sort of a priori knowledge of synthetic truths that we were looking for. Instead, it is a simple empirical fact about *appearance* that nothing can appear to have two 'competing' qualities simultaneously.

This reply will not do, for two reasons. First, it begs the question to claim that we can know by experience that two qualities compete in the relevant way. Experience tells us that no object is both red and green all over at the same time. But what is it about experience that reveals the further fact that no object *can* be like this? It would be more plausible to say that the exclusiveness of colours is not revealed by experience, but simply created by the way we distinguish between different colours. We so distinguish between red and green that we allow nothing to count as both red and green simultaneously. Hence the exclusiveness of colours is an artefact of our conceptual scheme rather than a reflection of the way the world is (and must be).

But what are we to say about the feeling that we don't invent colour exclusiveness for our own purposes, but simply mirror in our use of language (or our conceptual scheme) an exclusiveness which we find in the world? Perhaps in the case of colours it could be argued that colour is a matter of appearance, hence of a relation between us and the world, and so that colour exclusiveness is as much a fact about us – about the way things can appear to us – as about the world around us. This is to restate the position mooted three paragraphs ago.

The second objection to that position is that there are other examples of the sort of exclusiveness with which we are here concerned, which cannot be held to concern *appearance* in the same way. For instance, what about the obvious fact that a cow is not a horse? Nothing can be both a cow and a horse in the same respect and at the same time. But whatever sort of a fact this is, it is not a fact about appearances. Nor is it very convincing to say that it is a fact about our conceptual scheme rather than about cows and horses.

Is it perhaps part of the *meaning* of 'is a cow' that cows are not horses, so that 'is a cow' entails, among other things, 'is not a horse'? If it were, the truth that cows are not horses would be analytic, and so we would not here have an example of a synthetic truth known a priori. But if this were part of the meaning of 'is a cow', presumably anyone who knew that meaning would know that cows are not horses. And could there not be someone who knew nothing about horses, and did not know the meaning of 'is a horse' either, but who knew the meaning of 'is a cow' perfectly well? To be persuaded of this we only need to remember the myriad other things that cows are not – televisions, butterflies and porridge, for instance. If the meaning of 'is a cow' somehow contained all these exclusions, it would be impossible for anyone to learn it, particularly when we remember that the other words would contain their own exclusions too. So the proposition that nothing is both a cow and a horse is not analytic. But it is not about appearance, as the parallel propositions about colours might be held to be; and our knowledge of it cannot be held empirical on that account. We seem to know it a priori, if at all, because no further experience is necessary for its verification than that required for us to know what it is to be a cow and what it is to be a horse. Here, then, we seem to have a priori knowledge of a synthetic truth.

A similar argument can be run for the even more difficult problem of our knowledge of mathematical truth. If we grant that mathematical knowledge is a priori, are we to claim that mathematical truths are analytic or synthetic? Is '7 + 5 = 12' true in virtue of the meanings of the symbols alone? Kant used the term 'analytic' in a rather different way from ours, defining it not in terms of meaning but of concepts. He held that a judgement is analytically true if the concept occurring as predicate is contained within the concept occurring as subject; a good example is 'a brother is male' (Kant, 1961, Introduction 4; B10 – 14). In this sense of 'analytic', he once held that simple mathematical truth was analytic. But he later came to doubt this (Kant, 1967, pp. 128 – 31). 12, for instance, is the sum of 7 and 5; and one might be tempted to say that knowledge that this is so is required for possession of the concept 12. But 12 is also the sum of infinitely many other numbers, the product of others and so on. All of these facts have an equal claim to be required knowledge for anyone possessed of the concept 12, and since we cannot admit them all we can admit none. (The only truth which might possibly have a special claim is '12 = 11 + 1', 12 being defined as the successor of 11.) Mathematical truth is therefore synthetic, in Kant's sense.

The same argument, expressed with our definition of 'analytic' in terms of meanings, will be equally effective. Just as there are too many properties excluded by satisfaction of 'is a cow', so there are too many interrelationships between one number and other numbers for any of those interrelationships to be contained within the meaning of '12'. Mathematical truth is therefore synthetic, in our sense, even if knowable a priori.

So far the argument has run in terms of examples. Each is effective in its own way but still disputable. Kant, however, approaches the question in a way which if successful would render the appeal to examples more or less redundant. We saw that classical empiricists such as Locke claimed that all our concepts (or ideas, for Locke) are derived from experience, and attempted to establish this by enumeration. Kant does not argue directly against any part of the enumeration, but rather argues that there are some concepts which cannot be derived from experience because they are necessary for any possible experience. Anyone who lacked these concepts would be unable to have any experience at all. The argument here is extremely complex, but a basic idea is that the world is experienced as ordered spatially, temporally and causally. For instance, the experience of a ship moving down a river is an experience of a train of events which is ordered in space, in time and in the causal links between its various parts. (This example comes from Kant, 1961, B237 – 8.) Those elements of the ordering, however, are not things of which our original knowledge could be derived from some experience (maybe this one). Rather, one can only have an experience of this or any other sort if one is already in possession of the concepts which constitute the causal, temporal and spatial matrix within which the events we experience are presented. So these concepts are not empirical; although they are discernible in experience, they cannot be acquired by being extracted from the content of some experience. Such extraction, if possible at all, can only be achieved by someone who already possesses them, for only such a person can have an experience from which to extract them.

We might reply to this suggestion of Kant's that he has failed to distinguish between the claim that all concepts are empirical and the claim that all knowledge is empirical. Concepts are constituents of propositions, and our knowledge that propositions are true may be empirical even when those propositions have as constituents concepts which are not empirical. But it is at this point that the distinction between concepts and propositions begins to look dubious (if not before). For that distinction amounts in the present context to the suggestion that it is possible somehow to possess concepts such as those of space, time and causation without knowing true any propositions of which those concepts are constituents. And this is highly implausible. To have the concept of causation is to know the difference between events that are causally connected and those that are not – to understand what it is for two events to be causally connected. To have the concept of time is to be able to place events in a linear order. And so we find that someone who possesses the concept of causation already has some propositional knowledge; Kant claims, indeed, that such a person already knows that any event is preceded by another, on which it follows according to a rule (Kant, 1961, B238 – 41). Similarly, if you have the concept of space you know, according to Kant, that space is infinite, homogeneous and

Euclidean, and if you have the concept of time you know that time is linear. So conceptual knowledge requires propositional knowledge, for Kant, and so the propositions involved in our examples are known a priori, if at all. They are not analytic, however, since they constitute substantial knowledge about the empirical world, the world we experience.

We could complain about Kant's version of the propositional knowledge required for the possession of the concepts of space, time and causation, but it is hard to dispute the claim that conceptual knowledge requires some relevant propositional knowledge. A reply to Kant should therefore concentrate on his argument that some of our concepts are not empirical.

What we have seen so far, then, is that if we admit the distinction between a priori and empirical knowledge, the empiricist will find it difficult to maintain his claim that none but analytic truths can be known a priori. It seems that a more effective empiricism will deny the distinction between empirical and a priori, holding that no knowledge is distinctively one rather than the other. This is Quine's position. We shall approach it by asking what the subject matter of a priori knowledge is. What is the nature of those truths, if any, which can be known without appeal to experience? Kant held that any truth knowable a priori must be both universal and necessary (Kant, 1961, B3 – 4). We examine each of these claims in turn.

14.4 A PRIORI KNOWLEDGE AND UNIVERSAL TRUTH

Why did Kant hold that a priori knowledge must be knowledge of universal truth? The reason is that if our knowledge is of the nature of some particular object, it must depend upon examination of that object, and so must be empirical. Kant in fact saw no real distinction between necessity and universality, and supposed therefore that since a priori knowledge is of necessary truth, it must be of universal truth. We can grant for the moment that a priori knowledge is of necessary truth, and use this to argue that it need not for this reason be universal.

Kant need not deny that it is possible to know necessary truths about particular objects, so long as those truths are known by inference from parent universal truths. Thus I can perhaps know that the object before me cannot be both square and not square, but such knowledge is to be acquired only by inference from the universally true Law of Non-Contradiction: no proposition is both true and false. Universal necessary truths may perhaps have particular necessary truths as consequences, but the direction of discovery must always be from universal to particular, if the knowledge is to be a priori rather than empirical. For if our universal knowledge is to be a priori, it must be knowledge which is not reached from knowledge of particular cases; since the particular knowledge has to be empirical, the universal knowledge inferred from it would be.

The weakness of Kant's view here is in the claim that all knowledge of necessary truth about particular objects must be empirical, because it stems from examination of those objects. There may be a way in which we can acquire a priori knowledge which, though concerned with the nature of a particular object, is acquired not by examination but rather by reflection on its nature.

It is important to be clear about what we are trying to show. There are two stages. First, we might find an example of a necessary truth about a particular object which *is* not known empirically, though it might have been. Second, we might find an example of a necessary truth about a particular object which is known but cannot be known empirically. In the first case, we have an example of something which can be known either empirically or a priori; in the second we have an example which can only be known a priori. In either case we have an example of a priori knowledge, for a priori knowledge is knowledge that *can* be acquired 'without appeal to experience'. Whether the same proposition can be known in other ways as well is irrelevant. So the person who claims that his experience shows the truth of the causal law that every event follows upon some other according to some rule can be right. But our knowledge of this law is still a priori.

Kripke provides an example of the type we are looking for (Kripke, 1971). In a lecture he asked his audience to consider the wooden table at which he was standing. They knew, empirically, that the table was wooden. Now, he asked, could *that* table have been made of ice? Certainly there could have been an ice table there instead of a wooden one, but that would not provide what was required. What Kripke was asking was whether the table which is in fact wooden could instead have been made of ice, and we have a very strong intuition that any table made of ice would not have been the (wooden) one about which Kripke was asking. We can see, by reflecting on this table, that being made of wood it could not have been made of ice instead. Now this knowledge is not empirical. We (or the audience) knew empirically that the table was wooden, (*p*), and we saw that this meant that it could not have been made of ice, ($\Box q$ – necessarily it was not made of ice). So we have this situation:

1   we know empirically that p,
2   we know that $(p \rightarrow \Box q)$,
3   we know that $\Box q$.

Our knowledge that $\Box q$ is empirical, because it is derived by inference from our empirical knowlege that p. But what about our knowledge that $(p \rightarrow \Box q)$? Is this empirical or a priori? It does not seem to be empirical, because we cannot conceive of an experience which would verify it or falsify it (as Kripke argues, *ibid.*, pp. 152 – 3). So this conditional is known a priori, and is a necessary truth.

But now we face the question whether the necessary truth $\Box (p \rightarrow \Box q)$, which is a truth about a particular object, is known by reflection on the nature of the particular object or by subsumption as a simple instance of a universal truth. Do we know the universal truth that wooden objects could not have been made of ice directly, and infer from it that this object, being wooden, could not have been made of ice; or are we able to infer the universal truth from our knowledge of the particular case?

I think that Kripke's audience, at least, realized that $\Box(p \rightarrow \Box q)$ by reflection not upon the universal consequences of being made of wood but upon *that* table and upon whether any table made of ice could have been identical with that one. Of course, having seen it of that table, they could see that similar reflections would be equally effective in any relevantly similar case. So what they discovered a priori was recognizably true universally, and the particular truth was, in a sense, a consequence of the universal truth. But it was not by that route that they discovered it. They discovered it as a necessary truth by reflection on the nature of the particular case; their a priori knowledge was not then universal, and need not have become so if they had decided to think no further.

What this example of Kripke's is suggesting is that just as an ordinary contingent universal truth (for example, that all ravens are black) can be known by inference from contingent particular truths (about this raven and that raven), so equally a necessary universal truth (for example, that no table made of wood could have been made of ice instead) can be known by inference from particular necessary truths (necessary truths about particular tables). But this still would not make the universal knowledge empirical; it is a priori still, because the particular knowledge from which it is inferred is a priori. Kant was wrong, then, to suppose that truths about particular objects can only be known empirically. Some necessary truths about particular objects can be known a priori.

In fact we could try to tighten Kripke's screw a little. For we have admitted so far that the necessary truth that this table, being wooden, could not have been made of ice can be known either directly or by inference from the universal truth that no wooden object could have been made of ice instead. But perhaps there are some particular necessary truths which can only be discovered from particular cases; and if so the universal truths inferrable from them cannot be recognized except as they figure in particular cases.

Kripke's example may be of this sort. For our knowledge that no wooden table could have been made of ice instead can perhaps only be reached by confronting questions about particular tables (real or imaginary). And further examples may concern our knowledge of moral truths. Such truths may be necessary, for if actions are the better for being generous it seems hard to imagine a world in which they would be the worse for it. (They might all be wrong for other reasons.) But it may be impossible to know the necessary truth that an action is the better for being generous except by reflection on particular cases; this is what ethical theorists call intuitive induction (see Broad, 1930, p. 271 for an account).

14.5 A PRIORI KNOWLEDGE AND NECESSARY TRUTH

Kant was wrong, then, to say that a priori knowledge must be of universal truth. Particular truth can be known a priori. But our argument that this is so has assumed that Kant was right in his further claim that a priori knowledge must be of necessary truth. Contingent truths cannot be known a priori. And this is because a contingent truth is one which might be or might have been false; a contingent proposition is one which might or might not be true, and might or might not be false. But if it might be false, we cannot avoid empirical investigation if we want to discover whether it is in fact false or not. Contingent truth, then, can only be known empirically.

This point can be expressed using the terminology of possible worlds (see 3.3). A contingent proposition is one which is true in some worlds and false in others. If we want to know whether it is true in the actual world, we can only do this by determining empirically whether the actual world is one way or the other; that is, by determining which class of possible worlds contains the actual world.

Contingent truth, then, can only be known empirically. But the reverse is not true, as we showed in the last section. Some necessary truths can be known empirically; for instance, our knowledge that this table could not have been made of ice.

Here we are not saying that sometimes, where p is necessarily true, we can know empirically that p is true. The claim is rather that where p is necessarily true, we can know empirically that p is necessarily true.

But the example offered was of a necessary truth which was known empirically because it was known by inference from two propositions one of which was known empirically. Can we find a different example of a necessary truth which is known empirically other than by inference? Can necessities sometimes be experienced? This question is part of one raised earlier, about the range of perceptual knowledge. Can we, for instance, *see* that something must or cannot be true?

The sort of example we might offer here would perhaps be like this. We see two people walking down the street, one behind the other. Can we see that if he wants to overtake her, he will have to go faster? The question is, if not, why not?

14.6 QUINE AND THE DISTINCTION BETWEEN A PRIORI AND EMPIRICAL

So far we have decided that, although all a priori knowledge is of necessary truth, some necessities can be known empirically, even if only by inference from the contingent via a conditional known a priori. Quine argues that there is no other way in which necessities can be known; no necessity can be known other than empirically.

This makes it appear that Quine accepts the distinction between empirical and a priori knowledge in some way, but assigns no role or content to the a priori side. But in fact Quine is taking the line which we concluded in 14.3 was most promising for the empiricist; he is denying that the distinction is tenable at all. There is no dividing line, no reason for us to worry our heads about whether this or that knowledge is a priori or empirical. There may be distinctions of degree here, but all knowledge is more or less empirical.

Quine's route to this conclusion is not dissimilar to the route by which he demolished the distinction between analytic and synthetic truth (6.3). In fact the link between the two distinctions a priori/ empirical and analytic/synthetic is so close that any acceptance of the former would resurrect the latter. In both cases the argument starts from Quine's holism and the indeterminacy of sentential meaning. From this Quine argued that no sentence in our theory is completely immune from revision. Recalcitrant experience causes a revision among the observation sentences which form the periphery of our theory, and a consequential revision somewhere in the interior. Sentences nearer the periphery are more easily revisable than are sentences further in, but there is no way of telling in advance what sort of revision will turn out to be the most effective. This being so, even our firmest knowledge is susceptible in some degree to empirical results. But a priori knowledge must be immune to empirical results, because we need pay no attention to those results in order to acquire it. There can therefore be no such thing as a priori knowledge; all knowledge is to some degree empirical.

Quine's attitude to the distinction between necessary and contingent truth is now predictable. Necessary truth is conceived of as truth which could not be otherwise, and therefore must be immune to revision. If there were necessary truth there could be a priori knowledge of it, perhaps. But since no sentence is immune to revision, there is no necessary truth either.

A qualification is necessary here. The sort of necessity Quine is here rejecting is logical necessity or conceptual necessity, necessity thought of as guaranteed true by logic or by the nature of our conceptual scheme or the meanings of our words. Such necessary truths would be unrevisable, if there were any, and so Quine denounces them. But there is another sort of necessity, natural necessity, which he can and does admit. The naturally necessary is that which science tells us could not be otherwise; paper has to burn when lit, and water has to freeze below a certain temperature. Natural possibilities are those which are allowed by science. This sort of necessity and possibility is acceptable to Quine, because the propositions concerned are not unrevisable any more than science is unrevisable. But there is no further notion of logical possibility, with which we can say that some things which are naturally impossible (being incompatible with the laws of science) are still logically possible.

The difficulty with Quine's position here is his ambivalent attitude to the Law of Non-Contradiction. In one mood Quine asserts that this law too is technically subject to revision, even if only in the most extreme and inconceivable circumstances. This is the mood of his 'Two Dogmas of Empiricism' (Quine, 1953, p. 43). Later, however, Quine is more willing to admit vestiges of unrevisability. He argues (Quine, 1960, pp. 57 – 61) that the logical connectives do have a determinate meaning, and this makes it possible for him to allow (Quine, 1970, ch.6) that the logical laws are true in virtue of the meanings of the logical connectives in them. People who disagree about the laws of logic are not talking the same language. And this is to admit that those laws are unrevisable analytic truths.

14.7 A COHERENTIST APPROACH

A rather different account of a priori knowledge and necessary truth is given by Blanshard.

The extreme empiricist refuses to accept the notion of natural necessity. There is no necessity in the world, for him, but only regularities and our response to them. Hume held (Hume, 1955, ch. 7) that our sense that heavy objects could not help falling, or that a glass window was bound to break when a brick hit it, was to be explained not by the thought that there are some ways in which the world just happens to be and others in which it cannot help being, but by the suggestion that our experience of perfect regularities creates in us an irresistible habit of expectation. Natural necessity, then, is more a fact about us, the observers, than about the world we observe. Logical necessity, however, is admitted and explained by appeal to the Law of Non-Contradiction (see Hume, 1955, ch. 4.1).

Quine takes the opposing view. For him, logical necessity is rejected in favour of natural necessity, conceived of as that required by the laws of science. Quine, then, revives the distinction between necessary and contingent within the natural world, rather than as a distinction between the natural and the logical.

Blanshard's view is rather different. He rejects the old empiricist claim that all necessity is logical necessity, arguing rather as we did in 14.3 that there are large numbers of synthetic necessary truths whose necessity seems to be a fact about the world rather than derived from the intricacies of logic (Blanshard, 1939, chs 28 – 30). But he extends the domain of natural necessity farther than Quine would, for two reasons, both of which stem from his coherentism.

The first reason concerns the distinction between knowledge and understanding. As enquirers, we seek not just to know the truth but to understand, and to understand is to see why things should be the way they are. In understanding, then, we move from recognizing something as happening to be true, contingently true, to recognizing that it has to be true, that it is necessarily true (cf. remarks about the coherentist attitude to induction in 13.5). The domain of natural necessity extends, then, as far as understanding can reach.

The second reason is even more far-reaching. For a coherentist in the tradition of Bradley, truth and system coincide (see 8.2). The systematic and the coherent are the same, and coherence is defined in terms of the mutually explanatory. As our system grows in coherence, the interrelations between its parts become tighter and tighter. The explanatory power of the system becomes so great that we can no longer see any sense in which this or that part just happens to be true. Instead we begin to see each part as necessary to the whole, and in this we recognize that what at an earlier stage was seen as contingent truth has become necessary truth (cf. remarks in 8.1 about the difference between entailment and mutual explanation). So, if Blanshard is right, at the limit contingent truth vanishes, leaving only necessary truth. But since this necessity has been growing, necessity like truth is a matter of degree.

This conclusion leads to a rejection of the distinction between a priori and empirical knowledge. Blanshard writes (Blanshard, 1939, vol. 2, p. 424):

> The perception that necessitation is thus a matter of degree is inconsistent with the sharp line between a priori and empirical which the positivists are wont to draw. In the face of such insights as that anything red must be coloured and extended, or that orange falls in the colour-series between red and yellow, it is idle to say that judgements about empirical fact are *completely* without necessity. It is also idle to say that any judgement whatever possesses, with exactly its present meaning, so absolute a necessity as to be incapable of modification by any extension of knowledge.

FURTHER READING

Kant (1961, Introduction) and Kripke (1971).
Putnam (1977) on the relation between Quine on the analytic/synthetic distinction and on the a priori/empirical distinction.

Stroud (1969) on Quine on the unrevisability of logic; see also Quine's reply in the same volume.

Pears (1966) on the incompatibility of colours.

Locke's epistemology is in J. Locke (1961, Bk 4). Hume makes a distinction analogous to the analytic/synthetic distinction in Hume (1955, ch. 4.1). Locke's empiricism falters at J. Locke (1961, Bk 4 ch. 3.25); Hume's at Hume (1955, ch. 12.3). Hume's views on causation and natural necessity are at Hume (1955, ch. 7).

15
Is Epistemology Possible?

In this final chapter we consider the charge that the enterprise of epistemology, as conducted in this book, is impossible. Not just any sceptical argument will support this charge. Most sceptical arguments suggest that though we can start the construction of a theory of knowledge or justification, we can never complete the task; at least, not if completion includes establishing that we do have perceptual knowledge, scientific knowledge or whatever. This has been the role of the argument from error so far, and we have as yet found no answer to it. But the sceptical arguments we are now interested in claim instead that the enterprise of epistemology cannot even get started, and hence *a fortiori* cannot be successfully completed. One way of putting the point is that arguments of the first sort claim that though we may be able to construct a theory of what knowledge would be like if we had any, we cannot actually claim any knowledge (and so in particular we cannot claim to know that our theory is true). Arguments of the second sort claim that we cannot begin to construct a theory at all, because to do so involves some form of vicious circularity or the making of unjustifiable assumptions.

Hegel starts the introduction to his *Phenomenology of Mind* by considering the charge that in epistemology the task of knowledge is to examine itself rather than other things, and that this is impossible. Knowledge is not itself an object for us, but the instrument with which we approach our objects or the medium through which they appear to us. We cannot examine that medium itself, because it is always that by which we are related to our objects, and to turn it into an object is to cause it to cease to be the relation in which we are interested. This way of putting the point is suggestive, but Hegel immediately rejects it because it involves notions such as those of an instrument or medium which have not yet been made clear. He then reconstructs the problem in his own way. His first reformulation is that in the study of knowledge we cannot start without a criterion by which we are to distinguish between true knowledge and counterfeit substitutes. But no criterion that we may adopt can have justified itself at the outset of our enquiry, since the justification of a criterion is precisely among the results we are hoping to achieve at the end. But if there is no criterion for us to use at the outset, we cannot even begin.

Before providing his answer to this problem, Hegel elaborates. Knowledge is a relation between ourselves and the object of our knowledge. That object, when we know it, exists *for us*. But the object of our knowledge is independent of us, and as such exists *in itself* also. It is as it exists *in itself* that we call it truth; in knowledge our aim is to become aware of our object, truth, as it is *in itself*. But how is this possible? How can our knowledge be of the truth? For what we know, in so far as we know it, is *for us*, not *in itself*. And the criterion of what exists *for us* lies in us and comes from us, while that which we judge by that criterion, existing *in itself*, need not acknowledge our criterion as relevant or suitable. The criterion is our imposition upon an independent object. So there is nothing in what we can do that can ensure that our criterion fits our object as it is *in itself*.

In this way the problem of the criterion becomes in Hegel's hands an aspect of the more general problem of how our efforts to know our object as it is *in itself* can ever be successful. And this is a radical way of putting the already familiar difficulty that no matter how firm and well justified our beliefs there always remains the possibility that the world is not the way we take it to be. This difficulty, which lay at the basis of the sceptical argument from error, has become an argument that the theory of knowledge cannot begin, rather than that it cannot be successfully completed.

Hegel begins his resolution of the problem by pointing out that in epistemology the object of our enquiry is our awareness or consciousness. But this object is of such a nature that the distinction between what exists *for us* and what exists *in itself* is not here a distinction between what is available to us in consciousness and what is not. Both sides of the distinction fall within the grasp of consciousness. For our question is how in consciousness we are related to our object, and when our object is our own consciousness it is clear that there is no danger that our consciousness should have an existence *in itself* which is in principle hidden from us and separate from that consciousness as it exists *for us*. In epistemology, then, we are comparing the object we are conscious of with our consciousness of it, but this does not mean that the enterprise is impossible. For the crucial distinctions between consciousness and object or between the *for us* and the *in itself* are distinctions within what is available to us rather than between what is within and what lies beyond our grasp.

But though there is no general impossibility about the attempt to compare consciousness and object, there is always the possibility that in the comparison we should discover that the object as it is *in itself* is one thing to consciousness, while our knowledge of that object, the object as it is *for us*, is another; and that the two when compared should fail to correspond. When this happens what options are available to us? One is to attempt to alter our knowledge to make it fit the object. But this would not have the desired effect, for an important reason. Our knowledge here is that state of consciousness which best fits the criterion we are using. Even so, it failed to fit its object. And the criterion by which it failed to fit its object is found by consciousness in the nature of the object, not imposed arbitrarily from outside as was suggested before. So we cannot hope to gain anything by 'altering' our knowledge unless we also change the criterion; and we cannot change the criterion without changing the object. Altering our knowledge would mean changing our object; when knowledge and object fail to correspond, both collapse, and with them we lose the criterion which we were using to determine whether they correspond.

What has happened then is that at a certain level of consciousness what Hegel would call a contradiction has emerged. But Hegel's attitude to these contradictions is not one of despair. Instead he supposes that the result of these contradictions is that the nature of the contradiction we have exposed can teach us where to go from here. For when knowledge and object fail to correspond, we are not left with nothing. Our attempts to alter our knowledge lead to a change in the object, and thus a new pair to examine, to see whether they correspond. And this is so because the negation contained in the contradiction is not an *abstract* negation in which each side destroys the other, leaving nothing left, but what Hegel calls *determinate* negation, which has a certain form. And by its form it drives us up from the contradiction to a new level, where we have a new object and a new enquiry.

To take an ordinary example (not one of Hegel's): suppose that in our examination of sense-perception as a form of consciousness we determine that sense-perception, as we conceive it, fails to fit its object; that the object as it is *in itself* fails to correspond to the object which exists *for us*. One response to this is scepticism about our empirical knowledge. Another is to say that from this failure to fit (the contradiction) a new form of consciousness emerges, with its own object, requiring a new examination. And this progression from one form of consciousness to another will continue until we reach a form where the distinction between the object *for us* and the object *in itself* collapses completely, because we have reached a consciousness whose object can only exist *in itself* in so far as it exists *for us*. Here at last consciousness lays aside the appearance of being hampered by what is foreign to it; we have reached a level where consciousness can be and is its own object.

This progression from one form of consciousness to another is the mark of Hegel's conception of 'phenomenology'. It differs in two important ways from the approach we have taken hitherto. First, it treats sceptical arguments not as a danger to be defused or rebutted, but as a source of discovery. For it is only by means of sceptical arguments that the contradictions inherent in a particular level of consciousness will be revealed; it is the sceptic who shows that *here* our knowledge cannot correspond to our object, and hence it is the sceptic who drives us from one form of consciousness to the next until we reach a form where consciousness and object coincide. It is the notion of determinate negation which is crucial here; it is with this sort of negation that scepticism is properly concerned, and this is what drives the phenomenology. Second, epistemology for Hegel is possible, but only if it takes his route, progressing from one form of consciousness to the next. Any form of epistemology that does not progress in this way (Kant's, for instance) is destroyed by the vicious circularity. Appeal to that progression was the only means Hegel saw of solving the problem of the criterion and of overcoming the separation of the *in itself* and the *for us*.

15.2 CHISHOLM AND THE PROBLEM OF THE CRITERION

Is there a response to Hegel's problem of the criterion which does not take us so far away from the analytic tradition with which this book has been concerned? Few writers in that tradition have faced up to this methodological problem, but Chisholm has not only exposed it but attempted to provide an answer to it (Chisholm, 1977, ch. 7).

Chisholm begins by considering a general difficulty. In epistemology we tend to start with certain intentions; for instance, we intend to show that empirical and mathematical knowledge is possible. There are, then, certain types of knowledge, certain examples, which we expect our theory to validate; and if it does not this reflects badly on our theory rather than on the examples. There are other more dubious knowledge claims, for instance claims to moral or religious knowledge, whose eventual fate we may allow the best theory to decide. But there will be some that we insist upon. And what we do as philosophers is to extract from the agreed examples certain criteria which will validate those examples retrospectively and also give us a decision about the disputed examples. This is the 'common sense' approach which Chisholm's own theory of knowledge exemplifies. Accepting that empirical knowledge is possible, and being persuaded by the regress argument (4.1) that our theory must have some foundationalist structure, he simply writes a series of epistemic principles which have the desired effect. The justification of the principles is simply that they do have that effect; and we then accept their verdicts about the disputed examples.

An alternative approach is to adopt certain criteria at the outset, leaving it open which knowledge claims those criteria will eventually validate (if any). For instance, we might set down as our criterion the claim that all knowledge be somehow derived from sense-experience. But it might turn out that we are unable to show how any interesting knowledge (for example, of unseen objects, of the past or of mathematical truth) is derived from sense-experience, and in that case we simply abandon those areas. On this approach, then, we have more confidence in our criterion than in any examples, and we allow the possibility that none of our favourite examples will live up to the demands of our criteria.

Both of these approaches involve making assumptions which they themselves provide no means of validating. The common sense approach is manifestly an expression of philosophical prejudice, while the alternative 'criterial' approach is likely to hit on criteria at the outset with no chance of an explanation of what justifies our choice of these criteria rather than others. It may be, of course, that the common sense approach leaves no room for philosophical scepticism. But since this is merely a matter of prejudice, it can hardly be claimed as an advantage.

Surprisingly, since his own theory takes the common sense approach, Chisholm suggests that there is a way between the horns of this dilemma. This third approach he calls *critical cognitivism*.

Suppose that instead of fixing on certain examples (perceptual knowledge, memory knowledge, etc.) and insisting that our theory show that we do have such knowledge, we instead agree in advance on certain 'sources' of knowledge: perception, memory, reason and self-awareness, maybe. When we come to consider a contested concept such as that of ethical knowledge, it may seem that we have only two choices. Either we stick to our original list of sources and claim that since there is no further source there is no ethical knowledge, or we allow that there must be a further source (intuition, perhaps) in order to make ethical knowledge possible. This is the original dilemma, expressed now in terms of sources. But there is a third possibility, critical cognitivism. The critical cognitivist allows that none of the sources is itself a source of ethical knowledge directly, but tries to show that what those sources provide us with serves to enable us to know ethical facts. Our sources give us knowledge which serves as a *sign* of ethical truth, which *expresses* ethical truth to us and *through which* we can know it. For instance, our detestation of an action serves to make an evil known to us; the behaviour of another can express that person's pain to us, and so we can know their pain through their behaviour.

There may be merits in this proposal in general. It seems to offer greater flexibility to those struggling with the concept of moral perception or trying to account for our empirical knowledge of the mental states of others without introducing a further source called sympathy. But as it stands it is not so much a theory as a promissory note for a theory. To get any further we would want to know what it is for one thing to express another, what it is to see one thing as an expression of another, and whether there are different sorts of expression in different areas, for example in ethics and other minds.

But the problem really is why Chisholm should think of critical cognitivism as a third possibility which escapes the dilemma as he originally posed it. Critical cognitivism seems to be concerned mainly with our approach to the disputed cases, particularly of moral or religious knowledge (perhaps knowledge of the future too). But the problem of the criterion did not really concern our attitude to the disputed cases, but our attitude to the undisputed ones. The problem was that the initial selection of four sources of knowledge was nothing more than philosophical prejudice, and nothing in critical cognitivism answers this complaint.

Hegel would think of an epistemology which started from the acceptance of the four sources as simply ludicrous (an uncritical cognitivism), both because it takes as its starting point something which nothing in the procedure offers a chance of validating, and because if the distinction between different sources of knowledge is taken seriously as the beginning of a genuine theory of the mind and of cognition, it collapses in contradictions. None of the sources is individually able to provide knowledge. Consciousness in each case fails to correspond to its object; each level of consciousness creates its own criteria, and analysis shows that it cannot satisfy the criteria so created. So if Hegel's problem is a real one, we can only conclude that Chisholm has not answered it.

15.3 QUINE AND THE NON-EXISTENCE OF FIRST PHILOSOPHY

Hegel and Chisholm consider the charge that epistemology must either assume a criterion which it is in no position to justify, or take as given certain examples whose choice is a matter of simple prejudice. This matter is also confronted by Quine. The holism which results from Quine's acceptance of Duhem's thesis has among its consequences the abandoning of the analytic/synthetic distinction, that is the distinction between those sentences true in virtue of their meaning alone and those whose truth depends at least to some extent on how the world is (see 6.3). Although, for Quine, there is a difference of degree between sentences to whose truth we are very firmly wedded and those which we are more easily persuaded to abandon, there are no completely unrevisable sentences. Thus all sentences, in a way, count as synthetic; but some are more synthetic than others. And this brand of holism forces us to abandon the hope of a *first philosophy*, a philosophical system which stands apart from, is independently justifiable, and adjudicates on the claims of the special sciences such as physics or, more mundanely, of sense-perception. Philosophy (and epistemology, in particular) is continuous with or even part of natural science. It is not a peculiar investigation of concepts, nor a separable enquiry into the meanings of crucial words such as 'know' or 'justify'. If there were a first philosophy, this would perhaps be its subject matter. Instead, philosophy is only distinguished from other aspects of human enquiry by its generality; it tackles more general and broader questions than those investigated by the special sciences of physics and psychology.

On this Quinean approach, then, philosophy is the study of science from within science. But this seems to raise problems of circularity.

In studying science within science, the philosopher is not able to question the whole of science at once; rather he has to assume the general validity of scientific procedures and results if he is going to find reasons within science for questioning, and accepting or rejecting and replacing, particular aspects.

This is why Quine is so fond of Neurath's parable of the mariner who has to rebuild his boat while staying afloat in it. We have to keep the boat of science generally intact while we examine it and repair such parts as we find defective. We cannot take the boat into dry dock and get off it, nor can we suppose that the discovery of contradictions within science could enable us to rise above science, leaving our boat on a Hegelian helicopter.

What then persuades Quine that his conception of the relation between philosophy and science enables him to avoid the Hegelian charge of circularity? It looks as if, with the abandoning of a first philosophy, that charge simply recurs in a more vicious form.

One suggestion Quine makes is that the problem of circularity only arises within the philosophical tradition of the search for certainty and the attempt to deduce science from sense-data (Quine, 1969, pp. 83 – 4). But this suggestion will not hold water by itself (nor keep it out *à la* Neurath). It is true that if we were attempting to deduce science from sense-data, we would be involved in a vicious circularity if we assumed science in order to do so. But it is a fallacy to suppose that therefore all is well so long as we drop the hope of deduction.

Quine's suggestion here only begins to make sense within his more general approach. Since, in the absence of first philosophy, we have no alternative but to examine science from the inside, there is no danger that philosophy should adopt and impose a criterion from outside. The criteria to be used are the criteria of science, and this involves no circularity or prejudicial assumption, but rather a simple recognition of what the enterprise of epistemology is. Second, the only sceptical doubts that are possible are also those that derive from science rather than attempt to criticize science from some arbitrary 'rational' perspective. Our question should not be 'what is it that enables our scientific beliefs to count as knowledge?', for this question makes us suppose that our answer cannot itself appeal to any scientific results without circularity. Instead, we should ask 'If our science were true, how could we know it?'. Here the epistemological question is asked within the scope of the hypothetical, and since the question therefore assumes the truth of current scientific results, the answer can do so as well. Here epistemology is taking place within science. So the dangers that Hegel points to only arise, for Quine, in systems which separate philosophy from science. Once, as holists, we give up that separation and draw in our horns, there can be no general methodological objection to the practice of epistemology.

The reason, then, why Quine supposes that the danger of circularity is removed when we abandon the search for certainty is that that search only made sense within the attempt at a first philosophy, of which it was traditionally a central part.

15.4 EPISTEMOLOGY NATURALIZED

What then becomes of philosophy once it is thought of as part of science rather than as the separate study of science? Are we able to ask (and hope to answer) the same questions as before, but within the new perspective? And what attitude should we adopt to scepticism now? Is there still room for the sceptic?

Traditional epistemology studied the relation between data and belief, between evidence and theory. It attempted to show how our beliefs (for instance, the belief in an external world) are justified by the data from which they spring; how our scientific theories are justified by the evidence which supports them. Is this study to be abandoned and replaced, or can it be continued within the new perspective? Quine seems to vacillate between these two alternatives. Sometimes he suggests that the old questions smack of first philosophy, and that anyway the attempt to discover a relation between evidence and theory which would make the theory justified has proved to be unsuccessful. Why not then, he asks, simply study how we do go about moving from our data to the formation of belief? This factual study, squarely within the bounds of psychology, is what he calls *naturalized epistemology*. It leaves aside questions of justification and considers only the genetic, causal questions. We cease to worry about the gap between evidence and theory, and study instead the causal relations between the two.

Quine has a suggestion about one way in which that investigation could proceed. He finds in the practice of language-learning a mirror or model of the practice of theory-building. Observation sentences are basic on each side; they are the evidence on which our theories rest and the point at which language confronts reality directly enough for single sentences to be individually learnable (see 7.2). So an empirical substitute for the study of the relation between evidence and theory is the study of the ways in which language-learners actually move from an understanding of simple observation sentences to an understanding of the more complex sentences (expressing dispositions and tendencies or the consequences of unfulfilled conditions) of which theories are constructed.

Quine is suggesting here that naturalized epistemology does not involve a change of subject but rather offers a new way of studying the old subject. The old problem was the gap between 'meagre input' and 'torrential output'. But this gap can be studied in two ways, either by the study of the relation between observation sentences and theoretical sentences, as mentioned above, or more directly by the study of the relation between the physical input received by the human subject − retinal disturbance, for instance, constitutes the information received by the eye − and the beliefs which the subject is thereby caused to form; those beliefs being studied physicalistically, that is by studying the neurophysiology of the brain-activity which constitutes them. It is this latter approach, perhaps, which is the most characteristic of naturalized epistemology, and Quine holds (Quine, 1969, p. 83) that we are prompted to study it

> for somewhat the same reasons that always prompted epistemology; namely, in order to see how evidence relates to theory, and in what ways one's theory of nature transcends any available evidence.

As far as sceptical arguments are concerned, we have already seen that Quine is willing to admit the general epistemological question 'If our science were true, how could we know it?'. Within this question, the sceptic is allowed to find a role. He will have to find reasons within science for questioning whether scientific truth can be known; our science will have to show itself unknowable. This is not impossible, according to Quine, but it is very unlikely. There are two standard sceptical moves which are ruled out in advance by his requirement that the sceptic work from within science.

The first is any version of the argument from error which starts from the claim that it is logically possible at any time and in any circumstances that one's present belief should be false. Quine wants to nip any argument of this sort in the bud, by refusing to allow the notion of logical possibility which it uses. The only sort of possibility he is willing to admit is physical possibility, that which our science admits as possible. To allow another sort of possibility, one impervious to the results of physics, would be to re-create the analytic/synthetic distinction. And it is not physically possible at any time and in any circumstances that one's present belief should be false. If the only room for falsehood is logical room, it is no room at all. So this general sceptical argument does not get going.

In a similar vein, the sceptic might try to argue that, for all we know, reality may be entirely different from the way we take it to be; the world need not recognize our theory, or our object as it exists *for us* need not correspond to that object as it exists *in itself*. All these remarks, in Quine's view, rely on the supposition that there is an object, the world, which is separate from our theory and which provides a criterion by which our theory may be determined as false (not by us, of course, but simply in fact). But with Quine's account of the relation between epistemology and science, this supposition is senseless. The only criterion of reality is the one which science provides; the only reality is the one which science describes. So again there is no danger that our criterion should fail to fit our object, for science provides both criterion and object: a situation which should hold some attractions for Hegel.

These two sceptical approaches are ruled out, then, but any sceptical argument that uses science to confute science is, methodo- logically at least, acceptable. And Quine himself provides us with one. For he takes it to be a deliverance of science that we receive a 'meagre input' from which there is somehow generated a 'torrential output'. And surely this contrast between the meagre and the torrential is all that is needed for the sceptic to mount an argument from within science against the possibility of any scientific or theoretical knowledge. For if the gap is as great as all that, how can there be sufficient in the input to make justified the output we provide in response to it?

I think the response Quine would make here is one he makes in a similar context elsewhere (Quine, 1981, p. 475), that the sceptic here is overreacting. Instead of leaping immediately to enormous sceptical conclusions, we should wait to see what the naturalistic study of the relation between input and output turns up. It may seem to us in advance that the input is disproportionately small to ground such a fluent output, but empirical psychology may yet find ways of redressing the balance. So the contrast between input and output is not yet a deliverance of science; it may be and it may not be.

There seems, however, to be a misconception here. Quine is supposing that the question whether there is a disproportionate gap between input and output is empirical, and it is to be resolved by the naturalistic study of the causal relations between input, conceived of as sensory stimuli, and output, conceived of as the neurophysical states of the brain that are the physical correlates of beliefs. But viewed in these terms there is no contrast between meagre and torrential. The input is (together with other things) sufficient to cause the brain states which are its effects, and in following this causal story we are not any more studying a gap between input and output, if that gap is thought of as analogous to the gap between evidence and theory. The contrast between meagre input and torrential output, like the gap between evidence and theory, is not a *causal* matter but an *inferential* one. It belongs to what Sellars calls "the logical space of reasons" (cf. Sellars, 1963, ch. 5.1). The evidence is not conceived of as causally insufficient to ground the theory; it is insufficient (if at all) in the sense that it does not provide sufficient reason for, or fails to justify, the theory. So Quine is faced with a choice. Either he is ruling out this inferential question as not amenable to naturalistic epistemology, or he accepts it but fails to provide any method of answering it. (This point is well made by Stroud, 1984, ch. 6.)

But what would justify taking the first horn of this dilemma? Quine might wish to claim, or admit, that in studying the causal relation between input, which he sometimes tendentiously calls information, and output we have abandoned the epistemologist's traditional interest in evidential questions. Viewed naturalistically, the crucial gap has ceased to exist. But what in his position justifies this renunciation? The mere fact that epistemology for him has become naturalized, or is now a part of science rather than a superior court of reason, does not itself mean that questions of justification are ruled out of court. Science itself is not wholly naturalistic. It contains its own evaluative criteria, and those criteria can be used within science to tackle evaluative questions such as those of justification. It looks, then, as if naturalized epistemology contains no answer to the sceptic, nor even a method whereby an answer might be found.

The distinction we have been using here between evidential and causal questions might itself be questioned. Why should not causal enquiries be themselves enquiries into justification? After all, among possible accounts of justification considered earlier one prominent possibility was the causal theory of justification, which holds that beliefs are justified iff they are caused in a certain way. Perhaps Quine would wish to use this avenue to show how an interest in causal matters can both make sense of and hope to answer questions of justification. But if this is his answer to the sceptic, it is merely another form of externalism in the theory of justification. We have seen, so far, no reason to accept externalist answers; it is internalism that has the backing of intuition (9.2 – 3). But whether this is so or not, a Quinean adoption of externalism would be an independent stance, justified by neither of the distinctive theses considered here. Neither the absence of a first philosophy nor the naturalization of epistemology yields an independent argument for externalism. So if we still want an internalist answer to the questions of epistemology, Quine provides no answer and no substitute.

15.5 CONCLUSION

At the beginning of this chapter we distinguished between arguments that the enterprise of epistemology could never start, and arguments that it could never be successfully completed. (Some arguments were of both sorts.) We have seen that Hegel provides a conception of epistemology as the progression from one state of consciousness to other higher states, under which the arguments for the impossibility of epistemology are defused. Chisholm's notion of critical cognitivism failed to provide any answer at all, but Quine's rejection of first philosophy did yield a non-Hegelian perspective which escaped the charge of vicious circularity. The difference between Hegel and Quine, however, is that Hegel's perspective contains the promise of an answer to the sceptic, conceived now as someone arguing that the epistemological enterprise will never be successfully completed. Quine's views, however, seem not to offer any strategy to defeat the sceptical arguments that will arise naturally within the confines he accepts, i.e., sceptical arguments from within science. So we are still left with a sceptical argument which we have not seen how to escape from or rise above without taking the plunge with Hegel.

This commits me to offering my own suggestion. An attractive idea about how to reply to the sceptic (made, for example, in Stroud, 1984, ch. 7) is that we must find some means of preventing him from generalizing from his chosen examples. We might, that is to say, admit that we don't know that we are not brains in a vat, but hope to avoid being driven by this to admit that we don't know much else either. This was the strategy which Nozick followed but in chapter 3 we found it to be unsuccessful. It leaves us asserting counter-intuitively that we can know what we will do tomorrow but cannot know that there will be a tomorrow. But there is another sense in which the sceptic is generalizing from admitted instances, on which we might focus instead. This sense can be plainly seen in standard versions of the argument from illusion, and is also the central move in the argument from error.

The argument from error holds that if your present cognitive state is, as far as you can tell, relevantly indistinguishable from another which was not a state of knowledge, you cannot now claim to know. And it's not just that you can't claim to know; you don't know, because your present state is relevantly indistinguishable from (similar in all relevant respects to) one in which you don't know.

This argument relies on an epistemological analogue of the principle of universalizability familiar in ethical theory (see 1.2). In my view that principle is mistaken, and showing this seems to me to be important in the fight against the sceptic. (Everyone says piously that the aim should be to learn from the sceptic, but their practice only rarely fits their preaching.)

The principle of universalizability is mistaken in ethics because it ignores the ability further properties may have in a new case to defeat what were sufficient reasons for a moral judgement in a previous case, without causing us to return to the previous case and revise our judgement there (see Dancy, 1981). Because of this ability, we can never be driven from case to case by the universalizability of moral judgements. The fact that this case is indistinguishable from the first in all characteristics relevant to the moral value of the first does not ensure that the second has no other morally relevant characteristics; and so no choice we make in the second case can require us to alter our opinion of the first, unless we decide that the two cases are similar in all relevant respects (in all respects relevant to either). But someone who thinks they are morally different will not make that decision, and hence cannot be caught by universalizability. His position is consistent so long as he maintains that there is a morally relevant difference, even if he is not yet in a position to point to that difference.

The analogy with epistemology suggests that it is not possible to show that we don't know now by showing that we cannot point to a relevant difference between our present case and one in which we don't know. So long as we assert (as we will) that there is a relevant difference, our inability to point to it is no proof that we don't know, nor even that we are wrong (inconsistent) to claim to know.

This conclusion is not a form of externalism, however. For someone who knows now, despite being unable to point to a relevant difference between his present situation and one in which he doesn't know, is or may still be in possession of the factors in virtue of which his cognitive state is one of knowledge. This is because the fact that there is a relevant difference (and the relevant difference which there is) is not one of the features in virtue of which he knows now. It *allows* him to know now when he didn't then, but the properties in virtue of which he knows now do not include this *allower*. If there were no allower, he would not know now; but this does not show that the facts in virtue of which he knows now include the allower. The properties in virtue of which he knows now are more ordinary properties about the present case, not arcane relations between this case and others. And these more ordinary properties are properties which he (probably) can point to. For instance, I know that today is Wednesday even though I cannot say that I have not made or could not make mistakes in relevantly similar situations. I may not be able to distinguish my situation from those actual or possible ones, but I can say how I know that today is Wednesday. And this is all that internalism in the theory of justification requires.

There is considerable similarity between the argument I offer here and the externalist response (in the other sense of externalism, externalism in the philosophy of mind) to the argument from illusion (11.4); that argument also relies on a version of the universalizability principle. Whatever its merits, I cannot claim that my argument is wholly secure. This means that the title I originally intended for this book is doubly apt. That title, 'Feet of Clay', was dropped because it was too allusive. But it expressed the sense in which coherentism maintains that we can have empirical knowledge without a solid base to stand on: without foundations. It also expresses the fact that scepticism may continue more durable, more seductive and more secure than any reply we have found so far.

FURTHER READING

Hegel (1931, Introduction), Chisholm (1977, ch. 7), Quine (1969, ch. 3, and 1973, pp. 1 – 20), and Stroud (1984, ch. 6).

Taylor (1972) argues that Wittgenstein's private language argument is a good example of what Hegel means by determinate negation.

Chisholm's notion of critical cognitivism is similar to an idea scouted in McDowell (1982).

Rorty (1980) is a more recent attempt to show the impossibility of epistemology, for which I have failed to find room. (Be careful to watch what he means by 'foundationalism'.) Rorty suggests the need for a different conception of philosophy, a new approach.

This book has been firmly within the tradition which Rorty criticizes. For work within the continental tradition, a start could be made on the following primary and secondary sources: Habermas (1972, appendix and ch. 1); on Habermas, McCarthy (1978) and Ottmann (1982); Foucault (1972); on Foucault, Taylor (1984) and Cousins and Hussain (1984, pt 1); lastly, Bernstein (1983) offers a general account.

References

Albritton, R. (1959) 'On Wittgenstein's use of the term "criterion"', *Journal of Philosophy*, **56**, 845–57. (Reprinted in Pitcher, 1966.)

Alston, W. P. (1971) 'Varieties of privileged access', *American Philosophical Quarterly*, **8**, 223–41. (Reprinted in Chisholm and Swartz, 1973.)

Alston, W. P. (1976) 'Two types of foundationalism', *Journal of Philosophy*, **85**, 165–85.

Aristotle (1962) *De Interpretatione*, edited with the *Categories* by J. L. Ackrill (Oxford: Clarendon Press).

Armstrong, D. M. (1961) *Perception and the Physical World* (London: Routledge and Kegan Paul).

Armstrong, D. M., (1968) *A Materialist Theory of the Mind* (London: Routledge and Kegan Paul).

Armstrong, D. M. (1973) *Belief, Truth and Knowledge* (London: Cambridge University Press).

Austin, J. L. (1962) *Sense and Sensibilia* (Oxford: Clarendon Press).

Ayer, A. J. (1946) *Language, Truth and Logic*, 2nd edn (London: Gollancz).

Ayer, A. J. (1950) 'Basic propositions', in M. Black (ed.), *Philosophical Analysis* (Englewood Cliffs, NJ: Prentice-Hall) pp. 60–74. (Reprinted in Ayer, 1965, and in Chisholm and Swartz, 1973.)

Ayer, A. J. (1954) 'Can there be a private language?', *Proceedings of the Aristotelian Society*, supp. vol. **28**, 63–76. (Reprinted in Pitcher, 1966.)

Ayer, A. J. (1965) *Philosophical Essays* (London: Macmillan).

Ayer, A. J. (1969) *The Foundations of Empirical Knowledge* (London: Macmillan).

Ayer, A. J. (1976) *The Central Questions of Philosophy* (London: Penguin Books).

Baker, G. and Hacker, P. M. S. (1984) *Scepticism, Rules and Language* (Oxford: Blackwell).

Barker, S. F. and Achinstein, P. (1960) 'On the new riddle of induction', *Philosophical Review*, **69**, 511–22. (Reprinted in Nidditch, 1968.)

Berkeley, G. (1954) *A New Theory of Vision and Other Writings*, edited by A. D. Lindsay (London: Everyman Library, Dent/Dutton); contains also his *Principles of Human Knowledge* and *Three Dialogues*; first published 1709, 1710 and 1713 respectively.

Berlin, I. (1939) 'Verification', *Proceedings of the Aristotelian Society* 1938-9, **39**, 225-48. (Reprinted in G. Parkinson (ed.), *The Theory of Meaning* (Oxford: Oxford University Press) pp. 15-34.)

Bernstein, R. (1983) *Beyond Objectivism and Relativism* (Oxford: Blackwell).

Black, M. (1954) *Problems of Analysis* (London: Routledge).

Black, M. (1958) 'Self-supporting inductive arguments', *Journal of Philosophy*, **55**, 718-25. (Reprinted in Swinburne, 1974, and Nidditch, 1968.)

Blanshard, B. (1939) *The Nature of Thought* (London: Allen and Unwin).

Bonjour, L. (1980) 'Externalist theories of empirical knowledge', in French *et al.* (1980) pp. 53-73.

Bradley, F. H. (1914) *Essays on Truth and Reality* (Oxford: Oxford University Press).

Brandt, R. (1955) 'The epistemological status of memory beliefs', *Philosophical Review*, **64**, 78-95. (Reprinted in Chisholm and Swartz, 1973.)

Broad, C. D. (1930) *Five Types of Ethical Theory* (London: Routledge and Kegan Paul).

Cahn, S. M. (1967) *Fate, Logic and Time* (New Haven, Conn.: Yale University Press).

Carnap, R. (1967) *The Logical Structure of the World* (London: Routledge and Kegan Paul).

Chisholm, R. M. (1948) 'The problem of empiricism', *Journal of Philosophy*, **45**, 512-17. (Reprinted in Swartz, 1965.)

Chisholm, R. M. (1977) *Theory of Knowledge*, 2nd edn (Englewood Cliffs, NJ: Prentice-Hall).

Chisholm, R. M. and Swartz, R. J. (1973) (eds) *Empirical Knowledge* (Englewood Cliffs, NJ: Prentice-Hall).

Cornman, J. W. (1975) *Perception, Common Sense and Science* (New Haven, Conn.: Yale University Press).

Cornman, J. W. (1977) 'Foundational versus non-foundational theories of empirical justification', *American Philosophical Quarterly*, **14**, 287-97. (Reprinted in Pappas and Swain, 1978.)

Cousins, M. and Hussain, A. (1984) *Michel Foucault* (London: Macmillan).

Dancy, J. P. (1981) 'On moral properties', *Mind*, **90**, 367-85.

Dancy, J. P. (1984a) 'On coherence theories of justification: can an empiricist be a coherentist?', *American Philosophical Quarterly*, **21**, 359-65.

Dancy, J. P. (1984b) 'On the tracks of the sceptic', *Analysis*, **44**, 121-6.

Davidson, D. (1974) 'Belief and the basis of meaning', *Synthese*, **27**, 309-23. (Reprinted in Davidson, 1984.)

Davidson, D. (1984) *Inquiries into Truth and Interpretation* (Oxford: Clarendon Press).

Dennett, D. (1978) *Brainstorms* (Montgomery, Vt: Bradford Books).

Descartes, R. (1955) *The Philosophical Works of Descartes*, 2 vols, edited and translated by E. S. Haldane and G. R. T. Ross (Cambridge: Cambridge University Press).

Dretske, F. (1971) 'Conclusive reasons', *Australasian Journal of Philosophy*, **49**, 1–22. (Reprinted in Pappas and Swain, 1978.)

Dummett, M. A. E. (1978) *Truth and Other Enigmas* (London: Duckworth).

Edwards, P. (1949) 'Russell's doubts about induction', *Mind*, **68**, 141–63. (Reprinted in Swinburne, 1974.)

Ewing, A. C. (1934) *Idealism: A Critical Survey* (London: Methuen).

Feigl, H. and Sellars, W. (1949) (eds) *Readings in Philosophical Analysis* (New York: Appleton-Century-Crofts).

Firth, R. (1964) 'Coherence, certainty and epistemic priority', *Journal of Philosophy*, **61**, 545–57. (Reprinted in Chisholm and Swartz, 1973.)

Føllesdal, D. (1975) 'Meaning and experience', in Guttenplan (1975), pp. 25–44.

Flew, A. G. N. (1954) 'Can an effect precede its cause?', *Proceedings of the Aristotelian Society*, supp. vol. **28**, 45–62.

Foucault, M. (1972) *The Archaeology of Knowledge*, translated by A. M. Sheridan (London: Tavistock).

French, P. A., Uehling, T. E. and Wettstein, H. K. (1980) (eds) *Midwest Studies in Philosophy*, vol. 5, *Studies in Epistemology* (Minneapolis, Minn.: University of Minnesota Press).

Garrett, B. J. (1983) 'Nozick on knowledge', *Analysis*, **43**, 181–4.

Gettier, E. L. (1963) 'Is justified true belief knowledge?', *Analysis*, **23**, 121–3. (Reprinted in Phillips Griffiths, 1967.)

Goldman, A. I. (1967) 'A causal theory of knowing', *Journal of Philosophy*, **64**, 355–72. (Reprinted in Pappas and Swain, 1978.)

Goldman, A. I. (1976) 'Discrimination and perceptual knowledge', *Journal of Philosophy*, **73**, 771–99. (Reprinted in Pappas and Swain, 1978.)

Goldman, A. I. (1979) 'What is justified belief?', in Pappas (1979) pp. 1–23.

Goldman, A. I. (1980) 'The internalist conception of justification', in French *et al.* (1980) pp. 27–51.

Goodman, N. (1952) 'Sense and certainty', *Philosophical Review*, **61**, 160–7. (Reprinted in Chisholm and Swartz, 1973.)

Goodman, N. (1973) *Fact, Fiction and Forecast* (Indianapolis, Ind.: Bobbs-Merrill).

Gordon, D. (1984) 'Knowledge, reliable methods and Nozick', *Analysis*, **44**, 30–3.

Grandy, R. (1973) 'Reference, meaning and belief', *Journal of Philosophy*, **70**, 439–52.

Grice, P. (1961) 'The causal theory of perception', *Proceedings of the Aristotelian Society*, supp. vol. **35**, 121–52. (Reprinted in Swartz, 1965.)

Guttenplan, S. (1975) (ed.) *Mind and Language* (Oxford: Clarendon Press).

Habermas, J. (1972) *Knowledge and Human Interests*, translated by J. J. Shapiro (London: Heinemann).

Hacker, P. M. S. (1972) *Insight and Illusion* (Oxford: Oxford University Press).

Hamlyn, D. W. (1970) *The Theory of Knowledge* (London: Macmillan).

Hare, R. M. (1963) *Freedom and Reason* (Oxford: Oxford University Press).

Harman, G. (1970) 'Induction', in Swain (1970) pp. 83–99.

Harré, R. and Madden, E. H. (1975) *Causal Powers* (Oxford: Blackwell).

Hegel, G. W. F. (1931) *The Phenomenology of Mind*, translated by J. B. Baillie (London: Allen and Unwin; first published 1807).

Hempel, C. G. (1942) 'The function of general laws in history', *Journal of Philosophy*, **39**, 35–48. (Reprinted in Feigl and Sellars, 1949.)

Hookway, C. (1978) 'Indeterminacy and interpretation', in C. Hookway and P. Pettit (eds) *Action and Interpretation* (Cambridge: Cambridge University Press) pp. 17–41.

Hume, D. (1955) *An Inquiry Concerning Human Understanding*, edited by C. W. Hendel (New York: Bobbs-Merrill (Library of Liberal Arts); first published 1748).

Hume, D. (1967) *A Treatise of Human Nature*, edited by L. A. Selby-Bigge (Oxford: Clarendon Press; first published 1739).

Hylton, P. (1982) 'Analyticity and the indeterminacy of translation', *Synthese*, **52**, 167–84.

Jackson, F. (1977) *Perception* (Cambridge: Cambridge University Press).

Kant, I. (1961) *Critique of Pure Reason*, translated by N. Kemp Smith (London: Macmillan; first published 1781).

Kant, I. (1967) *Philosophical Correspondence 1759–99*, edited and translated by A. Zweig (Chicago, Ill.: University of Chicago Press).

Kripke, S. (1971) 'Identity and necessity', in M. Munitz (ed.) *Identity and Individuation* (New York: New York University Press) pp. 135–64.

Kripke, S. (1981) 'Wittgenstein on rules and private language', in I. Block (ed.) *Perspectives on the Philosophy of Wittgenstein* (Oxford: Blackwell) pp. 238–312.

Kripke, S. (1982) *Wittgenstein: On Rules and Private Language* (Oxford: Blackwell).

Kvanvig, J. L. (1984) 'Subjective justification', *Mind*, **93**, 71–84.

Lehrer, K. (1974) *Knowledge* (Oxford: Clarendon Press).

Lehrer, K. and Paxson, T. (1969) 'Knowledge: undefeated justified true belief', *Journal of Philosophy*, **66**, 225–37. (Reprinted in Pappas and Swain, 1978.)

Levi, I. (1980) *The Enterprise of Knowledge* (Cambridge, Mass.: MIT Press).

Lewis, C. I. (1946) *An Analysis of Knowledge and Valuation* (LaSalle, Ill.: Open Court). (Chapter 7 is reprinted in Chisholm and Swartz, 1973; chapter 8 is reprinted in Swartz, 1965.)

Lewis, C. I. (1952) 'The given element in empirical knowledge', *Philosophical Review*, **61**, 168–75. (Reprinted in Chisholm and Swartz, 1973.)

Lewis, D. (1973) *Counterfactuals* (Oxford: Blackwell).

Lewis, D. (1974) 'Radical interpretation', Synthese, **23**, 331–44.

Locke, D. (1971) *Memory* (London: Macmillan).

Locke, J. (1961) *An Essay Concerning Human Understanding*, edited by J. Yolton (London: Everyman's Library, Dent/Dutton; first published in 1690).

McCarthy, T. (1978) *The Critical Theory of Jurgen Habermas* (Cambridge, Mass.: MIT Press).

McDowell, J. (1982) 'Criteria, defeasibility and knowledge', *Proceedings of the British Academy*, **68**, pp. 455–79 (Oxford: Oxford University Press, 1983).

Mackie, J. L. (1976) *Problems from Locke* (Oxford: Clarendon Press).

Malcolm, N. (1958) 'Knowledge of other minds', *Journal of Philosophy*, **55**, 969–78. (Reprinted in his *Knowledge and Certainty* Englewood Cliffs, NJ: Prentice-Hall, 1963) and in Pitcher, 1966.)

Martin, C. B. and Deutscher, M. (1966) 'Remembering', *Philosophical Review*, **75**, 161–96. (Reprinted in Chisholm and Swartz, 1973.)

Mill, J. S. (1867) *An Examination of Sir William Hamilton's Philosophy*, 3rd edn (London: Longmans).

Nidditch, P. H. (1968) (ed.) *The Philosophy of Science* (Oxford: Oxford University Press).

Nozick, R. (1981) *Philosophical Explanations* (Oxford: Oxford University Press).

Ottmann, H. (1982) 'Cognitive interests and self-reflection', in J. B. Thompson and D. Held (eds) *Habermas: Critical Debates* (London: Macmillan) pp. 79–97.

Pappas, G. (1979) (ed.) *Justification and Knowledge* (Dordrecht: Reidel).

Pappas, G. and Swain, M. (1978) (eds) *Essays on Knowledge and Justification* (Ithaca, NY: Cornell University Press).

Peacocke, C. (1983) *Sense and Content* (Oxford: Clarendon Press).

Pears, D. (1966) 'Incompatibilities of colours', in A. G. N. Flew (ed.) *Logic and Language*, 2nd series (Oxford: Blackwell) pp. 112–22.

Phillips Griffiths, A. (1967) (ed.) *Knowledge and Belief* (Oxford: Oxford University Press).

Pitcher, G. (1966) (ed.) *Wittgenstein* (London: Macmillan).

Plato (1973) *Theaetetus*, edited and translated by J. McDowell (Oxford: Clarendon Press).

Pollock, J. L. (1979) 'A plethora of epistemological theories', in Pappas (1979) pp. 93–113.

Prichard, H. A. (1967) 'Knowing and believing', excerpts from his *Knowledge and Perception* (Oxford: Clarendon Press, 1950), reprinted in Phillips Griffiths, 1967.

Putnam, H. (1975) *Mind, Language and Reality; Philosophical Papers*, vol. 2 (Cambridge: Cambridge University Press).

Putnam, H. (1977) 'Two dogmas revisited', in G. Ryle (ed.) *Contemporary Aspects of Philosophy* (London: Oriel Press) pp. 202–13.

Quine, W. V. O. (1953) *From a Logical Point of View* (Cambridge, Mass.: Harvard University Press).

Quine, W. V. O. (1960) *Word and Object* (Cambridge, Mass.: MIT Press).

Quine, W. V. O. (1969) *Ontological Relativity* (New York: Columbia University Press).

Quine, W. V. O. (1970) 'On the reasons for indeterminacy of translation', *Journal of Philosophy*, **67**, 178–83.

Quine, W. V. O. (1973) *The Roots of Reference* (LaSalle, Ill.: Open Court).

Quine, W. V. O. (1975a) 'The nature of natural knowledge', in Guttenplan (1975) pp. 67–81.

Quine, W. V. O. (1975b) 'Reply to Chomsky', in D. Davidson and J. Hintikka (eds) *Words and Objections* (Dordrecht: Reidel) pp. 302–11.

Quine, W. V. O. (1981) 'Reply to Stroud', in P. French, T. E. Uehling and H. K. Wettstein (eds) *Midwest Studies in Philosophy*, vol. 6, *The Foundations of Analytic Philosophy* (Minneapolis, Minn.: University of Minnesota Press) pp. 473–5.

Reichenbach, H. (1952) 'Are phenomenal reports absolutely certain?', *Philosophical Review*, **61**, 147–59. (Reprinted in Chisholm and Swartz, 1973.)

Rescher, N. (1973) *The Coherence Theory of Truth* (Oxford: Clarendon Press).

Ring, M. (1977) 'Knowledge: the cessation of belief', *American Philosophical Quarterly*, **14**, 51–9.

Rock, I. (1984) *Perception* (New York: Scientific American Library).

Rorty, R. (1980) *Philosophy and the Mirror of Nature* (Princeton, NJ: Princeton University Press).

Russell, B. (1907) 'On the nature of truth', *Proceedings of the Aristotelian Society 1906–7*, **7**, 28–49.

Russell, B. (1921) *The Analysis of Mind* (London: Allen and Unwin).

Russell, B. (1926) *Our Knowledge of the External World*, 2nd edn (London: Allen and Unwin).

Russell, B. (1959) *The Problems of Philosophy* (Oxford: Oxford University Press).

Ryle, G. (1949) *The Concept of Mind* (London: Hutchinson).

Schlick, M. (1936) 'Meaning and verification', *Philosophical Review*, **45**, 339–69. (Reprinted in Feigl and Sellars, 1949.)

Sellars, W. F. (1963) *Science, Perception and Reality* (London: Routledge and Kegan Paul). (Chapter 5 is reprinted in Chisholm and Swartz, 1973.)

Sellars, W. F. (1973) 'Givenness and explanatory coherence', *Journal of Philosophy*, **70**, 612–24.

Sellars, W. F. (1979) 'More on givenness and explanatory coherence', in Pappas (1979) pp. 169–82.

Shoemaker, S. (1963) *Self-knowledge and Self-identity* (Ithaca, NY: Cornell University Press).

Shope, R. (1983) *The Analysis of Knowing* (Princeton, NJ: Princeton University Press).

Shope, R. (1984) 'Cognitive abilities, conditionals and knowledge: a response to Nozick', *Journal of Philosophy*, **81**, 29–48.

Small, K. (1961) 'Professor Goodman's puzzle', *Philosophical Review*, **70**, 544–52.

Snowdon, P. (1981) 'Perception, vision and causation', *Proceedings of the Aristotelian Society 1980–1*, **81**, 175–92.

Strawson, P. F. (1952) *Introduction to Logical Theory* (London: Methuen).

Strawson, P. F. (1974) *Freedom and Resentment* (London: Methuen).

Strawson, P. F. (1979) 'Perception and its objects', in G. F. Macdonald (ed.) *Perception and Identity* (London: Macmillan) pp. 41–60.

Stroud, B. (1968) 'Transcendental arguments', *Journal of Philosophy*, **65**, 241–56. (Reprinted in T. Penelhum and J. MacIntosh (eds) *The First Critique* (Belmont, Calif.: Wadsworth) pp. 54–69).

Stroud, B. (1969) 'Conventionalism and translation', in D. Davidson and J. Hintikka (eds) *Words and Objections* (Dordrecht: Reidel) pp. 82–96.

Stroud, B. (1977) *Hume* (London: Routledge and Kegan Paul).

Stroud, B. (1984) *The Significance of Philosophical Scepticism* (Oxford: Clarendon Press).

Swain, M. (1970) (ed.) *Induction, Acceptance and Rational Belief* (Dordrecht: Reidel).

Swain, M. (1974) 'Epistemic defeasibility', *American Philosophical Quarterly*, **11**, 15–25. (Reprinted in Pappas and Swain, 1978.)

Swain, M. (1981) 'Justification and reliable belief', *Philosophical Studies*, **40**, 389–407.

Swartz, R. (1965) (ed.) *Perceiving, Sensing and Knowing* (Berkeley, Calif.: University of California Press).

Swinburne, R. G. (1974) (ed.) *The Justification of Induction* (Oxford: Oxford University Press).

Taylor, C. (1972) 'The opening arguments of the *Phenomenology*', in A. MacIntyre (ed.) *Hegel: A Collection of Critical Essays* (Garden City, NY: Anchor Books) pp. 151–87.

Taylor, C. (1984) 'Foucault on freedom and truth', *Political Theory*, **12**, 152–83.

Urmson, J. O. (1953) 'Some questions concerning validity', *Revue Internationale de Philosophie*, **25**, 217–29. (Reprinted in Swinburne, 1974.)

Van Inwagen, P. (1975) 'The incompatibility of free will and determinism', *Philosophical Studies*, **27**, 185–99. (Reprinted in Watson, 1982.)

Watson, G. (1982) (ed.) *Free Will* (Oxford: Oxford University Press).

Weiskrantz, L. (1980) 'Varieties of residual experience', *Quarterly Journal of Experimental Psychology*, **32**, 365–86.

Wittgenstein, L. (1953) *Philosophical Investigations* (Oxford: Blackwell).

Wittgenstein, L. (1969a) *On Certainty* (Oxford: Blackwell).

Wittgenstein, L. (1969b) *The Blue and Brown Books* (Oxford: Blackwell).

Woodfield, A. (1982) (ed.) *Thought and Object* (Oxford: Clarendon Press).

Woozley, A. D. (1953) 'Knowing and not knowing', *Proceedings of the*

Aristotelian Society, 1952–3, **53**, 151–72. (Reprinted in Phillips Griffiths, 1967.)

Wright, C. J. G. (1984) 'Second thoughts about criteria', *Synthese*, **58**, 383–405.

Index

adverbial theory of sensation, 170
Albritton, R., 84
Alston, W. P., 65
analytic/synthetic, Quine's rejection
  of the distinction, 95, 223, 236;
  and empiricism, 213–14; the
  synthetic a priori, 214–18; and
  logical truth, 223–4; a coherentist
  account, 224–5, cf.112; analytic
  justification of induction, 203–5
antecedent security, 122–5, 176
anti-realism, introduced, 19–21, cf.
  22; as a response to scepticism,
  19–21, 89–91, 192–4; but an
  incomplete response, 139; in the
  theory of meaning, 89–90, 91–2,
  cf.19–20; and foundationalism,
  108; types of, 136–7; compatible
  with but not required for coherentism, 137–9; committed to an
  unsound theory of perception,
  179–80; metaphysical/perceptual,
  144–5, 179–80; and the past,
  193–4; and the future, 200–2; and
  the justification of induction,
  204–7
a priori knowledge, 212–26 *passim*;
  the synthetic a priori, 214–18; of
  universal truths only? 218–21; of
  necessary truth only? 221–2;
  Quine's rejection 222–4; and
  coherentism, 224–5; of principles
  of inference, 188–9, 212
argument from analogy (other
  minds), 68–73
argument from error, introduced
  12–15; not refuted by Nozick,

44–6; internalist, 46; and other
  minds, 67–8; easily rebutted by
  externalism, 131; anti–realist
  answers, 18–21, insufficient 139;
  coherentism contains no answer,
  136–9; used against indirect
  realism, 165; and memory-
  knowledge, 191–3; relies on the
  principle of universalizability,
  12–15, which is false, 239–41
argument from illusion, introduced,
  153; and indirect realism, 164;
  and memory 184; a direct realist
  response, 169–73, cf. 151, 153;
  rejected by externalism in the
  philosophy of mind, 175; its
  relation to the argument from
  error, 240; and internalism, 241
Aristotle, 201
Armstrong, D. M. 31, 133, 158,
  171
asymmetries, and foundationalism,
  99, cf.55–7, 63; semantical and
  epistemological, in Quine, 99–101;
  incompatible with holism, 102–3,
  which is preferable, 103–8;
  coherentism does not contain the
  asymmetries, 110, rightly, 118; the
  asymmetry of empiricism is compatible with coherentism, 120–5;
  genetic/continuing, 123
atomism, cf. holism
Austin, J. L., 64, 65
Ayer, A. J., 58, 65, 78, 87–91, 95–6,
  158–9, 168, 190, 213–14

Baker, G., 76–82, 84